C Programming Guide
Second Edition

Harold Mar
973-2846 (WORK)

Jack J. Purdum

Que Corporation
Indianapolis

Library of Congress Catalog No.: LC 85-60689
ISBN 0-88022-157-7

89 88 87 86   8 7 6 5

Interpretation of the printing code: the rightmost double-digit number is the year of the book's printing; the rightmost single-digit number, the number of the book's printing. For example, a printing code of 87-4 shows that the fourth printing of the book occurred in 1987.

Editorial Director
David F. Noble, Ph.D.

Editor
Virginia Noble, M.L.S.

Technical Editor
Chris DeVoney

Dedication

To my family:
Karol, Katie, and John Paul

Composed by Que Corporation
in Megaron

Cover designed by
Patterson / Thomas, Inc.
Listenberger Design Associates

About the Author

Jack Purdum

Dr. Purdum received his B.A. degree from Muskingum College and M.A. and Ph.D. degrees from Ohio State University. He was a university professor for 18 years before becoming president of Ecosoft, a software house that specializes in microcomputer software. Dr. Purdum has received many teaching and research awards, including a National Science Foundation grant to study microcomputers in education. He has published a number of professional articles; a BASIC programming text; and magazine articles in *Byte*, *Personal Computing*, and *Interface Age*. He is also author of *C Self-Study Guide* and coauthor of *C Programming Library*, both published by Que Corporation.

Table of Contents

Appendix 2: Binary, Octal, and Hexadecimal Numbering System

3 Writing Your Own Functions

7   Structures and Unions

8   Disk File Operations

Appendix 8: A Closer Look at File I/O

9 Common Mistakes and Debugging

Appendix A: ASCII Codes

Appendix B: Commercial C Products

Appendix C: Syntax Summary

Appendix D: Prototyping

Foreword

The programs and functions in this book were tested on several different C compilers running under the CP/M operating system. Most programs and examples will run on any C compiler that is compatible with UNIX version 7. Less sophisticated compilers may also be used. Programs in the later chapters (5 through 9) involve floating-point variables; these may not be available on less sophisticated compilers.

Because the implementation of C's standard library varies among compiler publishers, you should review your documentation for any peculiarities, differences in function calls, or additional program lines that should be added to the program examples for your compiler. One example is the inclusion of `stdio.h`. Some compilers demand that this file be included with every program file, whereas others require this file for only specific operations, such as reading and writing disk files. (The `stdio.h` file is covered in Chapters 4 and 8.)

To increase legibility, the programs, examples, C keywords, and variables are set in a font called digital. This font is reproduced below.

```
ABCDEFGHIJKLMNOPQRSTUVWXYZ
abcdefghijklmnopqrstuvwxyz
0123456789
!"#$%&'()*+,-./
:;<=>?@[]\^_{|}~
```

A ruler line is provided below to help you count the spaces in a program line.

```
    0   1   1   2   2   3   3   4   4   5   5   6
12345678901234567890123456789012345678901234567890
```

Preface to the Second Edition

This text is designed to teach you how to write programs in the C language. The fact that you are reading this preface suggests that you already know some of C's advantages over other languages. With its extensive set of operators and data types, C is a flexible language that lets you write anything from operating systems to accounting packages. The many other advantages will become clear as you read this text.

The book was written with two underlying assumptions: (1) the only way to learn a language is to write programs with it, and (2) learning is made easier if you can visualize what a program statement does. This text explains in an easy-to-read manner how to use C and why. Several appendixes explore certain topics in greater depth for the interested reader.

Each chapter contains program examples that introduce additional elements of the C language. Each program is kept as simple as possible but still conveys the topic at hand. The text encourages you to experiment with each program. Sometimes questions are asked that can be answered only if you run the program. In this sense, the text may be used as a self-study guide. In a formal classroom setting, these questions can be used for lab projects to reinforce the content of the chapters.

To build on previous knowledge, the book occasionally presents comparisons with the BASIC programming language. This strategy makes the transition to C easier for those who have worked with BASIC. Even if you do not know a programming language, you can learn C. Simple graphic representations are also used so that you can "see" what a particular instruction does. This is particularly helpful if you do not already know a programming language.

I have also tried to minimize for you the cost of experimenting with C. All the program examples in the first five chapters can be run with C compilers that are priced under $50. (Many of the program examples in subsequent chapters can also be run with these compilers.) By the time you read the later chapters, you should be convinced of the virtues of C and will probably want to invest in a full C compiler.

This book was a joint effort; many individuals contributed to the final product. In particular, I would like to thank Steve Browning and Chris DeVoney for their suggestions and critical attention to detail; Tim Leslie, who can always find one more detail to criticize; the publisher and editorial staff at Que, who don't know what a 40-hour week is; and finally, Ron Cain for his public domain C compiler that has done so much to popularize C.

There has been both a maturation and an increased interest in C since the first edition was written. At that time, relatively few C compilers were available for personal computers. Now, several dozen compilers are available, many at reasonable cost. C has also undergone changes. The language is being standardized by the X3-J11 ANSI committee. The new standard will produce many changes in the language. The second edition includes a discussion of the major changes that seem certain to be implemented, plus several others that are presently in a state of limbo.

The second edition also reflects a maturation in my own coding style and experience with the language. Many of the past readers of the first edition convinced me to change both the style and substance of many of the example programs. To them, my thanks and the presentation of the second edition.

Jack Purdum

Trademarks

Que Corporation has made every effort to supply trademark information about company names, products, and services mentioned in this book. Trademarks indicated below were derived from various sources. Que Corporation cannot attest to the accuracy of this information.

Application Programmer's Toolkit is a trademark of Shaw * American Technologies.

Aztec C is a trademark of Manx Software Systems.

C86 is a trademark of Computer Innovations.

CP/M is a registered trademark of Digital Research, Inc.

Greenleaf Functions is a registered trademark of Greenleaf Software, Inc.

Hewlett-Packard is a registered trademark of Hewlett-Packard Company.

IBM is a registered trademark of International Business Machines Corporation.

Intertec is a trademark of Intertec.

Lattice is a registered trademark of Lattice, Inc.

Microsoft, Microsoft BASIC-80, and MS-DOS are trademarks of Microsoft Corporation.

Q/C 88 is a trademark of The Code Works.

TeleVideo is a registered trademark of TeleVideo Systems, Inc.

UNIX is a trademark of Bell Laboratories, Inc.

Windows for C is a trademark of Vermont Creative Software.

Z80 is a registered trademark of Zilog, Inc.

Zenith is a registered trademark of Zenith Electronics Corporation.

1

An Introduction to C

This text is designed to help you learn to write programs in C as quickly as possible. Simple examples are used to illustrate each aspect of the C language. You can run many of these programs by using inexpensive C compilers available for many microcomputers. Therefore, you don't need to invest much money if you are just "investigating" C at this point. The programs, however, can be run on any computer—from a micro to a mainframe.

In any case, you will need access to a C compiler as you read this text. Appendix B lists several moderately priced C compilers available for a variety of personal computers. Even if you use the least expensive compiler (less than $20.00) on the list, you will be able to run all the programs in the first five chapters of this text. The programs in later chapters require a full-featured C compiler, but you should find C worth the investment by then.

Why C?

C has many advantages over other programming languages. It is a robust language whose large variety of operators and data types can be used to write anything from operating systems to accounting packages. In fact, many of the C compilers on the market today were written in C.

C is a portable language. With little or no modification, a C program written on one computer can be run on any other computer with a C compiler. The idea of "write it once" takes on real meaning with C.

Another advantage of C is its execution speed. If you have never worked with a compiler and are used to an interpreted language such as BASIC, you're in for a pleasant surprise. For example, one program in Chapter 2 does nothing more than increment a variable from 0 to 30000. In a completely unfair test, the interpreted BASIC version took 96 seconds, but the C version took less than 2 seconds.

The advantages of portability and speed combine to form another subtle advantage. On occasion, execution speed is critical, as in the task of sorting. Before C was widely used, coding the program in assembly language was the usual solution. But as new Central Processing Unit (CPU) chips were introduced, the programmer was forced to learn a new instruction set for each CPU. Retraining costs were so high that many commercial software houses (including a major supplier of BASIC interpreters) switched to C for in-house development.

This logic also applies to you. Although you'll have to spend some time to learn C, you won't have to waste time learning a new language whenever another CPU comes on the market. With a good C compiler, the difference in execution speed between C and an assembler will go unnoticed in all but the most demanding cases.

Another advantage of C is that it lends itself well to structured programming techniques, forcing you to think of function modules or *blocks*. Each block has a specialized purpose or *function*. A C program involves little more than arranging these modules to perform the overall task of the program. This modular approach makes program debugging and maintenance easier.

Finally, C is an enjoyable language—not necessarily because it's easy to learn, but because it's flexible. By creating your own function modules, you can make C do just about anything you want. You can even create your own language in C! But before you set off in that direction, let's continue with the task at hand: learning C.

Some Assumptions about the Reader

Several assumptions are made about the reader. The first assumption is that you have access to a computer, a text editor (for entering the programs into the computer and saving them on disk), and a C compiler. The exact compiler doesn't matter at this point.

The important thing is for you to try the examples *as they are presented in the text.* You cannot learn a language by reading about it; you have to plunge right in.

The second assumption is that you are familiar with some elements of programming. (The text contains several references to the BASIC programming language because of its widespread use.) This assumption should *not* be viewed as prohibitive. Even if you do not know a programming language, you should be able to learn C. However, the technique of showing a program or routine in C with the corresponding one in BASIC is used as a learning tool in this text. The BASIC that appears in this book will help you build on any programming knowledge you may have of that language.

A third assumption is that you are under no pressure to master C by tomorrow evening. Some chapters may dwell on a point longer than you think is necessary. This approach is used because C is like a pyramid that must rest on a solid foundation. Take the time to master the contents of a chapter before proceeding to the next one. Working each example is a step in the right direction. The *C Self-Study Guide* (available from the publisher) contains questions and answers that may be used to supplement this text.

Finally, be sure to experiment and enjoy yourself while you're learning. Keep in mind that understanding what is written in this text is not the same as writing your own programs. At every opportunity, try to write programs of your own.

Fundamental Characteristics of C Programs

Just as a child uses toy blocks to build things, the C programmer builds programs from "blocks" called functions. Children (and parents) like toy blocks because they can be reused to build new and different things. C programmers like functions for the same reason. Indeed, functions form the base from which all C programs are built and on which our understanding shall rest.

Functions in C

A C program can be viewed as a group of building blocks called *functions. A function is one or more C statements designed to accomplish a specific task.* Study program 1.1.

```
/*                    C                    */
/* this C program prints a message on the screen */

#include <stdio.h>

main()
{

    printf("This is my first program.\n");

}
```

```
10 REM This BASIC program does the same thing
20 PRINT "This is my first program."
30 END
```

Program 1.1.

This program is written first in C and then in BASIC. Both versions print the message "This is my first program." In C, a program *comment* or *remark* begins with a slash-asterisk combination (/*) and ends with the two characters reversed (*/). Everything between these marks is ignored by the C compiler. The comment serves the same purpose as the REM (REMark) statement in BASIC. Both are nonexecuting program statements.

Hint: Because the compiler ignores everything between /* and */, these comment characters are useful for debugging. If you want to remove a line from a C program for testing, surrounding the line by comment characters will have the same effect. You can remove an entire program section this way without having to retype it later. When the comment characters are removed, the "commented out" line is restored.

Remember that the compiler ignores everything between /* and */. Because comments do not affect a program's size or execution speed in any way, you should use comments liberally in your programs. Code that seems obvious today may look weird two months later. Liberal use of comments can help jog your memory at a later date.

#include <stdio.h>

The first task for the C compiler to process is the #include preprocessor directive. The details of the preprocessor are covered in a later chapter. For now, think of a #include as an instruction telling the compiler to "go search for a file named stdio.h and place whatever that file contains at this point in the program." In program 1.1, the file to be located is stdio.h. This is a special file that comes with all C compilers. The file name is an abbreviation for *standard input-output header* file. It is used whenever a program is expected to use input routines (such as getting a character from the keyboard) or output routines (such as displaying something on the screen). Because most programs do involve some form of input and output (hereafter called I/O), virtually all programs #include the stdio.h file.

Notice the angle brackets that surround the header file. On some compilers, you may have to use two sets of quotation marks, as in

    #include "stdio.h"

The difference between the use of brackets and quotation marks is explained in a later chapter. For now, you should use whichever works with your compiler. Details about #include and other preprocessor directives will also be supplied later. For the time being, think of the #include directive as a file containing some "overhead information" that the program needs and don't worry about the details.

The main( ) Function

The special function main() marks the point where a C program begins execution. Every program *must* have a main() function to show the compiler where the program starts. This function can be used only once in a program. If you use several main() functions, the compiler cannot tell which main() marks the start of the program.

One more point about main() should be noted. Because C does make a distinction between upper- and lowercase letters, Main() and main() are not the same function. The main() function discussed here should be written in lowercase letters only. C programmers generally do not use uppercase letters in a function name, nor do they mix upper- and lowercase letters in a single function or variable name.

Throughout this text, any reference to a function name has opening and closing parentheses immediately after it to help you recognize the name as a function. The function name also appears in
digital type. The parentheses and the special type help you distinguish the function named main() from the word *main*.

Braces

The opening brace ({), located in program 1.1 directly below the
letter m in main(), marks the *beginning of the function body*. The
function body contains one or more program statements that are
used to perform a specific task.

Ignoring what printf() is for the moment, you can see a closing
brace (}) at the bottom of the C program. This brace marks the *end
of the function body*. The opening and closing braces, therefore,
"surround" the statement (or statements) that forms the function
body. Figure 1.1 highlights what we have covered so far. Dots are
used to represent statements within the function body.

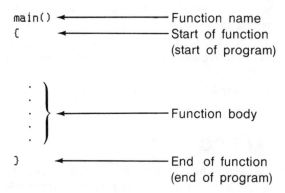

Figure 1.1.

The closing brace serves another purpose when it is used with
main(). Just as the opening brace of main() marks the start of a C
program, the closing brace of main() marks the *end of the
program*.

Determining where a BASIC program starts execution is easy; it
begins with the lowest line number of the program. Unless told to
do otherwise, BASIC processes the program by ascending line
numbers until an END statement is found. The END statement in
line 30 of program 1.1 causes the program to terminate.

Because C programs do not use line numbers, the opening and closing braces for the main() function mark the start and end of a program even when other C statements follow the closing brace in main().

To reinforce this idea, let's suppose that we wrote program 1.2, which is a BASIC-like C program similar to program 1.1.

```
main()      /* this is a phony BASIC-like C program */
{

     X$ = "This is my first program.\n";
     GOSUB printf(X$);

}
END

printf(X$)      /* a call to a function */
{

     PRINT X$;
     RETURN;

}
```

Program 1.2.

If this program behaved like an actual program, it would start execution with the main() function. The function body of main() has two statements. The first statement assigns a string of characters to X$. The second statement is a GOSUB that calls another function named printf(), which prints the contents of X$. The RETURN statement in printf() sends control back to main() for further processing. Because no further statements are in main(), the program ends when the closing brace of main() is reached.

Although C functions behave like BASIC subroutines in many respects, differences exist between the two. One difference is that a return statement in a C function is optional, depending on the function's purpose. The RETURN statement in program 1.2 is not required in C; if RETURN were omitted, the closing brace of the printf() (or any other C function) would still cause the program to return to the main() function. This automatic return suggests an important distinction between main() and other C functions:

The closing brace of the main() function marks the end of the program. The closing brace of any other function marks the end of the function and returns control to whatever function called it.

One function can call another before going back to main(). In fact, a function can call itself. This process is a *recursive function call*. (Functions are discussed in detail in Chapter 3.)

The Standard C Library

Let's take a closer look at the printf() line from program 1.1:

```
printf("This is my first program. \n");
```

This C function call prints the message between quotation marks on the screen. The \n at the end of the message is called the *new-line* character. It causes anything printed after the message to appear on the next (new) line. However, the obvious question at this point is, Where is the code for the printf() function? We know that printf() is used in the program, but the code doesn't appear after the closing brace or anywhere else in main().

All C compilers have a *standard library*, which is a collection of commonly used C functions, such as printf(), that have already been written for you.

If a program uses a function that is not written as part of the program, the compiler will search through the standard library for the missing function. If the compiler finds the function in the standard library, the necessary code for that function is added to the program. (Technically, these operations are performed by the *linker*, which will be discussed in Chapter 3.)

The more functions you have in your compiler's standard library, the fewer functions you have to write yourself. You can add whatever new functions you like. As your library expands, programming in C becomes easier because you don't have to rewrite functions. Eventually, even highly complex programs become little more than a series of C function calls.

Note: The designers of your compiler can use whatever names they want for functions in the standard library. Function names are not restricted by any C syntax rules. One compiler, for example, has a function named putfmt() that serves the same purpose as `printf()` in most other compilers. Unfortunately, such naming practices reduce the portability of C programs.

What is meant by *portability*? It means that a program written on computer XYZ using Jones' compiler can be recompiled on computer ABC using Brown's compiler, with few changes, if any, required in the program. For programmers writing in a commercial environment, portability means that they can easily get their software running on a different computer. Program portability enhances a programmer's productivity and is an important driving force behind C's popularity. Throughout this text (and in the *C Self-Study Guide*), ways to make your code more portable will be described.

Review the documentation that came with your compiler to find out what functions are included in your standard library. Don't be concerned if you don't fully understand everything you read. That understanding will come soon enough. All you want now is to get some idea of the extent of your standard library. Try to categorize the functions into those that work with string data, those that work with numbers, and so forth. (Many compiler manufacturers group functions for you.) Make a note of common functions with "nonstandard" names [for example, `putfmt()` instead of `printf()`] as you encounter them in subsequent program examples.

Nothing is "standard" about the number of functions included in the standard library. Some compilers supply as few as a dozen functions, whereas others have more than a hundred. Many functions in the library, however, *behave* in a standard way [For example, see the full discussion of `printf()` in Chapter 5.] Because deviations do exist, you should review your compiler's documentation to determine how each function works.

In subsequent discussions the term *library* refers to those functions that are part of the standard C library. Let's assume that your compiler uses the common function names and that nonstandard function names are not a serious problem. (Fortunately, most manufacturers of C compilers are moving toward using standard function names. The use of nonstandard names should be less of a problem now than it used to be.)

Semicolons in C

Now that you know where the printf() function comes from, we can take a more detailed look at what this function does. Look at the following program line:

```
printf("This is my first program.\n");
```

Notice that the line ends with a semicolon. The semicolon marks the *end of a C program statement*. In BASIC, program statements end with a colon, a backslash, a new line number, or some other character, depending on the dialect of BASIC used. These characters have the same purpose in both languages: they mark where the program statement ends. Omitting the semicolon at the end of a program statement is a common mistake made by beginning C programmers.

Arguments of Functions

A function usually cannot perform a task unless the function is first given some information. This information is called an *argument* of the function. Arguments are listed between the parentheses that follow the function name. In program 1.1 the argument of printf() is "This is my first program.\n" This argument is simply a string of characters to be displayed on the screen. The printf() function treats any characters between quotation marks as a *string constant* for display.

Because each function has a specific task and each task is different, you should expect each function to have different information requirements for performing its task. Therefore, any number of arguments can be passed to a function. If more than one argument is passed, they form an *argument list* for the function. Arguments in the list *must be* separated by commas.

For example, a function calculating the volume of a cube needs the length, height, and width of the cube. Such a function may appear as shown in code fragment 1.1. In this code, the dots represent details of the function. These details will be discussed later. (Note: As you know, a program must have a main() function. Because there is no main() in the following example, it is called a "code fragment." Such nonexecuting examples will be referred to as code fragments from now on.)

Code fragment

```
volume(length, height, width)

{

                              /* statements necessary to */
                              /* calculate the volume */

}
```

Code fragment 1.1.

Figure 1.2 summarizes what has been discussed about functions thus far.

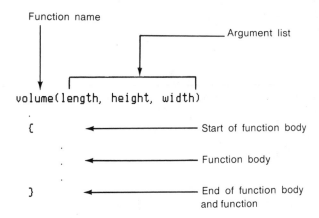

Figure 1.2.

Note that a function may have no arguments passed to it; in program 1.1, main() was used without arguments. You must still include parentheses, however, so that the compiler will know that you are using a function instead of a variable.

The use of the message "This is my first program.\n" as the argument passed to the printf() function in program 1.1 is not much different from the message's use in the BASIC version in the same example. In both cases the string constant surrounded by quotation marks gives printf() and PRINT the information to be displayed on the screen.

If you have written BASIC programs, you have used C-like functions with arguments before, but perhaps you didn't view them as such. For example, the function strlen(str) in C does the same thing as LEN(STR$) in BASIC: each function returns the number of characters in a string variable named str or STR$. Your library probably contains the strlen() function. If so, read your documentation to verify its purpose.

An Overview

Now that you know something about C functions, let's review program 1.1, labeling all of its parts. (See figure 1.3.)

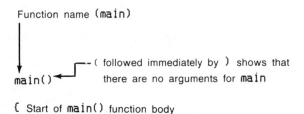

Function name (main)

main() ⟵ (followed immediately by) shows that there are no arguments for main

{ Start of main() function body

Function name (printf)

Indicates printf() as a function (start of argument list)

Argument for printf()

End of argument list for printf()

printf("This is my first C program. \n");

Statement terminator

} End of main() function body

Figure 1.3.

Remember that C functions can call other functions and that a function can call itself through a recursive function call.

Programming Style

In this section, we shall discuss style conventions that are used in writing C programs. Although several alternative styles are considered, you should select one style and use it in a consistent manner.

Lowercase versus Uppercase Letters

If you are accustomed to writing programs in BASIC, some parts of a C program may seem odd. For example, C syntax is different, and most C program statements are written in lowercase letters. Traditionally, uppercase letters are used for *symbolic names* and *constants* (which are discussed in Chapter 2), whereas everything else is written in lowercase letters. To program in C, you should develop the habit of writing in lowercase letters.

Placement of Braces and Indentation

C is a *free-form* language that doesn't care what style or format you use, as long as it is syntactically correct. The position of a statement is not important. Certain stylistic conventions, however, make a C program easier to read. For example, if program 1.1 were written as

```
main(){printf("This is my first C program. \n"); }
```

the program would compile and execute just as before. Although you are free to decide what style or format to use, some guidelines are offered in the sections that follow.

Braces and Functions

Braces group program statements together and mark the beginning and end of functions. The proper indentation and placement of braces make C programs easier to read (and debug!) than they would be otherwise.

The opening brace for a function is placed below (and aligned with) the beginning of the *function definition*. (For now, the terms *function definition* and *function name* will be used interchangeably.) The closing brace has the same alignment. For example, main() is a function that is defined in program 1.1. Note how the braces are aligned in program 1.3.

```
main()
{

    printf("This is my first C program. \n");

}
```

Program 1.3.

The definition of main() follows this convention because the opening and closing braces for the main() function are in vertical alignment. [In other words, they line up under the m in main().]

By indenting the statement that forms the body of main(), we can easily see where main() starts and ends just by looking at the braces. Legibility becomes more important as program complexity increases.

Using a different style, some programmers indent the braces one tab stop, as shown in program 1.4.

```
main()
    {

    printf("This is my first C program. \n");

    }
```

Program 1.4.

One reason for this style is that it makes the function name stand out more. Although you are free to choose either style, the one presented in program 1.3 is used throughout this text.

Braces *in* Functions

Braces can also group statements together in functions. Suppose that you want to add 1 to the variables x and y as part of a for loop. Program 1.5 suggests the style that should be used. (Dots represent the missing details.)

Notice the opening brace at the end of the for statement. The corresponding closing brace aligns with the f in for, just as the closing brace of the main() function aligns with the m in main().

Braces used in this way tell us two things: (1) for is not a function but rather a part of the C syntax (otherwise, the opening brace would be placed on the next line under the f in for); and (2) everything between the opening and closing braces is associated with the for loop. Braces group the statements that are controlled by the for loop into a single *block* of code. Because of the indentation of the code controlled by the for loop, you can easily see what statements are controlled by this loop. (The example in program 1.5 shows an inefficient way of incrementing the x and y variables and is not meant to represent good C coding practices. You will learn why later.)

```
main()
{
      .
      .
      .
    for (...) {          /* start of loop */
        .
        .
        x = x + 1;
        y = y + 1;
    }                    /* end of loop */
}
```

Program 1.5.

The space immediately following the word for also indicates that it is part of the C syntax but is not the name of a function. The compiler, however, doesn't care if the space is there or not. Although strong arguments can be made for including this space, many programmers omit it in day-to-day programming. You should decide whether to use such spacing or not. Be sure to select one style and use it consistently.

Program Variables

A *variable* is a data item that may assume any one of a set of values. Before a variable can be used in a C program, the programmer must state explicitly the type of variable being used. This statement is called the *definition* of the variable. All variables *must* be defined before they can be used in a program.

Note that in C precise meanings are given to the terms *define* and *declare*. If you declare a variable, you are simply telling the compiler what type of data is associated with the variable. If you define a variable, you not only declare what type of data the variable is to be, but you also allocate storage for the variable. The distinction between these two terms will become clear as we proceed through the book.

C has several data types, of which only int and char will be discussed here. (Some compilers may not support all the data types that C has to offer. These compilers may be called "subset" compilers. Because subset compilers are so widely available, the int and char data types are used so that the sample programs can be run on compilers that implement only a subset of C data types, as well as on other compilers.) A type int variable is used for integer numbers, and a type char variable is used for characters. Any variable used in a function *must be defined* before it can be used in a program statement.

For example, suppose a function named letter() uses a variable let_count to count the number of letters and uses delta_let to manipulate characters in the function. The function may appear as shown in code fragment 1.2.

```
letter()
{
      int let_count;      /* integer declaration */
      char delta_let;     /* character declaration */

      for (...) {
            .
            .
            .
      }
}
```

Code fragment 1.2.

In the function letter(), the variable let_count is defined as type int (an integer), and delta_let is defined as type char (a character).

A type int variable typically uses 16 bits when storage is allocated for it. An int data type is a signed value (that is, positive or negative) that normally is limited to the values -32768 through +32767 (roughly 2 raised to the 15th power, with one bit used as the sign bit). Because of this limitation, the programmer must give some thought to the range of possible values that type int variables may assume when the program is run.

You should know that some C compilers, particularly those on minicomputers or mainframe computers, use 32 bits for an int. Thus, the range of such ints is extended from -2,147,483,648 to 2,147,483,647. These compilers usually have a short int that requires 16 bits for storage and therefore has the same range as that of the int described in the previous paragraph. Let's assume, however, that an int uses 16 bits for storage for the remainder of this text.

The char variable definition, on the other hand, typically uses 8 bits for internal storage, of which only 7 are meaningful. The 128 (2 raised to the 7th power) unique values for type char variables describe the ASCII (American Standard for Coded Information Interchange) character set used for type char variables. Appendix A lists the ASCII character codes.

You can imagine the kind of trouble you can get into if you try to use a type char variable when you really want a type int. Compared to the reckless abandon of variables in most BASIC programs, a variable definition may seem a burden at first. You will quickly find, however, that a variable definition creates more efficient and maintainable code in the long run.

Variable Names

Variable names (or identifiers) consist of letters, digits, and the underscore (_), which counts as a letter. Names may be any length, but only the first eight characters (at most) are treated as significant by the compiler. The first character must be a letter, and upper- and lowercase letters have different significance. For example, the variable MAX is not the same as the variable max. Some examples of variable names are

    val3   red   screen5   high_bit   123_

Invalid examples include

    ?what   23rd   123   5th_bit   (sam)

You can use several conventions for selecting variable names. They are usually written in lowercase letters, with uppercase names reserved for symbolic constants. Use of the underscore may improve the readability of a variable name (for example, hat_size).

One convention is to use a single underscore (as in _bit) or a double underscore (as in __port) as the first letter for variable and function names in the standard library. The underscore reduces the chances of a "collision" between function and variable names in your library routines and those in a program (provided you follow this convention!). Be aware that many compiler manufacturers "reserve" variables with one or two leading underscore characters. To write portable programs, avoid using names with leading underscores.

Keywords

Certain identifiers are keywords and cannot be used as variable names. (See table 1.1.)

Table 1.1
C Keywords

auto	double	if	static
break	else	int	struct
case	entry	long	switch
char	enum	register	typedef
continue	extern	return	union
default	float	sizeof	unsigned
do	for	short	while
	goto		void

Each keyword will be explained as we proceed through the text. (An exception is entry, which is a reserved word but not yet implemented in C. enum and void will almost certainly become keywords in the near future, and they are discussed in later chapters.) Although C does not permit the use of keywords as variable names, a variable named auto_type is permissible because C treats it as one word and therefore does not consider it to be a keyword.

Simple Use of Variables and printf( )

Now that we know how to define numeric data in a program, let's write a simple program to print the sum of two integer numbers. Study program 1.6.

```
/* add two numbers and print result */

#include <stdio.h>

main()
{
    int sum, x, y;

    x = 20;
    y = 30;
    sum = x + y;

    printf("The sum of %d and %d = %d\n", x, y,  sum);
}
```

Program 1.6.

The three (type int) variables are defined with a single int definition in this program. The program can also be written as

```
int sum;
int x;
int y;
```

This multiple definition is common for line-oriented text editors, whereas the single definition in program 1.6 is normal for screen-oriented text editors. Pick the one you prefer.

Note that the type definition appears first because variables must be defined before they are used. A good programming practice is to leave a blank space between the variable definition(s) and the program statements that follow so that the type definitions will stand out.

The use of the printf() function in program 1.6 differs from that in program 1.1. printf() can do much more than just print strings. The general description of printf() is

```
printf("control string", argument1, argument2,...)
```

where the *control string* can be (1) ordinary text characters, such as "The sum of . . .", or (2) *conversion characters* to specify what and how data should be printed. The lead-in character for conversion is the percent sign (%). In program 1.6 the %d specifies that the conversion be an integer decimal number. The arguments that follow the control string match the conversion specifications from left to right. This alignment is shown in figure 1.4.

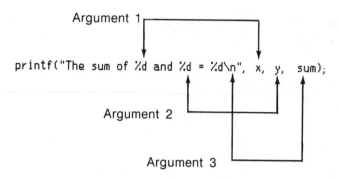

```
                Argument 1

printf("The sum of %d and %d = %d\n",  x,  y,  sum);

          Argument 2

          Argument 3
```

Figure 1.4.

The control string appears between quotation marks and contains three conversion specifications indicated by the three %ds in the string. These %ds signal that three integer arguments will follow the end of the control string, each argument separated by a comma. Because x is the first argument in the list, x is printed first, followed by y, and finally, by sum.

The variable values appear on the output device—usually a CRT (cathode ray tube, or screen)—at their respective places in the control string. For program 1.6 the output appears as

```
The sum of 20 and 30 = 50
```

Note how the value of each variable associates with its conversion specification (%d) in the control string. Equally important is the fact that the %ds are *not* printed as part of the output; their only function is to tell printf() how to print the values for the variables (in this example, integer decimal values).

If you look closely at the end of the control string, you will see the newline character (\n). This character causes the cursor to move to the extreme left of the screen and down one line. The character was added because some compilers leave the cursor exactly where the program ends, even after returning to the operating system. In program 1.6 the compiler might leave the cursor right after the 50, without the newline. With most compilers, however, positioning the cursor won't be a problem. You may want to leave out the newline to see whether it makes any difference in the cursor's position when the program ends.

In addition to decimal conversion, the variations in table 1.2 can be used with printf().

Table 1.2
printf( ) Variations

Numeric

%d	decimal (base 10)
%o	octal (base 8)
%x	hexadecimal (base 16)
%u	unsigned decimal
%e	scientific notation (double or float, 1.23E23)
%f	decimal (double or float, 123.456)
%g	%e or %f; select shortest

String

%c	single character
%s	string of characters

These variations (and others) will be used in later programs. [Chapter 5 presents a full discussion of printf().]

Some of the BASIC numeric counterparts are shown in table 1.3.

Table 1.3
BASIC Numeric Counterparts

C	BASIC-80	HP-3000
%4d	PRINT USING "####"	!%4I
%5. 2f	PRINT USING "#####.##"	!%7F2
%x	PRINT HEX$(X)	None

Style Summary

C is a free-form language. That is, braces don't have to line up, spaces can be used or left out after keywords, and so on. As mentioned previously, program 1.1 can be written as

```
main(){printf("This is my first C program. \n"); }
```

and it will compile and run exactly as before. Most people, however, find a "scrunched up" program more difficult to read. Adopting the style conventions in this chapter will help you write programs that are easier to read, understand, and maintain.

If you write in a commercial environment where more than one person is responsible for program development, all the programmers should agree at the outset on one style for writing C code. You'll then have a more productive shop in the future.

In a program of your own, try some of the `printf()` conversions presented in this chapter. Try rewriting program 1.6 so that it prints out the variables in hexadecimal and octal formats. Experiment by purposely leaving out a semicolon or a brace and using an undefined variable to see what happens. (Don't worry; it's difficult to "hurt" anything in hardware that is under software control.) Learning the kinds of error messages your compiler generates in a "controlled" situation will make program debugging easier later on. Devote as much time as you need to becoming comfortable with the C constructs in this chapter before proceeding to the next one.

2

Operators, Variables, and Loops

Operators are characters that designate mathematical or logical operations, such as +, -, etc. C makes available to the programmer an extensive set of these operators. Some are presented here, and others are discussed in later chapters.

Operators

C provides a full complement of arithmetic and relational operators. Arithmetic operators provide the basic mathematical operations to manipulate values. Relational operators perform logical tests on values. As you will see, arithmetic operators produce new arithmetic values whereas relational operators always resolve to a logical True (that is, 1) or a logical False (that is, 0).

Arithmetic and Relational Operators

Some of the more common arithmetic and relational operators are listed in table 2.1. (A complete list is found in tables 7.2 and 7.3 on pages 210 and 211.)

These operators are straightforward except for the equality/inequality operators. BASIC uses the equal sign both for assignment (X = X + 1) and as a test for equality (IF A = B THEN . . .), but C makes a distinction between the two uses.

Table 2.1

Operator Arithmetic:	Interpretation
+	add
-	subtract
*	multiply
/	divide
%	modulo (yields remainder of integer division)

Relational:	
>	greater than
>=	greater than or equal to
<	less than
<=	less than or equal to
==	equal to
!=	not equal to

The assignment operator is the same for both C and BASIC (for example, X = X + 1). In a test for equality, however, C uses a double-equal sign (==). With different operators, you can tell at a glance which operation is being performed.

The test for inequality in C is != as compared to <> in most BASICs. The exclamation point (!) means *not* in C.

if Statement

The use of a relational operator can be seen in an example of a simple if statement. The general form is

> if (*test criterion*)
>   *do this statement if test is True;*

Test criterion is used instead of the more formal "conditional expression" to reinforce the idea that a test is performed by an if statement to decide what the program will do next. The if statement in C does not correspond exactly to BASIC because C syntax does not use *then* as a keyword.

Program 2.1 illustrates how the if statement may be used.

In the example, we define *x* to be an integer variable and assign it a value of 3. We then use a printf() to print part of a message.

```
#include <stdio.h>

main()
{
    int x;

    x = 3;

    printf("\nThe variable x does ");

    if (x != 5)
        printf("not ");

    printf("equal 5\n");
}
```

Program 2.1.

Next, we execute the if statement with the relational operator != (not equal to) to test the value of x against the constant 5. Because x is equal to 3, it is logically True that x does not equal 5. Because the result of the test criterion "x != 5" is a logical True, the statement controlled by the if is executed and causes "not " to be printed on the screen. The program then prints the final message and displays the complete message as

```
The variable x does not equal 5
```

If we change the assignment of x to

```
x = 5;
```

you should be able to convince yourself that the message displayed becomes

```
The variable x does equal 5
```

Why? Because the if tests x against the value 5 and x now equals 5, the test criterion is now logical False, causing the statement controlled by the if to be ignored.

Now suppose that we want to control two statements with one if statement. Simply use braces to group the statements together, as in

```
if (g == h) {
    a = a + 1;
    b = b + 1;
}
```

Braces help if control multiple statements

Keep in mind that, without help, an if is designed to control one statement. The braces are used to group statements together so that the if can control multiple statements as though they were a single statement block.

Without the braces, only one statement is affected by the relational test associated with an if statement. Using the example in program 2.1, look at the following:

```
if (g == h)
     a = a + 1;
     b = b + 1;
```

Here the variable b will always be incremented even when g and h are not equal, because the statement

```
b = b + 1;
```

is not controlled by the if statement. The compiler sees the sequence as though it were written

```
if (g == h)
     a = a + 1;

b = b + 1;
```

Such mistakes can sometimes be difficult to spot because the syntax is correct, but the logic has gone astray. Braces must be used when a single if statement is to control two (or more) C statements.

if-else Statement

The if-else statement is an expansion of the simple if statement. The general form is

```
if (test criterion)
     do this statement if test is True;
else
     do this statement if test is False;
```

In C, an if-else statement functions like IF-THEN-ELSE in BASIC. Both provide a means of executing one of two possible sequences of code.

Let's suppose that we want to write a routine that prints Male if x is zero, but Female if x is other than zero. The BASIC program appears as

```
100 REM
110 REM    0= MALE      OTHERWISE FEMALE
120 REM
130 IF X=0 THEN PRINT "MALE" ELSE PRINT "FEMALE"
140 (rest of program)
```

The C version appears in program 2.2.

```
/* 0 = male otherwise female */

#include <stdio.h>

main()
{
    int x;

    if (x == 0)
        printf("Male\n");
    else
        printf("Female\n");
}
```

Program 2.2.

The if statement tests the value of x and prints Male if x equals zero. That is, if the test criterion (or conditional expression) of whether x equals zero is True, then the statement immediately following the if is executed; otherwise, the else statement is executed.

As previously shown, two or more statements can be grouped together with braces. The compiler treats multiple statements after if-else as a single statement when such statements are enclosed by braces and executes those statements as a single unit. For example, if we want to increment a variable to count the number of males and females, we can alter the routine in program 2.2, as shown in program 2.3.

If x does not equal zero (you don't know what x equals in program 2.2 because x hasn't been assigned a value yet), *neither* the printf("Male") *nor* the incrementing of is_male will be executed. If the braces were removed, is_male would always be incremented. In fact, the program would not compile because the else would no longer be tied to its if. Why? If braces are not used with an if-else statement, *only the first statement* after the if and else is affected by the *test criterion*. (The if-else behaves the same as a simple if statement in this case.) Also note the spaces before and after else (that is, } else { rather than }else{).

```
/* Ø = male otherwise female and count each */

#include <stdio.h>

main()
{
    int x, is_male, is_female;

    is_male = is_female = Ø;

    if (x == Ø) {
        printf("Male\n");
        is_male = is_male + 1;
    } else {
        printf("Female\n");
        is_female = is_female + 1;
    }
}
```

Program 2.3.

Placement of Braces with if-else

Program 2.3 illustrates several style conventions used in C. Notice how the braces are used when if-else has compound statements. One convention is to place the opening brace for the if statement on the same line as that of the if and to align the closing brace with the i in if.

The else statement follows the same format. The opening brace on the same line as the else, and the closing brace is aligned with the closing brace of the if. If no compound statement were with the if, the closing brace would align with the e in else, as shown in code fragment 2.1.

```
if (x == Ø)
    printf("male\n");
else {
    printf("female\n");
    is_female = is_female + 1;
}
```

Code fragment 2.1.

Following is a summary of the if-else style conventions for compound statements:

```
if (test criterion) {
        True: then do these compound statements;
} else {
        False: do these compound statements;
}
```

Try the routine in program 2.3 with and without the braces to see what happens. (Suggestion: Add a line that prints out the values of is_male and is_female.) How does the compiler handle the else?

A Common Mistake with if

Examine program 2.4 closely to find the error in coding.

```
#include <stdio.h>

main()
{
    int x;

    x = 5;

    if (x = 3)
        printf("x equals 3\n");
    else
        printf("x equals 5\n");
}
```

Program 2.4.

A quick glance at the program suggests that the programmer wanted the message x equals 5 to be displayed. However, because we used the assignment operator in the if test, x is in fact assigned the value of 3, and we end up printing x equals 3, which is just the opposite of what we wanted to do.

Why does the wrong message get printed? Keep in mind that a value of zero is treated as logical False in C, and any nonzero value is logical True. Because x now equals 3, which is not zero and therefore viewed as logical True, the wrong message is printed. Try changing the if statement to

```
if (x = 0)
```

and see what is printed. More importantly, explain why the message is printed.

Another common mistake is illustrated in program 2.5.

```
#include <stdio.h>

main()
{
    int x;

    x == 5;

    if (x == 3)
        printf("x equals 3\n");
    else
        printf("x equals 5\n");
}
```

Program 2.5.

In this example, we erroneously used the relational operator to test equality (x == 5) instead of for assignment (x = 5). This C syntax is perfectly valid, but testing for equality was probably not what we intended to do.

So what happens to x in program 2.5? The compiler will test to see whether x does equal 5 and will do nothing more. Now make the modifications as shown in program 2.6.

```
#include <stdio.h>

main()
{
    int x;

    x = 1;
    x = (x == 5);

    printf("The value of x is %d\n", x);
}
```

Program 2.6.

The program first assigns the value of 1 into x. The next line is a bit strange but will help explain what is going on in program 2.6. First, the program tests to see whether x equals 5 (that is, x == 5). Because this is a logical test, the result of the test will be either logical True (value of 1) or logical False (value of Ø). In the example, because x equals 1 and not 5, the test is logical False. Therefore, the result of the expression (x == 5) is Ø. The program now looks at the assignment operator (x =) and assigns the result of the *logical test* into x. Thus, x now equals Ø, which is the result of the logical test of x == 5. The sequence can be viewed as

```
x = (x == 5);
x = (1 == 5);
x = (logical False);      /* because 1 not equal to 5 */
x = (Ø);
x = Ø;
```

To prove to yourself how all of this works, run program 2.6 and observe the results. Now rerun the program after changing x = 1 to x = 5. Now go back to program 2.5 and explain what happens to x in that example.

Finally, does anything change if the statement is written as follows?

```
x = x == 5;
```

(Hint: You will need the help of tables 7.2 and 7.3 (pages 210 and 211) to answer this question.)

Keep these relational-arithmetic quirks in mind; they may save you some debugging headaches later on.

Logical Operators

C has a complete range of logical operators, as listed in table 2.2.

Our discussion centers on AND, OR, and logical negation. (The other logical operators are discussed later in the book.) Not all logical operators are available on subset compilers.

You must remember that, for logical operations in C, if a test criterion or conditional expression evaluates to 0, then the test is considered logical False. Any nonzero value is logical True. For an illustration, we can rewrite program 2.2 so that the routine appears as shown in code fragment 2.2.

The test criterion has been changed from x == Ø to just x. The interpretation, therefore, is that if x is True (nonzero), the value for x must be nonzero and female. This modification reverses the way

Table 2.2
Logical Operators

Operator	Interpretation
&&	AND
||	OR
<<	shift left
>>	shift right
!	logical negation
~	one's complement
&	bitwise AND
|	bitwise OR
^	bitwise exclusive OR
-	unary minus

```
/* male if Ø, female otherwise */

if (x)
     printf("Female\n");
else
     printf("Male\n");
```

Code fragment 2.2.

Male and Female are handled in the program; Female is now printed if the test criterion is True.

In its complete form, the routine might appear as it does in program 2.7.

```
#include <stdio.h>

main()
{
    int x;

    x = Ø;

    if (x)
         printf("Female\n");
    else
         printf("Male\n");
}
```

Program 2.7.

Because x has been assigned a value of zero, Male is printed. Why? The value of zero is a logical False value for x. When the test evaluates to logical False, the first statement following the if is skipped, and the else is executed.

Although using this format may seem to be a complicated way of doing things, you will see the format often in C programs. Try the routine in program 2.7 to verify that it works as described. Can you modify the program to use the NOT (!) operator but still preserve the logic? Give it a try.

Variables: Incrementing and Decrementing in C

Adding or subtracting the value one (1) from a variable is so common that C has a set of special operators for just this task. Program 2.8 shows how program 2.3 looks after it is rewritten, using these special operators.

```
/* program to print male-female and increment count */

#include <stdio.h>

main()
{
     int x, is_female, is_male;

     is_female = is_male = x = 0;
     if (x) {
          printf("Female-n");
          ++is_female;
     } else {
          printf("Male-n");
          ++is_male;
     }
}
```

Program 2.8.

The notation ++is_female is the equivalent of is_female = is_female + 1; thus, is_female is incremented by one. To subtract one from is_female, you use --is_female. Following is a summary:

```
++n;      increments variable n by 1
--n;      decrements variable n by 1
```

Note that incrementing/decrementing occurs *before* any other logical operation. Thus, the variable n is incremented or decremented before it is "used" in the program. For example, if is_female is 99 when the routine is entered, the program statement

```
x = ++is_female;
```

will assign x the value of 100 because is_female is incremented before its value is assigned to x. When ++ appears before the variable name, ++ is a *preincrement* operator. In other words, the variable is incremented before being used in another expression.

What happens if you want to increment is_female *after* x is assigned? The program statement

```
x = is_female++;
```

assigns the current value of is_female to x and *then* increments is_female. If is_female is 99 when the routine is entered, x equals 99, and is_female is 100. When ++ appears *after* the variable name, ++ is a *postincrement* operator. Thus, the variable is first used in an expression and *then* incremented.

The *postdecrement* operator works the same way and is written as

```
x = is_female--;
```

which decrements is_female after x has been assigned.

To test your understanding of how the pre- and postincrement and pre- and postdecrement operators work, answer this question: Would it make any difference which of these operators was used in program 2.8? [Try assigning any nonzero value to x and then adding a printf() to print the value of x, using the pre- and postdecrement operators.]

The compiler performs incrementing and decrementing operations according to the type of data being used. Most implementations of C use 16 bits of storage for each integer number. Let's suppose that the integer numbers are in an array named x. If we want to increment the contents of the x[1] array element, we can use the ++x[1] operation. The compiler will correctly increment the integer at x[1]. That is, the compiler increments the value found at x[1], not just the first byte of x[1].

C also allows you to increment/decrement memory addresses. (See Chapter 4 for more information.) If a variable x contains the address of p[1] and you want the address of p[2], a ++x will appear to increment x by 1. The variable x must actually be incremented by 2, however, because integer numbers require 2 bytes for storage. To get the next number in the array, you must increment the *address* by 2. Fortunately, the compiler takes care of this adjustment for you. For the moment, remember that increment/ decrement operations for variables with memory addresses are "scaled" according to the size of the type of data being used. More will be said about incrementing addresses in Chapter 4.

Loops

Looping is the repetition of a group of program instructions until a particular condition is reached. C provides for several loop constructs.

while Loops

A while loop executes a group of program statements as long as a test criterion is True. The basic format for the while loop is

```
while (test criterion True) {
    execute these statements;
}
```

Braces are needed only if compound statements (more than one) are controlled by the while statement. These braces serve the same purpose as those in if-else and if statements.

Program 2.9 uses the while construct to increment a variable from Ø to 30000.

The new statements in program 2.9 will be explained in the order of their appearance in the program.

#define

The #define preprocessor directive defines a *symbolic constant* for use in the program. In this case, the ASCII code that rings your computer terminal's bell (or buzzer) is defined as BELL. (See Appendix A for the ASCII codes.) The #define directive causes the

```
/* increment variable to 30000 */

#include <stdio.h>

#define  BELL 7         /* ASCII code for terminal bell */
#define  GOAL 30000     /* how many iterations          */

main()
{
    int x;

    putchar(BELL);

    x = 0;
    while (x != GOAL)
        ++x;

    putchar(BELL);
    printf("Loop finished\nat the bell.\n");
}
```

Program 2.9.

compiler to substitute an ASCII 7 into the program wherever the symbolic constant BELL is found.

Notice that a semicolon does not appear at the end of the line containing the #define. No semicolon is used for two reasons. First, a #define is a directive to the compiler for the preprocessor pass. As such, the #define is not a C statement but an instruction to the compiler. Second, a #define causes a literal text replacement for a symbolic constant. If a program has

```
#define  BELL   "\007";       /* note wrong use of semicolon */
.
printf(BELL);
```

the resulting textual substitution after the preprocessor finishes becomes

```
#define  BELL   "\007";       /* note wrong use of semicolon */
.
printf("\007"; );
```

which causes an error message because of the extraneous semicolon. Keep in mind that a #define is a textual substitution.

Similarly, we used a #define to set the value of GOAL to 30000. In this case, the number 30000 is substituted for GOAL wherever GOAL appears in the program. Although we could simply use 30000 directly for this example, the #define is easier to change if multiple occurrences of 30000 are in the program.

The #define statement can also be used to produce a single-byte bit pattern in octal or hexadecimal form. The general format is

```
' \nnn'        octal
' \xnnn'       hexadecimal
```

where nnn is the octal (base 8) or hexadecimal (base 16) number that corresponds to the desired bit pattern. (Appendix 2 explains both the octal and hexadecimal numbering systems.) For the ASCII bell code in octal, we could write

```
#define BELL '\007'          /* octal */
```

or

```
#define BELL '\x07'          /* hex */
```

The advantage of using #define is that you can change the constant's definition by changing the #define BELL (or GOAL), rather than searching through the entire program to alter each occurrence. Obviously, the #defines must appear in the source code before they are used. Normally, the #defines should appear at the beginning of your program.

putchar(c)

The putchar(c) function is a part of the C library and is used to write a single character (the argument c in the function) to the standard output device (usually the CRT). C does not provide for input or output statements as part of the language; they are library functions.

The printf() statement can also be used to ring the terminal bell, as in

```
printf("%c", BELL);
```

(Remember that the %c option to printf() is used to print a single character on the output device. In this case, the bell will sound on the terminal.)

Because the while statement controls one program statement (for example, ++x), braces are not needed. As the program executes, the test criterion (x != 30000) is checked after each pass through the loop. When the test proves False and x equals 30000, control passes to the putchar() and printf() functions, and the program ends.

If the test criterion is False on entry into the loop, the statements controlled by the while will not be executed. Therefore, statement(s) controlled by a while loop may not be executed at all.

To Be or Not To Be #defined

Consider the following situation: Your terminal uses an ASCII 12 to clear the screen of the CRT. You also know, however, that all your friends will want to run a copy of your program when you are finished with it, but they do not have the same terminal. How should you solve the problem?

Clearly, using a #define is preferable to using an ASCII 12 whenever you plan to use a clear-screen code in the program. The #define means that your friends only have to change the #define to their code instead of searching the entire file for ASCII 12's and making the changes.

Is there a better solution? Perhaps.

Suppose further that your "program" is not really one program, but ten programs that are all chained together. Even though you used a #define CLEAR 12 in each program, your friends must edit, recompile, and link all ten program files so that CLEAR is properly defined in each one.

Now suppose that you write a clear() *function* instead of using a #define. For your terminal the function may appear as shown in code fragment 2.3.

```
#define CLEAR 12

clear()
{
    putchar(CLEAR);
}
```

Code fragment 2.3.

Then whenever your program needs to clear the screen, you simply call clear(). Finally, you finish your program, give it to your friends, and warn them that they must change the clear() function to suit their terminal. Suppose that their terminal uses an ASCII ESC (that is, decimal 27) followed by an asterisk (*). They might change the clear() function, as shown in code fragment 2.4.

Note that because your friends' terminal takes two ASCII characters, the #define must be a string of two characters. Because putchar() can only handle one character at a time, your friends must use printf() rather than putchar().

```
#define CLEAR "\033*"

clear()
{
    printf(CLEAR);
}
```

Code fragment 2.4.

What does all of this save you? To answer, first ask yourself the question, Is there any longer a need to edit all ten program files, changing each #define and putchar(), or do my friends just need to edit the clear() function? Obviously, only the clear() function requires any editing. Your friends must still recompile and relink the programs, but less editing is involved.

Although changing the #define to a function call may not seem important, keep in mind that whenever you edit a file, you risk making a mistake. Whenever you can reduce the amount of editing needed, you lessen the chance of something being changed inadvertently. This advice is not etched in stone, but you should think about it when multiple programs are involved.

Special printf( ) Characters

If you look closely at the printf() statement in program 2.9, you will see \nat in the quoted string. When you run the program, the printed message is

```
Loop finished
at the bell.
```

The \n is an escape sequence for a character constant called a *newline* character, which sends a carriage-return, line-feed sequence to the output device. (The newline escape sequence serves the same purpose as a single PRINT statement in BASIC.)

Other common sequences are \t for a tab and \b for a backspace. To see their effect on the output, try substituting these two sequences for the first \n in the program. What happens and why?

Escape sequences are *single* characters. But the tab sequence, for example, looks as if it should be treated as two characters: the backslash and the t. But the backslash is a "lead-in" for the compiler, telling it that what follows is a special character. Without such a character, how could the compiler distinguish between a simple *t* and a tab in a quoted string (in other words, "\t this is a t")? [The backslash functions like the conversion character (%) in printf(). The % is there, but it's not printed by printf(). Both the backslash (\) and the percent sign (%) are only "attention getters" for the compiler.]

When encountering a backslash, the compiler reads the next character and substitutes the appropriate ASCII value for the character. For example, the \b (backspace) sequence is changed to a decimal 8 in ASCII, and the \t (tab) becomes a decimal 9. Both are single characters when the compiler is finished. After the backslash has served its "information" purpose, it is discarded by the compiler.

do-while Loops

The do-while loop is constructed much like a simple while statement:

```
do {
    statement(s);
} while (test criterion);
```

Because the test criterion is evaluated at the bottom of the do-while loop, the statement in the loop is *always executed at least once*. If the test criterion is True, then the statement is executed again.

The closing brace for the do-while loop is placed immediately before the while statement. This practice is recommended even when only one statement is controlled by the while loop; leaving out the braces makes it easy to forget about the do lurking above.

Now rewrite program 2.9, using a do-while statement. Does this revision have any effect on the program?

for Loops

The for loop in C differs from its BASIC counterpart in that all the relevant information is in one place. As a first step toward understanding this difference, let's write the BASIC equivalent of program 2.9:

```
100 X=0:REM                          (1)          (2)
110 FOR J=0 TO 30000:REM     STEP INITIAL & TERMINAL VALUES
120     X=X+1
130 NEXT J:REM               TEST FOR ANOTHER PASS
140 END:REM                          (3)
```

Three functional parts make up a FOR-TO-NEXT loop. The *first* part initializes the loop control variable J, which is set to 0 in line 110. The *second* part indicates the terminal value of J for the loop—30000 in this case. The *third*, and less obvious, part tests the loop control variable J to determine whether it has reached the terminal value.

The NEXT J statement in BASIC increments J. (With the STEP function, you can increment the loop control variable by some value other than one.) NEXT J then compares the loop control variable with the terminal value to determine whether the loop should be executed again. If so, control is sent to line 120 until the terminal value is reached.

→ The for loop in C places all three parts in the for statement itself and, as a bonus, makes them visible to the programmer in one place:

```
        (1)                (2)              (3)

for (initialized value(s); test criterion; loop increment) {
    statements controlled by loop;
}
```

The *first* part of the for loop uses an assignment expression for one or more variables. If more than one variable is initialized, each must be separated by a comma. The *second* part uses some form of relational operator (for example, !=, ==, <=, etc.) or test. The *test criterion* may be complex (involving a logical AND, OR, etc.). The *third* part of the loop often consists of incrementing one or more variables, but any other valid expression can be used.

The C equivalent of the loop in program 2.9 is shown in code fragment 2.5.

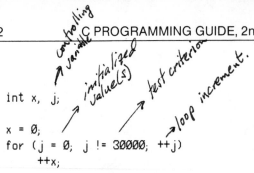

```
int x,  j;

x = 0;
for (j = 0;  j != 30000;  ++j)
    ++x;
```

Code fragment 2.5.

Referring to the assignment and relational operators, you can see that j is initialized to 0. (Assignment uses a single equal sign.) This expression is the equivalent of the first part of the FOR-TO-NEXT loop and establishes the initial value(s) for the loop.

The test criterion compares j to the terminal value 30000. (The operator != tests for inequality.) This comparison corresponds to the test performed by the NEXT of the FOR-TO-NEXT loop in BASIC.

The third part of the loop increments the controlling variable (++j). As long as j does not equal 30000 (in other words, the test is True), the statements controlled by the loop are executed. All three parts of the for C loop structure are visible to the programmer *in one place*.

Remember that the test criterion *must* be a relational operator or test. If the test is for equality, it must use the double-equal sign. From the preceding example, a common mistake made is

```
for (j = 0;  j = 30000;  ++j)
```

In this case, 30000 is assigned to j whenever the for loop is executed. As a result, the test criterion of the for loop (j = 30000) will always be True, the maximum value reached by j is 30001, and the for loop will execute forever. (Refer back to the discussion of the if statement if any of this is unclear.)

Most compilers cannot detect this error because j = 30000 is a valid expression. The test criterion should be written with the relational operator: j == 30000. This kind of error becomes less likely as you gain experience with C.

The for loop in C is more flexible than its BASIC counterpart. For example, you can move the incrementing of x into the for statement itself. The new lines are

```
for (j = 0;  j != 30000;  ++j,  ++x)
    ;                          /* note semicolon */
```

Now you increment x within the construct of the for loop itself. Note that multiple expressions like ++j and ++x must be separated by a comma operator. [You saw the comma used in Chapter 1 to separate multiple arguments in the argument list for volume(). Because arguments are viewed as expressions by the compiler, the purpose of the comma is the same in both examples: to separate multiple expressions.]

The statement terminator (the semicolon) is necessary because a for loop must control at least one program statement. In this case, it is a *null*, or "do nothing," statement.

When a for loop controls a compound statement, braces must be used. But when such a loop controls a single statement, no braces are needed.

Notice that the three major parts of the for loop are separated by *semicolons*, and that any additional arguments to a part of the loop are separated by *commas*. (The ++j and ++x must be separated by a comma.) Would code fragment 2.6 accomplish the same task?

```
int x;

for (x = 0; x != 30000; x++)
    ;
```

Code fragment 2.6.

Try it and see.

C also differs from BASIC in that more than one variable can be initialized at a time. If we want to preserve the distinction between the loop counter j and a variable x, we can rewrite the loop as shown in code fragment 2.7.

```
int j, x;

for (j = 0, x = 0; j != 30000; j++, x++)
    ;
```

Code fragment 2.7.

In this instance, both j and x are initialized by assignment expressions in the first part of the loop. As mentioned previously, each initialized variable must be separated by a comma.

You can also omit the expressions for all three parts of the loop in C. In this case, the test criterion always evaluates as True, resulting in an infinite loop. In other words, the statement for (;;) will execute forever, unless one of the statements controlled by the loop caused control to branch out of the loop.

One common bug you may encounter with the for loop is shown in code fragment 2.8 (assuming y is assigned before the loop).

```
int sum, x, y;

sum = Ø:
y = 5;
for (x = 1; x <= y; x++);     /* <-- big trouble */
        sum = sum + x * y;
```

indicates a do-nothing loop.

Code fragment 2.8.

The semicolon after the for loop essentially says that we have a do-nothing loop, when we really want to calculate the sum of the x and y products. With C's free-form syntax, it makes no difference where you put the semicolon when you enter the program. The formatting style—not the compiler—helps you read the code.

What the preceding code actually does becomes clearer when it is written as that in code fragment 2.9.

```
int sum, x, y;

sum = Ø;
y = 5;
for (x = 1; x <= y; x++)
        ;                     /* now it's more obvious  */
sum = sum + x * y;
```

Code fragment 2.9.

This code, however, is not what we actually want. sum equals 25 in this case. (Why?) The fact that the compiler gives a reasonable answer rather than an error message makes the bug just that much worse: the program runs and generates a nonzero value for sum. Never place a null statement on the same line as that of the for loop.

break: Exiting a Loop

Loops examine a set of data until a specified value causes the loop to be exited. The break statement allows us to exit a for, while, or do-while loop before the terminal value is reached.

Program 2.10 shows how the break statement is used.

In this example, the for loop is set up as an infinite loop, but it also increments x with each pass through the loop. The if statement tests whether x is greater than or equal to 30000 (the test criterion

```
#include <stdio.h>

main()
{
    int x;

    x = 0;

    for (; ; ++x) {
        if (x >= 30000)
            break;
    }

    printf("%d\n", x);
}
```

Program 2.10.

requires a relational, not assignment, operator) on each pass through the loop. If the test is False, the loop continues to increment x because the break statement is not executed.

Eventually, x will equal 30000, which causes the break to execute and sends control to the next statement "outside" the loop. (Note the use of braces with the for loop. Try running the program without them. What happened and why?) If all goes well, the printf() displays the value of x on the CRT.

continue: Ignoring Code within a Loop

Let's suppose that you have a home alarm system that is monitored by a C program and that a function called monitor() scans a number of alarm devices and reports to the program. In all cases except the number 999, everything is all right with the alarm system. When the number 999 is received, however, the program initiates a complex procedure that does everything from turning on the lights to calling the police.

In such a situation, we don't want a statement that breaks us out of the loop. We simply want to bypass the alarm section of the code—unless we receive a 999. Code fragment 2.10 illustrates how the continue statement might be used.

```
for (; ;) {
     if (monitor() != 999)
          continue;

     lights_on();        /* turn on lights */
     alarm();            /* sound alarm    */
     call_police();      /* call police    */

}
```

Code fragment 2.10.

An infinite loop continually monitors the alarm system by repeated calls to monitor(). Many modern office buildings use such a loop for automated heating and cooling.

The call to monitor() returns a number; only 999 indicates a problem. As long as monitor() does not return a 999, the if statement is True, and the continue statement is executed. The continue statement causes the next pass through the infinite loop, calls to monitor(), and bypasses the calls to the three alarm functions.

You can avoid the continue statement by rewriting the preceding program. (See code fragment 2.11.)

```
for (; ;) {
     if (monitor() == 999)
          break;
}
lights_on();        /* turn on lights */
alarm();            /* sound alarm    */
call_police();      /* call police    */
```

Code fragment 2.11.

In code fragment 2.11, we stay in the infinite loop as long as monitor() doesn't return a 999. When this happens, we execute the break statement, exit the for loop, and activate the alarm system. The break statement often makes the code more direct and easier to understand. For some uses, however, the continue statement is a better choice. You must make this decision yourself.

Because loops are used frequently in programming, try all the examples in this chapter before moving on. Experiment with different loop constructs (for example, leaving braces out and adding printf() statements) to get a "feel" for them. After you have tried variations of the routines provided, create some programs of your own. Check your compiler's library for any functions that may be useful in the programs you create.

Appendix 2
Binary, Octal, and Hexadecimal Numbering Systems

Despite all the things a computer can do, it only understands two things: on and off (or 1 and 0). In other words, a computer understands only data presented in base 2, or binary. Although this format is convenient for the computer, binary doesn't work well for people who are used to decimal (base 10) arithmetic.

Base 8 (octal) and base 16 (hexadecimal) numbering systems are often used for communicating with a computer. We saw in Chapter 2 that character constants can be represented in octal format. Before we discuss the octal and hexadecimal numbering systems, however, we must first consider binary numbers.

Binary Numbering System

Only two states are possible when working in binary: on and off. That is, each *binary digit*, or bit, can be only on or off at any given moment. The *on* state, represented as a 1, is usually some positive reference voltage in the computer (for example, plus 5 volts). The *off* state is represented as a 0 (for example, 0 volts). The following discussion uses the ASCII character set as a point of reference because ASCII characters are used frequently in C.

The ASCII (American Standard Code for Information Interchange) character set uses 7 data bits. With bit 0 defined as the least significant bit (LSB), ASCII characters use only bits 0 through 6, for a total of 7 bits. For example, a typical microcomputer uses an 8-bit data bus to communicate data throughout the system. However, when the microcomputer uses the ASCII character set, the most significant bit (MSB), which is bit 7, is usually ignored or stripped away. Therefore, when we talk about ASCII characters, we are actually concerned with bits 0 though 6; the MSB is not used.

Because a bit can be either on or off at any given moment, 256 (that is, 2^8) distinct patterns are possible in an 8-bit data word. Each bit can be thought of as 2 raised to a power, as shown in figure 2A.1.

Power	2^7	2^6	2^5	2^4	2^3	2^2	2^1	2^0
Binary	0	1	0	0	0	0	0	1
Decimal	128	64	32	16	8	4	2	1
Bit position	7	6	5	4	3	2	1	0

In this figure, each bit has a numeric value that equals 2 raised to a power equal to its bit position. The decimal values are listed to make the relationships clearer.

When the MSB is not used, the largest number we can represent in the ASCII character set is 127. Because 0 is also included in the set, 128 different bit patterns are available for the ASCII character set.

In table 2A.1, the bits in positions 0 and 6 are on (numbering starts with 0 and reads from right to left); thus, the decimal numbers 64 and 1 are "turned on," for a total of 65. If you look up this number in the ASCII table in Appendix A, you will find that decimal 65 is the ASCII code for the letter A. The binary representation for A is 01000001. (Notice that the MSB is off.)

In the "good old days" (?), programming was done in binary—not that programmers wanted to program in binary, but no alternative existed. No high-level languages were available for small computers. Many of the early small systems did not even have keyboards. Programming was done through switches that turned the various bit positions on or off. You could always tell the ardent programmers in those days by the "binary blisters" on their fingers.

Unfortunately, because people don't think in terms of binary numbers, communication with the computer is that much more difficult. In an attempt to make things easier on us (and to make programmers more productive), other numbering systems are often used: octal (base 8) and hexadecimal (base 16).

Octal Numbering System

The octal numbering system divides binary digits into fields of 3 bits each, starting with the LSB (0) data bit. If you refer to table 2A.1, you will see that 3 bits let us represent 8 numbers (0 through 7).

Table 2A.1

Binary	Octal
000	0
001	1
010	2
011	3
100	4
101	5
110	6
111	7

Obviously, we need to be able to count higher than 7. If we want a number larger than 7, we must "roll over" into the next field of 3 bits. The binary representations for 8, 9, and 63 are shown in table 2A.2.

To represent a number greater than 63, we must go to a third field. However, because 8 bits is the width of our data word, the third field can use only 2 bits. Therefore, the largest octal number possible in the third field is 3. The binary, octal, and decimal representations for the 3 fields are shown in table 2A.3.

Table 2A.2

Field 2	Field 1 = 6 bits total
001	000 = 8
001	001 = 9
111	111 = 63

Table 2A.3

	Field 3	Field 2	Field 1	=	8 bits or 1 byte
Binary	11	111	111		11111111
Octal	3	7	7		377
Decimal	128+64	32+16+8	4+2+1	=	255
Binary	01	000	001		01000001
Octal	1	0	1		101
Decimal	64	0	1	=	65

As you can see, binary 01000001 is 101 in octal and 65 in decimal. Again, both are the ASCII representation for the letter A.

To use the character constant A in C, you may write

```
#define LETTER_A    '\101'
```

Although you can define the letter A in this way, most C programmers prefer

```
#define LETTER_A    'A'
```

because here, more than in octal representation, you can easily understand what is being defined.

Appendix A lists the ASCII codes in the binary, octal, and decimal numbering systems. A significant advantage of octal over binary is that the same information can be conveyed in 3 octal digits rather than 8 binary digits.

Hexadecimal Numbering System

Hexadecimal (hereafter called *hex*) is a base 16 numbering system that uses 2 fields of 4 binary digits for each hex number. Because 4 binary digits are available, we can present 2^4 combinations, or 16 unique numbers. As always, because 0 is a valid number, the 4 binary digits can represent a number from 0 through 15.

Because we must be able to count from 0 through 15, we encounter a problem when we try to represent the numbers 10 through 15 as single characters. For this reason, the letters A through F are used to represent the numbers 10 through 15, as shown in table 2A.4.

Table 2A.4

Binary	Hex	Decimal
0000	0	0
0001	1	1
0010	2	2
0011	3	3
0100	4	4
0101	5	5
0110	6	6
0111	7	7
1000	8	8
1001	9	9
1010	A	10
1011	B	11
1100	C	12
1101	D	13
1110	E	14
1111	F	15

To represent a number larger than 15, we must again "roll over" into the next 4-bit hex field. The binary-hex representation for 16 is shown in table 2A.5.

Table 2A.5

Field 2	Field 1	
0001	0000	
1	0	= 16 (decimal)

Therefore, *a 10 hex is 16 decimal*. Note the base 2 power relationship, as presented in figure 2A.1. That is, 2 raised to the fourth power is 16.

Problems can arise, however. If you see the number 10 written somewhere in a program, how can you tell if the number represents 10 decimal or 10 hex? Octal is less of a problem, especially when all 3 fields are represented. (For example, 012 is 10 decimal.) Because of this potential area of confusion, C expects to find 0x before a hex number. To use a hex constant of 16, we write it in the program as 0x10.

If we want to define the same constant in octal, we must supply a leading 0. *In octal, a decimal 16 is defined as 020.* Therefore, an ASCII escape character is *27 decimal, 0x1b hex,* or *033 octal.* Representations of the letter A are shown in table 2A.6.

Table 2A.6

0100 0001	(binary)	=	A	(ASCII)
1 0 1	(octal)	=	A	
4 1	(hex)	=	A	
64 + 1 = 65	(decimal)	=	A	

The hex number 0x41 is the ASCII representation of the letter A. You should be able to verify that the largest 8-bit number in hex is FF, which corresponds to 255 decimal. It also follows that

11111111 (binary) = 377 (octal) = FF (hex) = 255 (decimal)

One advantage of hexadecimal numbers is that 2 hex numbers can represent 8 binary digits; hex numbers are shorter. Because hex numbers use fields of 4 binary digits, numeric representations in hex are easier, for computers use address and data fields that are even multiples of 4 bits.

You should review Appendix A to reinforce the concepts discussed here.

(If the question ever comes up in a trivia game, 4 bits are called a nibble, and 8 bits are called a byte. In the spirit of promoting standards, the following names are offered for larger bit patterns:

    12 bits = munch
    16 bits = chomp
    32 bits = gulp

In the future, we might talk about a kilochomp or megamunch of memory, gulp processors, byte-chomp addressing modes and other exciting things. Or you may want to forget this paragraph altogether.)

3

Writing Your Own
Functions

One of C's strong points is that new functions can be created and used over and over again in different programs. Once a function has been written and tested, it doesn't need to be written again. It becomes part of your "personal" C library. Some of the ground rules for writing and using functions are discussed in this chapter.

Form of C Functions

If you have a compiler that supports data types other than int and char, you probably noticed when you reviewed the functions in your standard library that they appear more "complex" than those discussed thus far. It is not that the functions are more complex but that we have only dealt with a simple call to the function. Until now, functions have been hidden in the dark of a "black box" called the standard library. Now is the time to bring them to light.

Obviously, you must create a function before you can use it. In more formal terms, you need to define the function. *All C function definitions have the general form* shown in figure 3.1.

Although this form may seem intimidating at first, it really is not. To make the definition more concrete, let's assume that we need a simple function to cube a number passed to the function. Let's use a crude function first, then make it more intelligent later. (See code fragment 3.1.)

The first line of the function gives us the information shown in figure 3.2.

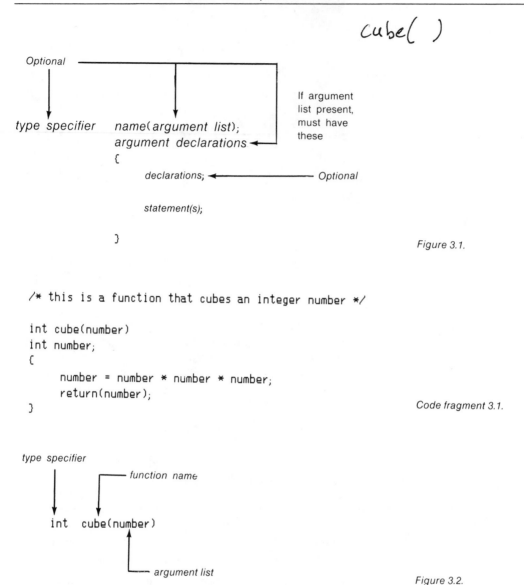

cube( )

Figure 3.1.

```
/* this is a function that cubes an integer number */

int cube(number)
int number;
{
    number = number * number * number;
    return(number);
}
```

Code fragment 3.1.

Figure 3.2.

Type Specifier

A *type specifier* indicates what type of data is returned to the calling function. You use a type specifier when the function returns a data type other than an integer. C provides for many data types (such as char, double, float, and long and short ints, as well as others). For the time being, we shall stick with the simple data types, int and char.

If you omit the type specifier from your function definition, the compiler will assume that you want an integer. When you write a function to return a character from the function, the compiler converts the character to an integer anyway. Therefore, the *default type specifier* for a function is int. Any function definition that does not include a type specifier defaults to a function that returns an int.

Given what you have just learned, you really do not need the type specifier for the function in code fragment 3.1. If we omit the type specifier, the function will default to an integer function. If the function is designed to return a floating-point number (that is, a number that might have a fractional value), a float type specifier is needed.

This default points out one potential trouble spot. If a function is to return something other than an integer, but the type specifier is left out of the function definition, you will probably get "garbage" back from the function. Even worse, the function may return reasonable values in one case but garbage in another. Remember that the absence of a type specifier may be the cause if a function seems to have a mind of its own! Because of the potential for creating problems by not declaring a type specifier, you should explicitly state the type specifier for all functions that you write.

Type Specifiers and Return Values

As you now know, the type specifier dictates the data type that is returned from a call to a function. Program control leaves a function in three general ways. First, the function can execute a statement that returns a specific value to the function. An example of how such a statement is used is shown in code fragment 3.2.

In this example, whatever the value of x may be, its value will be assigned as an integer into variable b after the return from the function. The programmer's responsibility is to ensure that x is within the permitted values of an integer number.

Throughout this text, the terms *calling function* and *called function* are used. In code fragment 3.2 main() is the calling function because it is calling func1() to perform some task for main(). The called function, therefore, is func1(). If func1() in turn called some other function, func1() would be a calling function. Can a calling function also be a called function? Yes, because C allows a function to call itself (that is, through a recursive function call).

```
#include <stdio.h>

main()
{
    int b;

    .                   /* the calling function  */
    b = func1();        /* for func1() is main() */
    .

}

int func1()             /* The called function   */
{

    .

    .


    return x;
}
```

Code fragment 3.2.

As expected, when a called function does its job, program control returns to the calling function. In code fragment 3.2, when the called function [func1()] finishes its job, control returns to the calling function [main()]. In code fragment 3.2, control returns to main() and prepares for the assignment of the return value from func1() into variable b.

The second way we can return control from a function is shown in code fragment 3.2.

In this example, the function tests variable i against some special value (perhaps a number that indicates the end of a table search) and returns control to the calling function. Note that no value is being returned from the function. Program *control*, not a value, is returned to the calling function.

Where's the problem? The problem is that an unspecified value gets assigned to variable b in main(). No specified return *value* is being returned from the function. Depending on the compiler, you may get a valid integer value (which is, after all, what the type specifier says we should get from the function) or simply two bytes of junk from the stack or somewhere else. Clearly, we should not use a function call in an assignment statement like the one shown in code fragment 3.3 when no value is returned from a function call.

```
main()
{
     int b;

     .
     .
     b = func1();
     .

}

int func1()
{
     int i;

     .
     .
     if (i < SPECIAL)
          return;

     .
}
```

Code fragment 3.3.

The second potential problem is similar to the first one and occurs when we "fall off" the end of a function. In other words, the function has no return statement. Code fragment 3.4 shows an example.

```
main()
{
     int b;

     .
     b = func1();
     .

}

int func1()
{

     .
     .
     .
}
```

Code fragment 3.4.

In code fragment 3.4 a series of statements are executed, but no return value statement (for example, return x) is in the function. The result is the same as that in code fragment 3.3; two bytes of junk will be assigned into b in main().

The message should be clear: Don't rely on just the type specifier to tell you what is returned from a function. If the documentation for a function omits the type specifier, don't assume that a valid integer value is returned from the function. Most compiler manufacturers will tell you exactly what is returned from a call to a function.

The risk of confusion relating to type specifiers and "fake" return values is sufficiently serious that many compiler manufacturers have created a new data type called void. Compilers that use void treat it as a keyword; therefore, void should not be used as a variable name in your programs even if your compiler does not follow this new convention. (If you do use void as a variable name and try to recompile the program on a compiler that does support the void keyword, the program will draw an error message.) If fact, void will almost certainly become a keyword in the future, and we will treat it as one now.

Compilers that do support void as a keyword will have functions that are defined as the following:

```
void      func.2()
{
          .

          .
}
```

The purpose of such a function definition is to tell the programmer never to use this function in an expression, as in the assignment statements illustrated in code fragments 3.3 and 3.4.

If your compiler does not support void as a keyword, you can use a simple #define, such as

```
#define void int
```

When the preprocessor sees the word void in a program, the preprocessor will substitute int in place of void. The programmer, however, will still see the word void as the type specifier and will be warned not to use the (junk) value returned from the function in an expression.

Function Names

In our "cube" example, we gave the function the clever *function name* of cube. Generally, the character representation of a function name follows the same rules for variable names: (1) the function name must start with a letter or underscore character, (2) digits are permitted after the first letter, and (3) only the first eight characters are significant.

This third rule may cause problems. Often three steps are required to produce an executable C program. The sequence can be viewed as the following:

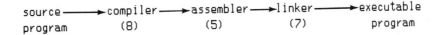

```
source ────────►compiler ────────►assembler ───►linker ───────►executable
program          (8)               (5)          (7)            program
```

This diagram indicates that the compiler recognizes 8 significant characters for variable and function names in the source program, but that the assembler is limited to 5 characters and the linker is limited to 7.

Now suppose that you have in your program the function declarations shown in code fragment 3.5.

```
on_val1(a)          on_val2(b)
int a;              int b;
{                   {

        .                   .
        .                   .

}                   }
```

Code fragment 3.5.

Perhaps the functions are used to turn on values 1 and 2 in some control process. The compiler can distinguish between the two function declarations because it has 8 significant characters for function names. Even the linker can tell the difference despite its limitation of 7 characters.

The assembler is the source of the problem because both functions appear to have the function name on_va. The assembler will issue a "duplicate definition" (or its equivalent) error message. You should check your compiler's documentation to determine what the actual limit is for function and variable names; the limit may be more or less restrictive than in the example presented here.

The function name has one additional requirement: the name must have opening and closing parentheses following it. The parentheses enable the compiler to distinguish between a variable and a function name. To the compiler, main is a variable, whereas main() is a function.

On a related matter, whether a blank space can appear between the function name and the parentheses is not clear. Consider the following:

```
func1 ()      /* first form  ???? */
func1()       /* second form (ok) */
```

Not all compilers will recognize the first form as a function, but all compilers will recognize the second form. To play it safe, you should use the second form. Because all compilers recognize the second form, it is the more portable of the two alternatives.

Function Definitions, Semicolons, and Declarations

When you define a function, the semicolon (;) should not appear after the function name. In omitting the semicolon, you are telling the compiler that you are *defining* the function, not using it.

The line

```
int cube(number)       /* correct way */
```

informs the compiler that you are about to define a function named cube. The line

```
int cube(number);      /* wrong way */
```

will produce a syntax error on some compilers—and even stranger errors on others.

Finally, the line

```
int func1();              /* note missing argument list */
```

is a valid statement in C and *declares* (not defines) that func1() is a function that returns an integer value. The line declares what comes back from func1(); it is a single statement. A function definition, on the other hand, describes the code that *is* the function. (Recall that a declaration does not allocate storage, but a definition does.) Program 3.1 will help illustrate this distinction.

```
main()
{
        double atof();          /* declaration */
        double x;
        char c[25];

        .
        .
        x = atof(c);
}

double atof(s)                  /* definition */
char s[];
{

        .
        .
        return d;
}
```

Program 3.1.

In main(), we declare that atof() (ASCII-to-float) is a function that returns a double data type. If we didn't have this declaration in main(), main() would think that atof() returned an integer value. Because the double data type (discussed in full in Chapter 6) requires 8 bytes, atof() will send 8 bytes back to main(), but main() would only use 2 of those bytes because it thinks atof() is (by default) an integer function. Therefore, we must *declare* atof() in main() as a double so that main() knows what data type atof() is sending back from the function call. The declaration of atof() in main() tells main() to grab 8 bytes, not just 2 bytes, from the call to atof(). Forgetting to declare functions that return noninteger values to the calling function is a common C programming mistake.

Now look at the definition of atof(). Because its type specifier is double, the compiler knows that the code which follows defines what atof() does and will allocate enough space (such as 8 bytes) to send back a double to main() when the function finishes its job.

Therefore, a function declaration gives us just enough information to know what type of data a function returns, whereas a function definition tells us how that data type is actually produced. The difference between a function declaration and definition is not only a fine one, but also an important one.

Declarations give you a glimpse. (No storage is allocated for the compiler to examine.) Definitions let you study the whole picture. (Storage is allocated.)

Argument List

An *argument list* contains the variables that pass to the function any information needed to perform the function's task. The argument list may contain zero or more arguments. In the examples presented thus far, we have seen `main()` use no arguments, `volume(length, height, width)` use three arguments, and `cube(number)` use one argument.

Whether a function needs an argument depends on the purpose of the function. A function that requires "outside" help probably needs an argument list. If the function is self-contained and needs no information other than what the function creates itself, no argument list is necessary. (You will learn later in this chapter why no list is needed.)

Argument Declarations

Each variable in the argument list of a function must have an *argument declaration*. If no argument list is provided for a function, no argument declaration is needed. Now let's compare the `main()` and `cube()` functions in code fragment 3.6.

```
main()      versus    cube()

main()                int cube(number)
{                     int number;
          .           {
          .
          .                   .
}                             .
                      .
          }
```

Code fragment 3.6.

Although `main()` has not needed any arguments thus far, `cube()` needs to know the number that is to be cubed. Because a number is "handed" to the `cube()` function from "outside" itself, `cube()`

needs to know what type of data it has just received. This communication is the purpose of the argument declarations.

Any variable in an argument list that is not explicitly declared defaults automatically to an int; such a declaration is known as a *default argument declaration*. To avoid future problems, however, you should develop the habit of explicitly declaring *all* arguments in a function call, even when they are integer variables. You are not as likely to forget to declare noninteger data types if you declare all variables. Therefore, you should ignore the default and declare all function arguments. In the program examples, all arguments are declared explicitly, even when they are integers.

A semicolon follows each line of an argument list declaration, as shown in code fragment 3.7.

```
    /* right */                          /* wrong */

int cube(number)                  int cube(number)
int number;   /* note semicolon */  int number  /* semicolon missing */
{                                 {

       .                                 .

}                                 }

int volume(l, h, w)               int volume(l, h, w)
int l, h, w;                      int l, h, w,   /* not a comma */
{                                 {

       .                                 .

}                                 }
```

Code fragment 3.7.

For the cube() function, a semicolon follows the single argument declaration. For volume(), we have declared l, h, and w to be integers and grouped them into one argument declaration. The last argument in the group, w, is followed by a semicolon. Omitting the semicolon or substituting a comma is unacceptable and will produce an error when the program is compiled.

(If you are familiar with the concept of a stack, you probably already know why argument declarations are necessary. These declarations tell the compiler how many bytes must be popped off the stack to "fill in" the variables that are being passed to the function.)

Finally, the argument declarations must occur before the opening brace of the function body. If we stretch things a bit, we can view everything between the opening and closing braces (that is, the function body) as being "created" by the function and everything else as being "handed to" the function. Logically, the arguments that have been handed to the function must be declared before the function body.

Function Body

The opening brace marks the beginning of the function body, and the closing brace marks the end of both the function body and the function definition. The declarations and statements needed to perform the function's task are located in the function body.

All variables in the function body that were not declared as part of the argument list declarations must be declared or defined in the function body itself before the variables are used. If, for example, a function uses variable j as a loop counter in the function body, an int j; definition must appear first in the function body before j is used, as shown in code fragment 3.8.

```
int junk(stuff) /* function name and argument list  */
int stuff;       /* argument declaration             */
{                /* start of function body           */

    int j;       /* internal variable definition     */
        .
        .
}                /* end function body and definition */
```

Code fragment 3.8.

The variable stuff is handed to the function as part of the argument list and must be declared before the start of the function body (before the opening brace). The variable j is used internally by the function; j does not need any "outside" help to do its task in the function body. Therefore, j is defined in the function body (between the opening and closing braces).

In our cube( ) example, number is the only variable used in the function body. Because number was declared as an argument declaration, the variable doesn't need to be defined or declared again. In fact, a second definition or declaration of number will draw an error message from the compiler.

The RETURN Statement in C

The RETURN statement in BASIC sends program control back to the point at which the subroutine was called. A simple return statement in C does the same thing. If a C function does not have a return statement in it, a return is performed when the closing brace of the function is encountered.

For example, if we want a simple function that will pause for the user to press a key before continuing, we can use either of the two versions presented in code fragment 3.9.

Code fragment 3.9.

```
void pause_1()
{
      int c;

      c = getchar();
      return;

}
```

```
void pause_2()
{
      int c;

      c = getchar();
}
```

Neither of these functions needs outside data passed to it to perform its task, so no argument list or declaration is present. We do, however, use variable c in the function body; therefore, c must be defined before it is used. (Is the variable c really needed? No, because we never use c in the function.)

The function getchar() is a common library function used to get a single character from the keyboard. [c is declared as an int rather than a char for several reasons, which will be explained in Chapter 8. For now, we shall abide by the compiler's documentation, which says that getchar() returns an int.]

Although the function pause_1() makes explicit use of the return statement, pause_2() does not. However, because the closing brace of the function body is found after the call to getchar(), pause_2() also returns control to the calling program. Both programs perform identically.

Returning a Value from a Function

The `return` in C is not limited to a simple return from the function; `return` can also pass a value back to the code that called the function. If we replace the `return` in `pause_1()` with the statement

```
return (c);
```

we can return whatever key was pressed by the user to the code that called `pause_1()`. Any expression can be contained between the parentheses [for example, `return (x + y)`]. The expression can be as complex as you want, but only one value will be returned.

We can omit the parentheses around the returned value in a simple expression; thus, we can write

```
return (c);
```

as

```
return c;
```

As you gain experience in C, however, you will find yourself writing return values as complex expressions. In those cases, you probably will need parentheses to make sure that the complex expression is evaluated correctly. Because a single rule is easier to remember than all the exceptions, you should develop the habit of placing parentheses around any and all return expressions, no matter how simple they are.

What data type is returned from `pause_1()`? (Hint: What does the type specifier for the function say? And if the type specifier doesn't say anything, what does that tell you?)

Keep one final rule in mind: You cannot define a function within a function. For example, writing the routine shown in code fragment 3.10 is illegal.

Now that you have some idea of what a function is, you may be wondering why an argument list is needed in the first place. After all, in our `cube()` example, `number` already exists in `main()`, so why all the mystery about passing arguments? The next sections provide an explanation.

```
int func1()
{
      int func2()          /* wrong */
      {



      }
}
```

Code fragment 3.10.

Scope, Storage Class, and the Longevity of Variables

Variables in C differ in behavior from those in most BASICs. In a BASIC program, a variable retains its value throughout the program. In other words, it is a "global" variable.

For example, if you set X to equal 3 at the beginning of a BASIC program, then call a subroutine that assigns X the value of 5, X will be "globally" changed to have a value of 5 throughout the BASIC program. Even if X is never used after its first assignment, x will still retain the assigned value for the entire program, and the value of x will be present everywhere in the program.

This "globality" of BASIC variables is also a fruitful area for program bugs. How many times have you changed the value of some variable only to find that it produced some other, undesired "side effect" (that is, a bug) elsewhere in the program? If you've ever written a BASIC program in which you felt you were running out of variable names, you've probably experienced such bugs. Such side effects can be minimized in C; this inherent protection is provided by the storage classes that variables may assume.

C has four *variable storage classes*: (1) external (extern), (2) automatic (auto), (3) static, and (4) register. The scope of variables will also be considered as we proceed. The *scope* of a variable refers to the part(s) of a program for which the variable is visible or available for use. To appreciate what scope actually means, however, we need to consider what a compiler does when it generates a C program.

Compiler and Linker

We cannot do justice here to the inner workings of a compiler. We can serve our purposes, however, by highlighting some of the operations performed by the compiler.

The first step in writing a C program or function module is to use a text editor to write the C program. After you finish writing the program, you can save it on disk as source.c, which becomes the source code for the program. The *source code* is really little more than an ASCII text file with statements that are (we hope) in agreement with the rules of C.

The text file source.c becomes the input file for the C compiler. The compiler checks the source file to make sure that the file agrees with the syntactic and semantic rules of C. If the file doesn't meet the rules, then the compiler will generate error messages to help you locate and correct the errors. For example, suppose you write a routine like that in program 3.2.

```
#include <stdio.h>

main()          /* not a good program */
{
    int sum, price;

    sum = price * quantity;
    printf("\nThe sum is %d\n", sum);

}
```

Program 3.2.

The compiler will generate an error message because the variable quantity has not been defined. We know that we want quantity to be an integer, but the compiler doesn't know that. The compiler must generate an error message because it doesn't know how to reference quantity. The compiler doesn't know what type of variable quantity is, what it should contain, or anything else about it.

If quantity were defined in the proper manner in program 3.2, where would the printf() function come from? We already know that printf() comes from the library of C functions, but how does printf() get "tied in" with the program? To simplify the process of finding printf(), the compiler tells itself, "I've found printf() and it's a function. I'll store some preliminary stuff about it now and let someone else worry about the details."

After the compiler finishes examining the source file and finds that everything is okay, it "outputs" an intermediate file. (Let's call it source.o.) The contents of the intermediate file will vary among compilers but may be assembly language or some form of intermediate language (for example, pseudocode or a relocatable format) developed by the designer of the compiler. You don't need to know the specific contents.

The intermediate file (source.o) becomes the input file for the linker. The primary purpose of the *linker* is to take all the information generated by the compiler and "link" that information to form an executable C program. The linker is the "someone else" for whom the compiler generated the preliminary information about printf().

What happens when the linker comes to printf()? Depending on the compiler, it will have generated the information needed by the linker to resolve the missing printf() function. Typically, the compiler will direct the linker to look in the C library for the code necessary to complete the printf() function.

The important thing to remember is that the compiler must communicate to the linker the way in which missing variables or functions needed in the program are to be handled. Keep this rule in mind when you read about the scope and storage classes of variables and functions in the next several sections.

External Variables

External describes a storage class that can be applied to either variables or functions. Any variable that is declared outside a function is an external variable. Because you cannot define a function in another function, all C functions have an external storage class. Consider program 3.3.

In program 3.3, variable x is an external variable that is available to func1() and func2(). This variable is declared as being type int and is globally available throughout the program in the same way that variables are global in a BASIC program, because the declaration of x comes before the rest of the program. The scope (or visibility) of x, therefore, is from the beginning to the end of the program.

```
#include <stdio.h>

int x;    /* external storage class because it is not */
          /* declared inside a function               */

void func1(), func2(), func3();

main()
{
    x = 1;
    printf("x = %d\n", x);
    func1();
    printf("x = %d\n", x);
    func2();
    printf("x = %d\n", x);
    func3();
    printf("x = %d\n", x);
}

void func1()          /* multiply x by 1 */
{
    x = x * 1;
}
void func2()          /* multiply x by 2 */
{
    x = x * 2;
}
void func3()          /* multiply x by 3 */
{
    x = x * 3;
}
```

Program 3.3.

In view of our discussion of the compile-link process, because x is defined outside the function, the compiler tells the linker that x is available to any function that needs the variable. Note that variable x is used in the func1(), func2(), and func3() functions, but that none of these functions has a definition for x. (In other words, an int x; definition does not appear in any of the three functions.) The linker has no problem with this lack of definition because the compiler told the linker that x is available to any function in the program. The scope of the external variable x is global throughout the program.

Note what this discussion means: x is available to each function without your having to pass x as a function argument. Furthermore, if func1() modifies the value of x, the new value of x will be available directly throughout the program; you don't have to use a return (x) in a function call. To verify this process, type in program 3.3.

Now consider program 3.4.

Program 3.4.

```
main()
{
      x = 4;
      .

}

int x;

func1()
{
      x = x * 1;
}
```

The compiler is going to have a problem with program 3.4, and the program is going to have another problem. First, when the compiler sees x = 4, it has not yet read what x is. The definition of x comes *after* we have used it. Thus, the compiler will issue an error message. The second problem for the programmer is that, even though func1() knows about x, the result of the multiplication will be zero because external storage class variables are (supposed to be) initialized to zero by the compiler.

The lesson here is consistent with what has already been presented: x is visible from the point of its definition to the end of the file. But because x was defined after main(), main() cannot use x.

Other possibilities for external variables are available. C lets you write individual functions and save them on disk for inclusion in other programs through the linker. Consider program 3.5, in which file 1 is the source program file [that is, file 1 has the main() in it], and file 2 contains a previously written function. [Only one file can have a main() in it. Otherwise, the linker wouldn't know which main() is the correct one for marking the start of the program.]

In program 3.5 variable x in file 2 is an external variable because x is defined outside the function. File 2 can be linked with file 1 to

```
File 1                          File 2

main()                          int x;
{
      extern int x;             func2()
                                {

}                               }

func1()
{
      int x;

}
```

Program 3.5.

form a complete program. *When two (or more) files are combined, however, the scope of an external variable will run from only the point of declaration to the end of the file in which the external variable is declared.* Thus, the x in file 2 is available to anything in file 2 that might need the variable, but file 1 doesn't know that the x in file 2 exists. Therefore, the external storage class for x in file 2 does make the variable available throughout file 2, but not in file 1.

If we want main() to have access to the external variable defined in file 2, we must use the extern declaration in main(). The

```
extern int x;
```

declaration in main() causes the compiler to generate instructions to the linker to look outside file 1 for x. Think of the "extern" part of the declaration as meaning to "look in some other file for." The declaration in main(), therefore, says to "look in some other file for int x."

The extern declaration of x is necessary, however. If we tried to use x in main() without any declaration for x, we would get an "undefined variable" error message from the compiler.

The x defined in func1() of program 3.5 is internal (and private) to the function func1(); the variable's scope is limited to func1(). x is a variable totally different from those found elsewhere in the program. Whatever is done to x in func1() has no impact on any other x used in the program. In other words, a variable declared within a function has priority over external variables with the same name in that file. Now study figure 3.3.

In figure 3.3, if main() wants to use variable x, it must be declared in main() as extern int x. The use of x parallels the discussion of

```
            main()
            {
                 extern int x;
            }
File 1──

            void func1()
            {
                 int x;
            }

            int x;      /* scope of x limited to file 2 */
            func2()     /* unless extern elsewhere       */
            {
File 2──     }

            void func3()
            {
            }

            void func4()
            {
File 3──         extern int x;
            }
```

Figure 3.3.

program 3.5. Obviously, only one variable named x can be exter-nally defined in a given program; otherwise, we would draw a "multiply defined variable" error from the compiler.

Any function in file 2 [func2() and func3()] can use the variable x without an extern int x declaration in the function because x was externally declared in file 2. The x is external because it was de-clared before func2() and func3() were defined. Because x is ex-ternally declared first in file 2, all functions located in file 2 have access to x. When file 2 is compiled, the compiler makes x globally available to all functions in the file. The compilation of file 2 par-allels the discussion of program 3.3.

The use of variable x in func4() must be declared. If the variable is declared extern int x, the external x from file 2 is used. When file 3 is compiled, the extern int x declaration causes the compiler to leave instructions for the linker to look outside file 3 to resolve the variable named x.

Don't forget that a simple int x definition in any one of the functions overrides the externally defined x from file 2. In figure 3.3 func1()

is one example of this process. Regardless of what func1() does to x, the function will not alter the externally declared x in the program.

The scope of the external variable x in file 2 is limited to func2() and func3(). Either function can use x without any declaration of x. That is, func2() and func3() can use the external variable x without using an int x or extern int x declaration.

To make x visible in any other file requires the use of the extern int x declaration in any function that needs x. The compiler-linker's job is to find the external variable (assuming the programmer has done things correctly).

One final point is that typically the linker will automatically search the library to resolve any undefined functions in the source file. If you have written and compiled a function but not yet included it in the library file, most linkers allow you to specify files to be searched that are outside the library. Check your linker's documentation for details on how this search is done.

Automatic Variables

The scope of an *automatic* variable is limited to the function in which the variable is defined. This means that the automatic storage class is the *default storage class* for C variables in a function. If a variable defined in a function has the same name as an external variable defined elsewhere in the same program, the automatic variable definition will have priority over that of the external variable.

Automatic variables have values that are "local" to the function in which the variables are defined. That is, if x is defined in a function, we can change the variable as much as we want in the function without having any effect on the value of x used elsewhere in the program. The local values of automatic variables minimize the side-effects, or bugs, mentioned previously.

Program 3.6 illustrates how automatic variables work.

In program 3.6 x is an (automatic) integer variable in both main() and prove_it(). Run this program and look at what is printed. What happened? Why? What value for x was printed in prove_it()?

```
/* show the effect of automatic storage class variables  */

#include <stdio.h>

void prove_it();

main()
{
    int i, x;

    for (i = 1, x = 0; i < 10; i++, x++) {
        printf("\n The value of x in main: %d\n", x);
        prove_it();
    }


}
void prove_it()
{
    int x;

    printf(" The value of x in prove_it: %d\n", x);
}
```

Program 3.6.

If we want, we can use the auto keyword for either definition of x. The definition

   auto int x;

is the same as

   int x;

when x is defined within a function. However, no commercial C code that I've seen has ever used the auto declaration because it is the default storage class for variables. As a general rule, you can safely use the default in this case and omit the auto keyword from definitions within functions.

Remove the definition of x in prove_it() and try to run the program again. Any problems? Now move the definition of x in main() so that x is an external variable and run the program again. What effect did the change have? Why? Try removing the definition of x in prove_it(). Any difference? You should experiment with a simple program like program 3.6 until you are sure that you understand the distinction between external and automatic storage classes as well as their scope.

Beginning C programmers are often tempted to make all variables external. Resist the temptation, for it will only lead to trouble as programs become more complex. Scoped variables are a real asset once you get used to them, and they make program debugging and maintenance much easier.

Values and Scoped Variables

External variables retain whatever value they currently have throughout the program or until they are assigned a new value in the function. C language specifications state that variables with the external storage class are initialized to zero. (Some subset compilers, however, do not provide for initialization of variables and may not initialize external variables to zero. Consult your documentation if you are in doubt.)

Automatic variables, on the other hand, "die" once the function is completed. Reentering the function does *not* mean that you can expect to find in the function any variable with the value it had when you left the function. Indeed, C can just about guarantee that all variables will have garbage in them until they are assigned some value in the program. The value of x printed in the `prove_it()` function in program 3.6 will be whatever happened to be in memory at that location when the program was run (in other words, garbage).

Automatic and `register` variables are *not* initialized to zero as in some BASICs. Variables with the external and `static` storage class are (supposed to be) initialized to zero by the compiler. If you want a variable to be zero, it is best to assign it explicitly as such.

Although storage class and scope may seem a burden, they do force you to be explicit about the initial values of variables. No doubt you've had bugs that were caused because you didn't initialize a variable to the proper value. You will find this type of bug much less frequent in C.

static Variables

`static` variables can be either internal or external. If a variable is defined to be `static` within a function, the variable is local to that function. Such a variable is like an automatic variable but with one important difference: *static variables remain "alive" even after a function is completed.* In other words, whatever value was in the static variable the first time the function was completed will be in the static variable the next time the function is called.

For example, suppose you need a variable to keep a running total of the number of times you enter a function. You can code the function in question with a static variable, as shown in code fragment 3.11.

```
int func1()
{
      static int x = Ø;

      .
      .
      ++x;
      return x;
}
```

Code fragment 3.11.

The declaration static int x in code fragment 3.11 causes the compiler to do things differently than if x were an auto variable. When func1() is compiled, the compiler generates a memory address for x and initializes it to zero. Because we have initialized the variable as part of the definition, the variable is *not* initialized again at run time. Therefore, when we first load the program that uses func1(), x has a known address and an initial value of zero. (We actually don't need to initialize x to zero; the compiler should do this for us. We're just playing it safe.)

When func1() in code fragment 3.11 is executed for the first time, the static int x definition is not executed because the compiler already took care of x when we compiled the program. It's as though the definition isn't even there at run time (that is, when the program is run). When the ++x is executed, the value of x is incremented to equal 1. On the next call to func1(), the memory address that holds x is now equal to 1 because the previous call to x set it to that value. Therefore, x will equal 2 when we leave the function this time. We can repeat the function call to func1() as many times as we want, and x will retain its previous value.

One small alteration, however, does change things. Consider code fragment 3.12.

In code fragment 3.12, we removed the initializing value of 0 from the definition of x to a separate statement. In this case, x can never

```
func1()
{
    static int x;

    x = 0;
    .

    .
    ++x;
    return x;
}
```

Code fragment 3.12.

have a value greater than 1 because we reset x to zero whenever we enter the function.

Clearly, code fragment 3.12 will do a poor job of keeping a running total of the number of times we execute func1(). Keep this in mind when you use an internal static variable.

An *external static variable* behaves in the way you expect: it is available to only those functions defined in the same file in which the static variable is defined. In figure 3.3 earlier, if x were defined as static int x; in file 2, only func2() and func3() would have access to x. An external static definition, therefore, makes the variable available to those functions in the same file but invisible to any other file. The scope of an external static variable is the file in which it is defined.

Think about the difference between an external static storage class and the external storage class previously discussed. The static external storage class has a scope that is limited to the file in which the class is declared. The external storage class permits the scope to extend to any other file that might need the variable.

Of what use is the external static storage class? Because both variables and functions can be defined as external *static*, this storage class makes those variables and functions "invisible" outside their source file. Thus, you can create in one file a function or variable that will not conflict with another function or variable outside that file, even when other files use functions or variables with the same name.

Note that we can use the static keyword as a type specifier for a function, as in the example

```
static int func1()
{

    .
    .
    .

}
```

Reasons for using. Static storage class

This function definition means that we can have a function named func1() defined in another file, but the compiler will view them as two distinct functions because the life of the static int func1() "lives" only within the file in which this function is defined.

There are two primary reasons, therefore, for using the static storage class. It is used (1) when a variable needs to "pick up" where it left off the next time the function is called (such a variable is called an internal static variable), or (2) when you want to limit the scope of an external variable or function to a particular file. static definitions also minimize the chance of collision with other functions or variables that share the same name but are defined in different files.

Finally, a technical point about internal static variables often improves execution speed relative to automatic variables. Because the compiler allocates space for internal static variables at compile time, the execution speed for internal static variables is somewhat faster than the speed for automatic variables. The reason is that automatic variables are usually referenced off the stack. Some address calculations are therefore necessary whenever an auto variable is referenced in a function. static variables, on the other hand, have a known address at run time; thus, no calculations off the stack are necessary. The amount of time saved will vary from one compiler to another, and the time is affected by how frequently the variable is used.

register Variables

Used when execution speed is important!

register variables in C are normally used when execution speed is important. The idea behind the register storage class is to tell the compiler to reserve one of the CPU (Central Processing Unit) registers for a variable. Because data manipulation in a register is faster than in memory, execution speed is enhanced. The register storage class is intended for variables that will be used intensively (for example, loop counters).

Obviously, the only declarations allowed for a register variable are data types (such as int and char) that can fit in a single register.

Because the number of CPU registers in a computer is limited, you have no guarantee that a `register` will actually be used. The compiler, however, will try to use a CPU register for the variable if a register is available.

Check your compiler's documentation to see whether the external, `static`, and `register` storage classes are supported. (All compilers must support automatic variables.) Some subset C compilers do not support the `static` and `register` storage classes. With the limited number of registers available (especially in a microcomputer), you have no guarantee that a `register` variable will actually be used, even if it is supported.

Privacy and Functions

At the beginning of the chapter, we saw that an argument list gives the function the necessary data it needs to perform its task and that the external storage class permits us to make variables available to a function without using an argument list. But what happens when an argument list is needed? (We are ignoring the external storage class for the moment.) For an illustration, let's suppose that the following statement appears in `main()`:

```
int cub_num;

cub_num = 5;
```

Because `cub_num` is defined in `main()`, `cub_num` is an automatic variable. Somewhere in memory an integer variable named `cub_num` is created and assigned the value of 5. Let's assume that the compiler uses memory locations 20000 and 20001 in which to store `cub_num`, as suggested in figure 3.4.

20000   20001

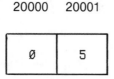

Figure 3.4.

What we have is the variable `cub_num` with a value of 5, which the compiler arbitrarily placed at memory locations 20000 and 20001. Now, let's say that we want to use `cub_num` in our `cube()` function, passing `cub_num` to `cube()`.

In main(), we might use the following line to print the cube of cub_num:

```
printf("The cube of %d is %d\n", cub_num, cube(cub_num));
```

This causes 5 and 125 to be displayed on the screen.

The function call cube(cub_num) is unique in C because, when the printf() is executed, the call to cube(cub_num) creates a temporary copy of cub_num for use by the function. In other words, the compiler causes some variable, such as temp_1, to be created and used in the call to cube(cub_num). Where the copy is created is up to the compiler, but let's assume that the location is 20100. Figure 3.5 shows what we would see in memory.

Figure 3.5.　　　　　　variable cub_num　　　　　variable temp_1

For the function main(), cub_num resides in memory, starting at location 20000. However, what the cube() function receives for cub_num is located at 20100. In effect, the function call seems to be cube(temp_1). Both variables have the same value, but they are *not* the same variable. The term *call by value* means that the function receives a *copy* of the value, not the variable itself.

If this illustration is taken a step further, when the return(cub_num) in cube(cub_num) is executed, the relevant memory locations appear as shown in figure 3.6.

Figure 3.6.　　　　　　variable cub_num　　　　　variable temp_1

In the printf() statement

```
printf("The cube of %d is %d\n", cub_num, cube(cub_num));
```

cub_num is printed with the same value that it had in main()— that is, 5. When cube(cub_num) is printed, temp_1 is actually printed.

Functions receive copies of the value(s) passed to them. As a result, a function cannot alter the value of the variable that appears in the function's argument list, because the function receives a call-by-value copy of the argument, not the actual variable itself. A function fiddling around with memory locations 20100-20101 cannot possibly alter the value stored at memory location 20000-20001. This restriction explains why variables are local to a function and not global like the variables in BASIC. Unlike BASIC, C has privacy, which is an advantage for the programmer.

At the risk of getting ahead of ourselves, how would you alter cub_num for further computations in the program? The astute reader has probably already figured out that all you have to do is give the function the *address* where cub_num resides in memory and tell the compiler *not* to use a copy of cub_num. (We shall see how to pass the address of a variable in Chapter 4.)

Arrays: A Privacy Exception

An exception to the privacy rule on function calls occurs when an array variable is used in the argument list. An *array* is a grouping of similar data types that share a common name. A *character array*, for example, is an array of alphanumeric characters grouped together under one name. Two examples of array declarations are

```
char message[10];
int num[10];
```

They permit up to ten different characters to be associated with the variable message and ten numbers to be referenced by the variable num.

To examine the first element of an array, use message[0] for the character array and num[0] for the integer array. Selecting an element of an array is much like subscripting in mathematics. The only difference is that *all arrays in C start with element zero*. Therefore, the fifth element in the character array is actually message[4]. (For those who aren't used to thinking about array element zero, just keep in mind that the element you want is one position lower than you might think!)

In C, arrays create an exception to the privacy rule discussed in the previous section. When an array variable is passed to a function, the function receives the location of the original array. In using the preceding example, if cub_num is an array that starts at memory location 20000, cube(cub_num) receives the address of the cub_num array (that is, 20000) with instructions not to create a copy of the array. The function will receive the memory address of cub_num[0], which means that functions can directly alter the data in any element of the array. This is true for any type of array.

Why the exception for arrays? One reason for this exception is the manner in which a compiler handles arrays. Another reason is the need to conserve memory. Given that arrays tend to be large collections of data, whereas other (nonarray) variables are discrete units, duplicating arrays in function calls might tend to chew up large chunks of memory quickly.

Bear the distinction in mind: Unless told otherwise, *functions receive copies of all variables except arrays.* Algorithms for programs in C should reflect this fact.

Designing a C Program

The variety of data types and function calls in C gives a programmer a greater degree of control over the code than is available in many languages. At the same time, this variety places some responsibility on the programmer to think through the code *before* it is written. The experienced programmer will begin writing a program with a block outline of what the program is to do. C allows you to write code in the same block structure but much more easily than in other languages.

Suppose that you want to expand the simple cube program to also calculate the square of the number. Founded on the cube program, the outline of the new program may be the following:

1. Get the integer value to be squared and cubed.

2. Print the integer value.

3. Square the number.
   Is it safe to square it?

   a) If okay, square it.
      Return square to calling function.

   b) If not, say it's too big and return zero.

4. Print the squared value.

5. Cube the number.
   Is it safe to cube it?

   a) If okay, cube it.
      Return cube to calling function.

   b) If not, say it's too big and return zero.

6. Print the cubed value.

7. End the program.

Many programmers will take the outline and translate it into pseudocode. *Pseudocode* is an imaginary language that is essentially English with some of the programming language's syntax added. Following is a pseudocode for the previous outline:

```
#include <stdio.h>

main()
{
        declare working variables;
        initialize variable;
        print() its original value;
        call() and assign square;      /* need square function */
        print() its squared value;
        call() and assign cube;        /* need cube function   */
        print() its cubed value;
}
```

The pseudocode should indicate any new functions you will need to write. It should also suggest what functions may be used from the C library [for example, printf(), which we'll need again.] You can then move to the functions you need and write the pseudocode for them. (Use the outline as a guide and try your hand at the pseudocode for the two needed functions.)

Pseudocode makes moving on to the actual C code much easier. (See program 3.7.)

The program begins with a simple comment that tells us what the program is designed to do. The #defines are used because they represent constants that may vary from one machine to another.

Integer variables use 16 bits on most systems. If the number of bits does change, all you have to do to adapt to any new integer specification is to change these two #define statements to the new values. You won't need to go looking through the entire program to locate and change the constants. For 32-bit integers, you can use 46340 for MAX_SQR and 1290 for MAX_CUBE. Always use #defines when you work with constants that may be changed.

Note that #defines are substituted throughout the source program wherever they occur. (The only exception is found within comment characters and quoted strings.) Also note that defines are declared outside any given function. Thus, #defines behave the same way externals do: their substitution is available to all functions in the source file. Put another way, a "global" substitution of symbolic constants is possible with a #define.

The main() function should look quite straightforward to you. The cub() function is a little different in that we are passing two arguments to the function rather than one. [The function is called cub() to distinguish it from the earlier cube() function. In fact, we could have used the "cube" function but purposely rewrote cube() to use two arguments.] A common mistake made by beginning C programmers is forgetting to declare the variables passed to the function. As previously mentioned, arguments passed to a function must be declared after the function name and before the opening brace of the function body.

cub(i, x) is a library function.

Look at the statement used to call cub():

```
i = cub(i, x);
```

You can think of this statement as being processed by the compiler in a "right to left" fashion. That is, the compiler (1) gathers together the arguments i and x, (2) calls cub() with the copies of these variables, then (3) assigns the value returned from cub() to i. If you prefer, you can accomplish the same operation with

```
printf("The value cubed is %d\n", cub(i, x));
```

As you saw in the original cube() function, arguments used in printf() can be functions. As far as the compiler is concerned, such arguments work in much the same manner, except that the assignment of the value returned from cub() to i is no longer needed. If you plan to do some more work with the cubed value, assignment is necessary. Because i is an automatic (that is, temporary) variable in cub(), the variable's value disappears when the program returns from the function.

For an exercise, change the program so that it prints the answers in decimal, hex, and octal formats. Afterward, change the program so that one printf() function is used, but the square and cube functions are treated as arguments to printf(). This last change is not as easy as it first may seem. (Hint: Keep in mind that we have "cascaded" the two functions. In other words, we need the result of sq() before cub() can work properly. Think about it.)

Now that we have reviewed some of the details about functions, you may want to read again your compiler's documentation on each library function. With the exception of the data types we have not discussed yet, you should be able to understand what the function expects to be passed in an argument list, how these arguments must be declared, and what the function returns.

Use these library functions to create some of your own programs. Then design several functions of your own that may be useful to you. Try experimenting until you have enough experience to be confident about using functions.

```
/* take an integer and print its square and cube */

#include <stdio.h>

#define MAX_SQR 181    /* number > 181 overflows square */

#define MAX_CUBE 32    /* number => 32 overflows cube    */

main()
{
    int i, x;

    x = 3;
    printf("The value being used is %d\n", x);
    i = sq(x);
    printf("The value squared is %d\n", i);
    i = cub(i, x);
    printf("The value cubed is %d\n", i);
}
```

```
/*****************************************************/
/* function squares integer, checking for overflow */
/*****************************************************/

int sq(i)
int i;
{
    if (i <= MAX_SQR)  /* MAX = 181 for squared integers */
        i = i * i;
    else {
        i = 0;
        printf("\nNumber too large to square. \n");
    }
    return (i);
}


/*********************************************************/
/* function cubes integer, using square and original value */
/*********************************************************/

int cub(i, x)
int i, x;
{
    if (x < MAX_CUBE)   /* CMAX = 32 for cubed integers */
        i = i * x;
    else {
        i = 0;
        printf("\nNumber too large to cube. \n");
    }
    return (i);
}
```

Program 3.7.

4

Using Pointers in C

Pointers are the most confusing aspect of C for the beginner, but they shouldn't be. Simply stated, *a pointer is a variable that points to another variable.* Pointers seem difficult at first because many programmers have had little or no experience with them. Every computer language has pointers, but most languages don't allow the programmer to use pointers directly. C, however, makes them available to the programmer. They are powerful tools once they are mastered.

To help you visualize how pointers work, let's consider how a hypothetical computer memory system might look, as shown in figure 4.1.

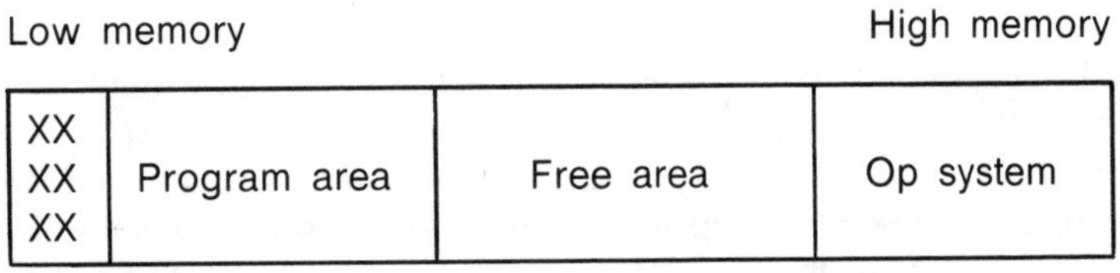

Low memory   High memory

Figure 4.1.

A compiled C program occupies the lower segment of memory address space, followed by a free area for dynamic data storage (for variables, constants, etc.). We'll assume that the operating system uses the higher memory addresses and that two bytes are used to store integers and memory addresses.

Let's also assume that a program has in it the definitions

```
int number;
char letter;
```

When the program is run on our hypothetical system, 16 bits (2 bytes) of memory are allocated somewhere in the data area for the integer variable number, and 8 bits (1 byte) are allocated for the character variable letter. Each variable is stored in a memory address in the data area.

For further clarification, let's say that the variable number starts at location 15000 in memory and that letter is located at address 15010. Let's also assume that number has been initialized to 3 and that letter contains an ASCII x. These variables may be defined and initialized somewhere in the program as

```
int number;
char letter;

number = 3;
letter = 'x';
```

If we enlarge figure 4.1 and use the preceding values, the memory system will appear as shown in figure 4.2.

Memory address:

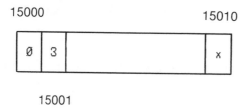

Figure 4.2.

Whenever you use the variable number directly, the compiler must know (1) the address of the variable (for example, address 15000), and (2) *how many* bytes [that is, 2] are required for storage. When you use letter, the compiler does not need to know *what* the letter is but merely the *value* (15010) for the letter's address and the *number* of bytes (1) required for storage. (Can this be one reason why all variables must be declared before they are used?)

Notice that the declaration for either data type tells the compiler how much storage is needed for the variable. Each variable, therefore, is scaled to the amount of storage needed for that data type. You must remember that *all data types in C have a scalar associated with them*. The scalar, usually 1 for a char and 2 for an int, reflects the amount of storage required for the data type. (Other data types and their scalars are discussed in Chapter 6.)

Keep in mind also that the compiler is responsible for deciding where the newly defined variable will reside in memory. Once the compiler has placed the variable in memory at some address the compiler has picked, the compiler will get rather cranky if you try to change that address for a given variable.

With this information in mind, let's explore what a pointer is. A *pointer* is a variable that *contains an address which points to some type of data*. Using our example, we can create pointer variables that point to the number 3 and to the letter x. What we need to know now is how to declare and use pointer variables.

Definitions and Pointers

Thus far, we have used only the data types int and char in the sample programs and routines, and we'll continue this practice until Chapter 6. Other data types (such as long int, float, and double) will vary in the number of bytes required for storage. Pointers are also a type of variable. A small computer typically uses 2 bytes for a pointer, whereas larger systems use 4 bytes. The underlying principles for pointers don't change in either case, however.

Because a pointer is a unique data type, we need some way of telling the compiler that we are defining a pointer rather than some other data type. The definition of the pointer variable must tell the compiler to do three things: (1) create an address for the pointer, (2) create a scalar for the pointer equal to the number of bytes associated with the data type being pointed to, and (3) mark this variable as a pointer.

As shown in figure 4.3, an asterisk (*) must be used when a variable is defined as a pointer.

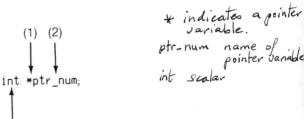

```
        (1)  (2)

         |    |
         |    |
         ↓    ↓
      int *ptr_num;
         ↑
         |
        (3)
```

* indicates a pointer variable.
ptr_num name of pointer variable
int scalar

Figure 4.3.

In this figure the definition tells the compiler the three things it needs to know about pointer variables: (1) I'm a pointer-type variable; (2) My name is ptr_num, and I need a memory address at which to reside; and (3) Create me with a scalar that is associated with a type int variable (for example, a scalar of 2). Until now, variable definitions conveyed only the data type and the variable name to the compiler. But now, the third item makes pointers different from other (nonpointer) definitions.

Sometimes imagery helps you recall important concepts. Think of the asterisk as an "eye" that lets you see into another variable. Actually, that's what a pointer is: a device that lets you see the value of some other variable. Given the two definitions

```
int *ptr;
char *let;
```

the first asterisk tells the compiler that you want a variable named ptr which is capable of looking at an int data type. The second definition says that you want a second "eye" which is capable of looking at a char data type. Note that both pointer variables (ptr and let) take the same amount of storage (for example, 2 bytes for small computers and 4 bytes for larger computers). The only difference between the two pointers is that the scalar for ptr is that of an int (such as a scalar of 2), and the scalar for let is that of a char (such as a scalar of 1). Both pointers are "eyes" but fitted with different glasses to look at different types of data.

Defining a pointer to a character rather than an int differs only in the scalar associated with the pointer. Of course, the specified data type determines what scalar is set for the pointer. The definition for a pointer to a char (see figure 4.4) is the same as that shown in figure 4.3, except for the data type that sets the scalar.

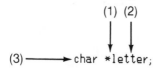

Figure 4.4.

The definition of a character pointer conveys the same three pieces of information discussed previously, except that a character pointer points to a char rather than an int.

Another important fact should be noted about pointers. If the value of a pointer is zero, the pointer is guaranteed *not* to point to valid data. This bit of information can be useful in many C programs. For example, if you call a function that is supposed to return a pointer, you can use a return value of zero to indicate that an error occurred in the function.

Initializing a Pointer

Before you can use a pointer, you must *initialize* it to point to something. A simple definition of a pointer will not cause the pointer to point to anything useful. An uninitialized pointer will most likely point to some random (that is, "garbage") place in addressable memory instead of where you want the pointer to point. Therefore, *before* you use a pointer, be certain that you assign to it a proper pointer address.

Suppose that we want to initialize a pointer variable to point to number. We can do this with the unary & operator in C. The syntax is

```
ptr_num = &number;
```

& – "address of"

The & operator can be verbalized as "address of." The preceding statement says to "take the address of number and store the address in ptr_num." What does ptr_num contain as its value? If we use the example presented earlier, ptr_num will have the value 15000. The pointer variable ptr_num is initialized to hold the *memory address* where we can find the value of number.

A common mistake is to think that a pointer contains the *value* of a data type, but a pointer contains only an *address* that points to a data type. Because the value of a variable and where it is stored in memory (in other words, its address) are different, we need a way of viewing this distinction.

lvalues and rvalues

Every data item in a computer language has an *lvalue* and an *rvalue*, which mean *left value* and *right value*, respectively. In the previous example, we created a variable number and initialized it with a value of 3. We also saw that the compiler placed number in memory starting at address 15000.

The lvalue (left value) of a data item is the address in memory *where* that item is located. For the variable number, its lvalue is 15000.

The rvalue (right value) of a data item represents *what* is stored at the data item's lvalue. In other words, the rvalue is what has been assigned to the data item. To visualize these two concepts, refer to figure 4.5.

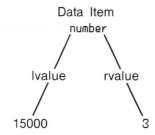

Data Item
number

lvalue   rvalue

15000   3

Figure 4.5.

In this example, a data item number is stored at memory location 15000 (its lvalue) and is assigned the numeric value of 3 (its rvalue).

Now let's see how lvalues and rvalues relate to pointer variables.

lvalues, rvalues, and Pointers

Let's suppose that code fragment 4.1 appears in a program.

```
int number, *ptr_num;        /* line 1 */

number = 3;                  /* line 2 */
ptr_num = &number;           /* line 3 */
```

Code fragment 4.1.

Using the data from the previous example, we'll assume that the compiler has placed number at memory location 15000. Let's further assume that the compiler created the pointer variable (ptr_num) to reside at memory location 16000. These locations are known to the compiler after line 1 in code fragment 4.1 has been processed. Thus far, the relationships are illustrated in figure 4.6.

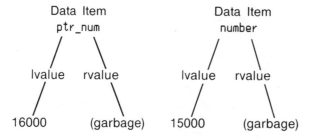

Data Item   Data Item
ptr_num   number

lvalue   rvalue   lvalue   rvalue

16000   (garbage)   15000   (garbage)

Figure 4.6.

Both variables now exist in memory. (They each have an lvalue but do not contain any useful information.) Their rvalues are whatever random bit patterns happen to exist there, because C does not initialize (automatic) variables to zero. If both variables were of the external storage class, their rvalues would be zero instead of garbage.

Figure 4.7 shows how things look after line 2 is executed.

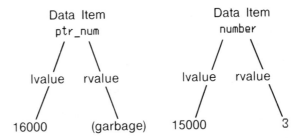

Figure 4.7.

The assignment statement establishes a value of 3 for number. Therefore, number now has both a valid lvalue and a rvalue. However, because we have not yet initialized ptr_num, it still contains random garbage for its rvalue.

The purpose of line 3 is to initialize ptr_num to point to number. After line 3 is executed, the illustration appears as in figure 4.8.

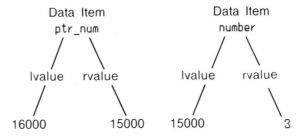

Figure 4.8.

Recall that the & operator takes the *address of* number, and the equal sign causes that address to be assigned into ptr_num. The pointer variable (ptr_num) now has a valid rvalue. Specifically, the rvalue of ptr_num is the lvalue of number. We can now say that ptr_num points to number.

In effect, we have tied ptr_num and number together, as shown in figure 4.9.

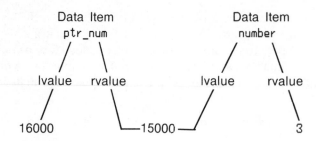

Figure 4.9.

Note the relationship between the pointer variable ptr_num and the variable number, to which the pointer points; the rvalue of ptr_num and the lvalue of number are the same. Figure 4.10 displays this relationship another way.

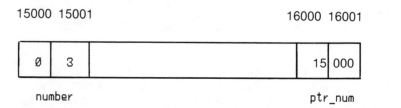

Figure 4.10.

Now let's consider the point of view of the compiler. It has two variables that can be used to access the same information. In other words, the compiler knows that (1) number is located at 15000 (lvalue) with the contents of 3 (rvalue), and (2) a pointer variable exists at 16000 (lvalue) with the contents of 15000 (rvalue).

Because the compiler knows that ptr_num is a pointer to number, the compiler can access the variable named number through a process called indirection. Indirection is the process of accessing the contents of a variable (its rvalue) through its pointer variable, again using the asterisk operator.

Consider the use of pointers in code fragment 4.2.

```
int number, *ptr_num, new_num;     /* line 1 */

number = 3;                        /* line 2 */
ptr_num = &number;                 /* line 3 */

new_num = *ptr_num;                /* line 4 */
```

Code fragment 4.2.

Using the same numbers as before, let's inspect each line as viewed by the compiler. Line 1 defines two integer variables (number and new_num) plus a pointer to an int (ptr_num). Line 2 assigns the value 3 to number, and line 3 initializes ptr_num to point to number. (Thus, ptr_num has an lvalue of 16000 and an rvalue of 15000.)

Line 4 shows the indirection process. The asterisk tells the compiler to (1) take the rvalue of ptr_num (15000), (2) get "scalar bytes" of data stored at that location (an integer 3), and (3) assign the value found there to the variable new_num. This variable (new_num) now contains the same value as that of the variable number: 3.

The definition of the pointer in the first line is important to the compiler. When you define ptr_num to be a pointer to an integer, the compiler can then tell how many bytes to examine in retrieving what is stored. As you probably guessed, the scalar of the pointer tells the compiler how many bytes of data must be used to retrieve what is stored at the address being pointed to. The definition also tells the compiler that it can treat the rvalue of the pointer variable ptr_num (15000) as a memory address. All properly initialized pointers have rvalues that are memory addresses.

Asterisks in Definitions versus Asterisks Elsewhere

If you're confused about the use of the asterisk, you're not alone. When the asterisk appears in a definition, such as

```
int *ptr_num;
```

the asterisk's only purpose is to inform the compiler that ptr is a pointer variable. The definition of a pointer creates an "eye," as previously suggested. So far, however, the eye can't see anything because it has not been initialized to point to anything useful.

When you use the asterisk in any other type of statement, you are asking for the rvalue of what the pointer is looking at. If we assume that the pointer has been initialized properly, as in line 3 of code fragment 4.2, then line 4

```
new_num = *ptr_num;                 /* line 4 */
```

says to use the rvalue of ptr_num (15000) as an address of a memory location, use the scalar of the pointer and fetch scalar bytes of data from that location, and then assign those bytes into new_num.

The asterisk in line 4 let's the "eye" go to a memory address, get what is stored at that address, and look at it. Because the statement also has an equal sign, what is being looked at is also stored in new_num by the assignment operator.

Simply stated, the asterisk in a definition tells the compiler to create a pointer (and fix the scalar size), but an asterisk anywhere else says to "go to the address to which I am pointing and get scalar bytes of data so that I can look at them."

Three simple steps must be followed when you use a pointer.

1. Define the pointer (using the *):

        int *ptr;

2. Initialize the pointer to point to something useful (using the &):

        ptr = &number;

3. Get whatever the pointer points to (using the *):

        printf("ptr is looking at %d\n", *ptr);

A few words of caution may prevent you from experiencing certain difficulties. First, you will create all kinds of trouble if you define a pointer for an int, then try to use it to fetch a different data type. For example, if you define a pointer to char but initialize the pointer to look at an int, the scalar for a pointer to char says to look at only 1 byte of data, but ints use 2 bytes. Your pointer will see only "half an int."

Don't mix data types.

Second, you should remember that an uninitialized pointer will never point where you want it to point. Always initialize a pointer before using it. Try to visualize what would happen if these rules were not followed.

Always initialize a pointer with &

The Importance of Pointers

You are probably wondering, Why use pointers when I can simply make the assignment new_num = number? Although you probably could make that assignment directly in the simple example shown previously, there are a number of good reasons for using pointers.

First, a function cannot access directly a variable defined in another function. As we saw in Chapter 3, all variables (except externals) are local to the function. Whenever a function receives "outside" values as an argument list, the function receives copies of the values (not the lvalue of the argument itself). So how can the programmer alter the original variable?

The only way to access a variable that "lives outside" a function is to use a pointer variable, which is part of the function's argument list. A function must use a pointer variable in the function argument list for any nonlocal variable that is to be altered by the function.

The only exceptions to this rule are external variables and arrays. External variables are globally available to all functions in the program, and arrays are not copied when they are passed to a function. (If you need to refresh your memory about these exceptions, review Chapter 3.) When an array appears in an argument list, the function receives the lvalue of the array. In all other cases where pointers are not used, the function receives a copy of the variable.

To simplify program writing, many beginning C programmers may be tempted to define all variables as externals. This practice gives rise to the *second* reason for using pointers: they minimize the "side effect" bugs mentioned in the previous chapter. *One function cannot directly access a variable in another function.* When pointers are used to access variables indirectly, the risk of contaminating other variables in the program is reduced. C forces you to use indirection (with pointers) in a very deliberate manner whenever a function alters a variable outside itself.

Finally, keep in mind that if you call a function to alter the "original" value of a data item in the calling function, you must use a pointer. If the function can perform its task simply by using a temporary copy of the variable, then you don't have to use a pointer. The only exception to this rule is an array variable. (If an array variable is used in the argument list of a function, the lvalue of the array is given to the function. In this sense, array names are actually pointers. Give it some thought.)

Although pointers may seem difficult to understand now, mastering them is well worth the effort. You will appreciate pointers when program changes or debugging are required.

A Program Using Pointers

To test your understanding of how pointers work, let's write a program that (1) accepts a line of input from the keyboard, (2) asks the user to enter a character to be counted in the line of input, and (3) displays how many times the character occurs. (See program 4.1.)

```c
#include <stdio.h>

#define MAXLEN 80          /* largest string size */

main()
{
    char string[MAXLEN+1], c;
    int count;
    void getline(), cnt_let();

    printf("Enter a line of text.\n\n");
    getline(string);

    printf("\n\nEnter a character to be counted: ");
    c = getchar();

    count = 0;
    cnt_let(string, c, &count);
    printf("\n\nThe letter %c occurs", c);
    printf(" %d times in the line.\n", count);
}

/*******
        Function fills a character array until the RETURN key
    is pressed, then adds the null to the end of the string.

    Argument list:      char s[]        character array to hold
                                        input characters


    Return value:       none

*******/

void getline(s)
char s[];
{
    int i;
```

```
        i = 0;
    while (i < MAXLEN) {
            s[i] = getchar();
            if (s[i] == '\n')
                break;
            ++i;
    }
    s[i] = '\0';
}


/*******
        Function receives the string (s), the character to
    count in the string (which), and the address of where to
    store the count.

    Argument list:        char s[]         character array that
                                           holds input string
                          char match       the character used for
                                           finding a match
                          int *num         pointer to variable
                                           that holds number of
                                           matches found


    Return value:         none

*******/

void cnt_let(s, match, num)
char s[], match;
int *num;
{
    int i;

    i = 0;

    while (s[i] != '\0') {
            if (s[i] == match)
                    *num += 1;
            i++;
    }
}
```

Program 4.1.

We'll need two new functions for this program: one function to enter a line of text, and a second function to count character occurrence. The rest of the program draws on elements we have used in previous programs.

What this program does first is #define the symbolic constant MAX-LEN for 80 characters. This symbolic constant is used in main() to reserve MAXLEN-plus-one elements in the character array variable named string[]. (Whenever we discuss an array variable, the variable name is followed by brackets.) One is added to MAXLEN so that we can add the character string terminator (' \0 ') to the end of the array. The getline() function limits the number of characters entered from the keyboard to MAXLEN (in other words, 80).

Notice how we have declared that both getline() and cnt_let() return the void data type. In other words, the line

```
void getline(), cnt_let();
```

tells the compiler that these functions return the void data type (that is, garbage). Such declarations also jog the programmer's memory that these functions, because they return garbage, should not be used with an assignment statement, such as

```
i = getline(s);
```

If such an assignment is made, i will not contain anything useful because getline() does not have anything useful returned from it. In the future, compilers will probably check such semantic errors.

The program then asks you to enter a line of text and performs a function call to getline(), using string[] as its argument. There are two important points to note here: (1) the variable name string can be used in the argument list without being referred to as string[], and (2) getline() receives the actual address where string[] is located in memory, because character arrays are not copied during a function call. For example, if string[] is located in memory starting at address 17000 (in other words, string[0] is at 17000), then that is the address of s[] in getline(). The addresses of string[0] in main() and s[0] in getline() are identical.

[By the way, the getline() function behaves virtually the same as the gets() function that is included in most C libraries. If you don't want to type the getline() function, you can leave it out and use gets() instead.]

The while loop in getline() gets one character at a time by function calls to getchar() and ends if you try to enter more than 80 characters (that is, MAXLEN). If you press the RETURN key before MAXLEN characters are entered, the program can detect the RE-TURN key by comparing it to the newline character (' \n'). The if statement then becomes True, and the break statement throws you out of the while loop.

Note: The getchar() used in this program is normally part of the standard library. However, some compilers use buffered I/O for getchar(), but others do not. As a result, the getchar() on some compilers forces you to press RETURN after each character is entered; therefore, getline() will only get one character. If your compiler uses buffered I/O, see whether an unbuffered getchar() exists in your library. A likely candidate is getch(), although it probably will not display the character on the screen as each character is entered. Furthermore, some compilers will use the carriage return character (' \r') to sense end of input instead of using a newline character (' \n'). Try these substitutions if you have problems with the program as shown.

The getline() function appends the null character (' \0') to the end of the character array so that it can be treated as a string. All character arrays that are to be treated as strings in C end with the null character. Because strings are treated this way, printf() knows that it has reached the end of a string when the null character is sensed.

Don't forget that an array isn't copied when passed as an argument to a function. Therefore, getline() is working with the character array string from main(), not a copy. Because we are interested in only the contents of the array, we don't need to return anything from the getline() function call.

After initializing count to 0, the program requests that you enter the character to be counted in the string. The function call to getchar() gets the character and assigns it to c.

After the character is assigned to c, the program does a function call to cnt_let() with three arguments. To illustrate this, let's assume that string[] begins at memory location 17000, the character to be counted (c) is stored at location 18000, and the number of occurrences of the letter (count) is stored at location 19000. This relationship is shown in figure 4.11.

```
              17000    x    19000 ◄────────Memory locations
```

Figure 4.11.   `cnt_let(string,  c,  &count);`

The letter x above the variable c is the assumed letter that is being passed to the function. Because the variable c is not an array or pointer, a copy of the variable is sent to cnt_let().

Note that the program specifies that the *address of* count (&count) is to be sent to the cnt_let() function. Therefore, the lvalue of count is sent to cnt_let().

If we look at this relationship from the function's point of view, cnt_let() sees the relationship shown in figure 4.12.

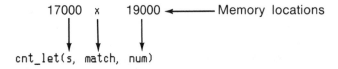

Figure 4.12.

Because the argument declaration for variable s is a character array (char s[]), it is the same array as string[] in main() and has the same lvalue in main() and in cnt_let().

The difference between how match and num are treated is important. The function cnt_let() sees the data as

```
void cnt_let(s = 17000, match = x, num = 19000)
```

The compiler then sees

```
char s[ ], match;
int *num;
```

and can now figure out what the arguments sent to cnt_let() mean. First, because the function knows that s[ ] is an array of chars, cnt_let() knows that 17000 is an lvalue. Second, because match is declared as a plain char, cnt_let() knows that it has a copy of something. The function will create a temporary variable named match and store x as the rvalue. (Let's assume that the function stored match at memory address 18100.) Finally, because num is declared to be a pointer, the function knows that it has been passed an lvalue. The compiler creates a temporary integer pointer variable named num (let's say at memory location 20000—nums lvalue) and shoves 19000 into num for its rvalue.

A diagram showing each argument with its associated lvalue and rvalue is presented in figure 4.13.

Note that num has an rvalue which is the lvalue of count in main(). Remember learning earlier that a pointer must be initialized to

Figure 4.13.

work properly? How did the pointer get properly initialized? Look what happened when we passed the address of count to cnt_let. Now refer to figure 4.14.

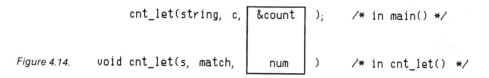

Figure 4.14.

If we turn the boxed-in part of figure 4.14 on its side, we have

    num = &count;

which is exactly the way to initialize a pointer, as shown previously in the chapter. Now that we know that all of our variables are properly declared, we are ready to see what the cnt_let() function does.

This function first assigns i to zero. The cnt_let() function uses a while loop to test for the end of the character array by looking for the null character (' \Ø'). On each pass through the loop, a comparison between the character in the string array (s[i]) and the letter being searched for (match) is made.

If the search is successful, the contents of memory location 19000 are incremented by 1. We used the += operator to increment what num is pointing to. The interpretation of the += operator is the following:

    *num += 1;   is the same as   *num = *num + 1;

Because we are using a pointer, the variable count from main() is actually being incremented each time the memory location is incremented. Recall that the asterisk lets us see the value being pointed to. Therefore, the line

    *num += 1;

or

    *num = *num + 1;

says to (1) get the contents of what num is pointing to (*num), (2) add one to whatever is currently stored there (+ 1), and (3) assign that new value back into what num is pointing to (*num =). The whole process is actually incrementing the variable count from main(), but the incrementing is done through the pointer num in cnt_let().

Note: Whenever you want to use pointers to alter the contents of a number, you must use the asterisk in front of the variable name. This is why *num += 1; must be used in the cnt_let() function.

Variable i is incremented (i++) after each comparison and causes the program to march through the character array s[ ]. When the null ('\Ø') is finally read, the while loop terminates, and control passes back to main(). Once again, no return is needed because we already have the number of successful comparisons stored in count. The program then prints out the results of the search and ends.

Enter this program into your computer and experiment with it. If your compiler supports the unsigned data type, try using the %u conversion character in printf() to print out the actual memory locations that your compiler uses for count, num, s, and string[]. For example, if you have a statement in main() that appears as

```
printf("\nAddress of count = %u\n", &count);
```

place a similar statement for s, match, and num in cnt_let(). Then reread this section, substituting the actual values you found.

Incrementing and Decrementing Pointers

Pointer variables can be incremented and decremented like any other data type. Remember, however, that the increment/decrement operators function according to the scalar of the data type being used. For example, suppose we define an integer array of three elements and initialize the array with the values 1 to 3. Let's also suppose that the array begins at memory address 15000 (the array's lvalue). This arrangement is represented in figure 4.15.

Because each integer requires 2 bytes for storage, when you increment a pointer to an integer variable, you actually increment the address held in the pointer variable by 2. Therefore, the scalar for our integer data type is 2. For example, if the variable ptr is a

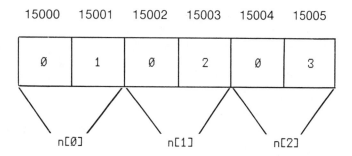

Figure 4.15.

pointer to the n array, ptr will contain the address 15000 after the variable is initialized. The statement

    ++ptr;

increases the address in ptr to 15002 and makes ptr point to array element n[1]. The compiler automatically makes the necessary scalar adjustment for you, provided that you have declared the pointer correctly. The variable ptr must have been declared as

    int *ptr;

in the program before ptr's use.

If we had mistakenly declared ptr as a character pointer, such as

    char *ptr;

and then used it to address the n integer array, the ++ptr statement would only increment the pointer address by 1 byte rather than the 2 bytes needed to access the next integer in the array, because the scalar for a char is 1. If a pointer points to a series of characters, the increment operation will add 1 to the address. The same operation on a pointer to a series of integers adds 2 to the pointer address. These rules also apply to the decrementing operation on pointers.

Other data types may require between 1 and 8 bytes for storage. (See Chapter 6.) The compiler must keep track of these requirements when pointers are used. The programmer must also make sure that the pointer actually points to the correct data type. If the pointer does not, then garbage data will creep into the program. Keep in mind, too, that all pointers have an associated scalar which is determined at the time the pointer is defined.

Another Example

To test further your understanding of pointers, study program 4.2. Try to determine what should be displayed, then enter the program to see whether you were correct.

Two functions [stuf() and mid()] are used in this program. The stuf() function fills a character array with the letters A to I. The mid() function prints a subset of the character array in the same manner that the MID$ statement works in many dialects of BASIC.

```c
#include <stdio.h>
#define SIZ 9                        /* maximum to look at */
main()
{
    int j;
    char letter[SIZ];
    void stuf(), mid();        /* don't do assignment with 'em */

    stuf(letter);              /* fill array with characters  */

    for (j = 0; j < SIZ; ++j)    /* print out the array */
        printf("%c ", letter[j]);

    printf("\n\n");

    mid(letter, 3, 3);
}

/******
        Function stuffs an array with letters A to I.

    Argument list:      char *c   pointer to a character array

    Return value:       none

******/

#define A      65     /* ASCII A = 65; easier to recognize */
```

```
void stuf(c)
char *c;
{
    int i, x;

    for (x = A, i = 0; i < SIZ; ++x, ++i)
        *c++ = x;
}


#undef A


/*******
        Function prints the contents of a character array
    and is of the following form:

    MID(string address, start of print, number to print)

    Argument List:       char p[]      array of characters
                         int start     where to start printing
                         int num       number of chars to print


    Return value:        none

*******/

void mid(p, start, num)
int start, num;
char p[];
{
    int i;

    for (i = 0; i < num; ++i)
        printf("%c", p[start + i]);
}
```

Program 4.2.

Program 4.2 begins with a #define statement that sets the maximum size of the array (SIZ). Because 9 is the value assigned to the symbolic constant SIZ, the array has valid elements: letter[0] through letter[8]. All arrays in C start with *element zero*, and the number of elements you "get" is determined by what you request in the array declaration. That is, the declaration

    char letter[9];

requests nine elements in the letter[] array, not ten. Likewise, the first element is letter[0], not letter[1], as in some BASICs.

The position of array elements follows an *N-1 Rule*. For example, the third element is actually letter[2]—that is, letter[N-1] = letter[3-1] = letter[2]. Thus, the maximum subscript for the letter[] array in program 4.2 is letter[8]. C has no default array size, nor is there boundary checking on array subscripts in C. (Unlike C, many BASICs default to ten elements without a DIM statement.)

Again, notice that we have declared that stuf() and mid() return the void data type.

The statement

```
stuf(letter);
```

calls the stuf() function to fill the array with the characters A to I. Note what has been done here. If we assume that the letter[] array resides at memory location 16000 (the starting address of letter[]), we can visualize the call to the stuf() function as shown in figure 4.16.

```
stuf(16000); ──────────────►  /* function call in main() */
    .
    .
    .
stuf(16000) ◄─────────────┘  /* in the function itself */
char *c;
    .
```

Figure 4.16.

The result of this call is that the stuf() function is passed the starting address of the letter[] array because arrays are not copied during function calls. Therefore, the lvalue is passed, not the rvalue.

Also note that we have declared the lvalue that comes in to stuf() to be a pointer to char. The declaration is

```
char *c;
```

instead of

```
char *c[];
```

Later in the chapter, you will see that these two declarations actually have the same meaning in C. You will also learn why pointers are used more often than arrays.

Notice that a #define is used to define the letter A with its corresponding ASCII value of 65. The #define will cause the value 65 to be replaced for the A when x is initialized in the for loop. Observe also that a #undef A is used, just after the end of the function. The #undef A does exactly what you might expect: it "undefines" the symbolic constant A in the file. This is done just in case a variable named A occurs later in the program.

In the for loop, the x variable is given the value 65 (an ASCII A) by the #define previously discussed. The statement

    *c++ = x;

says to take the value of x (which is 65) and place it in the rvalue of what c is pointing to. We already know, however, that c has the lvalue (16000) of letter[] in main(). Therefore, we are placing the character A in letter[0]. Understanding what this statement does is very important. Consider figure 4.17.

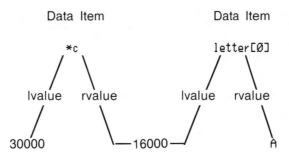

Figure 4.17.

We've assumed that the compiler placed variable c at memory location 30000 (the lvalue of c). The rvalue of c was given to the function as an argument in the function call and is 16000. However, the rvalue of c is the lvalue of letter[] in main(). Therefore, a simple

    *c++ = x;

causes c to take the value of x (the character A) and place it at address 16000. Thus, as we can see in figure 4.17, letter[0] now contains an A. Because the scalar for a pointer to char is 1, the postincrement on c means that we increment the rvalue of c by 1 *after* we assign the character A to address 16000. The rvalue of c is then 16001.

On the second pass through the loop, x equals 66 (the ASCII letter B). Because we postincremented c (*c++) on the first pass through

the for loop, B is placed in memory address 16001. Therefore, letter[1] now contains a B in it. This process continues for nine
passes through the loop. When the loop is finished, memory addresses 16000 through 16008 contain the letters A to I,
respectively.

No return statement was needed in the function because we were
working with a pointer. Control automatically returns to main()
when the closing brace of the stuf() function is reached. The program then resumes with the for loop in main().

The for loop in main() prints out the contents of the array, with
each letter separated by a blank space. Because j is initialized to
zero in the loop, the contents of the array, starting with element
letter[0], are printed. The loop then prints out the remaining
characters in the array. If we had added one more element to the
letter[] array and placed a null in that element, we could have
used the %s conversion of printf() to print the array as a character
string.

Remember that, as far as the compiler is concerned, it makes no
difference whether you refer to the character array by letter (its
name) or &letter[0]. Both references are identical and will yield
the lvalue of the array.

Note: The lvalue of a variable is a constant. If x is a variable (not a
pointer), we cannot say

```
  &x = &x + 1;      /* WRONG! */
```

because this line attempts to change the lvalue given by the compiler to the variable x. The compiler gets fussy if you attempt to
change its placement of variables and will let you know when this
happens.

To return to the discussion, the program prints two *newlines*, or
blank lines, by calls to the printf() function and then calls the
mid() function with the following arguments:

```
  mid(letter, 3, 3);
```

When the mid() function is reached, it may be viewed as

```
  void mid(16000, 3, 3)
  int start, num;
  char p[];
```

In this case, we have declared p[] to be an array. Because the
compiler knows it cannot copy arrays, it establishes p[] as an array

with an lvalue of 16000. In other words, p[] is simply the name given in mid() for the letter[] array from main(). Because p[] and letter[] have the same lvalue, they are one and the same.

How can we get away with declaring p[] as

    char p[];

without giving an array dimension? The reason is that we are not really defining the *size* of the array: that was already done for us in main() when letter[] was defined and storage was allocated for it. The only purpose of the declaration in the function is to let the function know what it has—the first element of some array. The function could care less how big the array is.

Only when two-dimensional arrays are passed to a function does the function need to know something about the size of the array. For example, if an array is defined as

    char c[5][10];

in one function and is then passed to a second function, the argument declaration in the second function will be

    func1(s)
    char s[][10];

This second declaration must have the second subscript to know where to "fold" the vector in memory. The first declaration says that 50 characters are divided into 5 elements of 10 chars each. The "fold" is every tenth character. The same information is conveyed in the second declaration, but the function doesn't care how many elements there are—only where the "folds" are.

(Question: What is the scalar of a pointer to a double-dimensioned array? Write a program that declares a double-dimensioned array and a pointer to it. Fill the array with numbers. Then initialize the pointer, increment it by one, and print out what the pointer points to. Surprised? Explain the results of your experiment.)

The variable start is the starting index of the array we want to print, and num is the number of array characters to be printed. These arguments are visualized in figure 4.18.

Remember that when start equals 3, we are asking for element s[3] of the array, *not* the third element (which would be s[2] because arrays start with zero). The two elements are not the same. (Refer to the N-1 Rule mentioned previously.) If your program ever

returns a list of data that is "off" by one, the chances are that you
have forgotten about the zero array element.

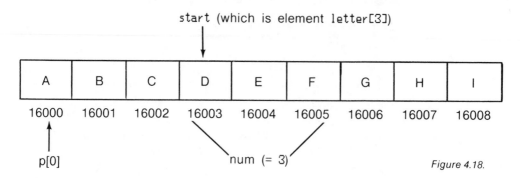

Figure 4.18.

Pointers versus Arrays

What happens if we define mid() as

```
void mid(16000, 3, 3)
int start, num;
char *p;
```

Everything is the same except that we now have declared p to be
a pointer to char. An illustration appears in figure 4.19.

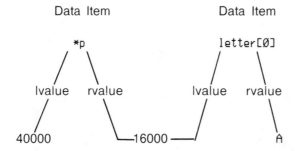

Figure 4.19.

Because p is now a pointer, it knows that it has been handed an
lvalue. Variable p is created with its own address (40000) and assumes the value of 16000 for its rvalue. Because we already know
that 16000 is the lvalue of letter[] in main(), we end up working
with letter[].

Conclusion: Whether we declare p to be a pointer (*p) or an array
(p[]) makes no difference; both declarations end up working with
letter[]. Therefore, *p does, in fact, equal letter[0].

If the variable p[] had been declared as a pointer in program 4.2, the statement

```
printf("%c", p[start + i]);
```

can also be viewed as

```
printf("%c", *p[16000 + i]);
```

which prints the contents of memory location 16003, or the letter D. The for loop increments i until the three characters (that is, num = 3) have been printed. Because no further statements are in the mid() function, the closing brace sends control back to main(). And because no statements follow the call to the mid() function in main(), the program ends.

Another test should be considered. What happens if we change the for loop in the mid() function to read as shown in code fragment 4.3?

Code fragment 4.3.

```
for (i = start; num; i++, num--)
    printf("%c", p[i]);
```

Try to determine what will happen and then run the program with the modification. Are the results what you expected? Why or why not?

Although program 4.2 is fairly trivial, it does point out one important aspect of the C language: If you need a statement that isn't provided in C, you can write a function to provide the statement. Then you can place the new function in the library and use that function in subsequent programs without having to rewrite it.

Other Reasons for Using Pointers

We have already stated that using pointers is the only way to affect the value of a variable that is passed to a function as an argument. True, arrays and external storage class variables are exceptions, and using externals to simplify coding is tempting. As previously suggested, however, the use of externals defeats the inherent protection of the data that C offers.

Other reasons for using pointers are evident. First, because of the way pointers are treated internally by the compiler, they are slightly more efficient than arrays. Pointers usually cause less code to be generated, which also means that execution speed is increased somewhat.

Another reason is that pointers can be used in ways that save data space. For example, suppose that you are writing a program containing a number of messages that must be displayed (for example, string constants that are parts of a screen menu). To keep the example simple, let's further assume that the messages to be displayed are the following:

```
Factorials, Permutations, and Combinations
ANOVA
Normal
```

The first message has 42 characters in it. We could declare the two-dimensional array

```
char menu[3][43];
```

which says that we have a three-element array of chars, each of which can hold 43 chars. (Don't forget space for the null terminator on strings.) If we wish to initialize the array as part of the definition, the array must be either an external or static array. If the array is external, it is defined and initialized as

```
char menu[3][43] = {
     "Factorials, Permutations, and Combinations",
     "ANOVA",
     "Normal"                        /* note: no comma */
     };
```

Notice the syntax for initializing arrays: (1) an opening brace, (2) the quote string constant, and (3) a comma. The last initializer does *not* have a comma following it and before the closing brace.

The total storage requirements for the menu[] array are 129 bytes. The storage looks like a "box" in memory. (See figure 4.20.)

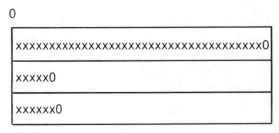

129

Figure 4.20.

Now consider the alternative of using pointers. Here we declare a single-dimensioned array of pointers to chars:

```
char *m[3] = {
    "Factorials, Permutations, an d Combinations",
    "ANOVA",
    "Normal"
};
```

The syntax for initialization is the same, except that we have defined a pointer to char, instead of defining an array of chars. The real difference, however, is in the storage requirements. The "box" for the pointer version is shown in figure 4.21.

0

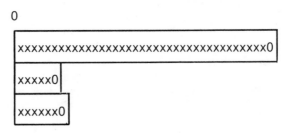

Figure 4.21.

The storage requirements in this case are 56 bytes for the strings plus 6 bytes (possibly 12 on large systems) for the pointers. The reason is that the compiler will allocate only the space required for the initialized strings when pointers are used. In the two-dimensional array, the compiler has no choice but to allocate what you requested.

For the pointer version, you print out the first string by using something like

```
printf(m[0]);
```

and the first message will be displayed. The memory savings can be substantial when pointers are used.

Look again at the library documentation that came with your C compiler, this time noting the functions that require pointer variables as part of the argument list. Try using several of these standard library functions in programs of your own. Pointers are a powerful feature of C when used correctly. If you practice using them now, your ability to use them efficiently will be well worth the effort.

5

Input and Output in C

For those used to programming in BASIC, it may come as a surprise that C has no inherent input or output (that is, I/O) statements. In other words, C does not provide the equivalent of PRINT or INPUT as part of its syntax. How useful can a language be if it doesn't allow you to do any I/O?

Of course, C does allow for I/O in the form of function calls. One of C's strengths is that you are not restricted to using predetermined I/O statements. In C, you can create whatever functions you need, or you can use the ones in the standard C library.

Using I/O Functions from the Standard Library

As discussed in Chapter 2, each C compiler has a number of *prewritten functions*. The printf() function, which we've used in most of our earlier sample programs, is one example. As you proceed through the book, you will be introduced to other functions that are usually part of the library.

The documentation provided with your compiler should describe the functions that make up your library. Because the library is a collection of functions, the documentation should also explain what arguments are expected when each function is called. For example, the documentation might include

```
int strlen(string)
char *string;
```

followed by a brief description of what the function does. In this example, `strlen()` returns an `int`, which is the length of a character string pointed to by `string`.

The `strlen()` function expects to receive a pointer variable named `string` that is a pointer to characters. The `int` before the function name tells us that this function returns an integer. (Is the type specifier needed?) The function description should tell us that the function returns an integer equal to the number of characters in the string. The length of the string does not include the null at the end. In other words, `strlen(x)` is the equivalent of LEN(X$) in BASIC.

Note that the description of the standard library functions is *permissive*, not *mandatory*. That is, you do not have to use a pointer named `string` for the function to work properly. In code fragment 5.1, the variable is a string array.

```
#include <stdio.h>

main()
{
      int numchar;
      char c[30];
      .            /* some statements that create the string */
      .
      numchar = strlen(c);
      printf("The length of the string is: %d\n", numchar);
      .            /* the rest of the program */
}
```

Code fragment 5.1.

As suggested in the example, any variable name can be passed to `strlen()` as long as the variable is a character array or pointer to characters; the variable does not have to be named `string`, as shown in the documentation.

After `strlen()` is called from `main()`, `strlen()` returns an integer, which we have assigned to `numchar`. Variable `numchar` contains the number of characters in the string. We could also have done the function call as

```
printf("The length of the string is: %d\n", strlen(c));
```

and left out the assignment of the string length to `numchar`. Which method is better depends on how the string length will be used in your program. If you will need to use the string length in subsequent calculations, the first version is better because the string length is assigned to the variable numchar, which can be used in subsequent calculations. If you want to print the length of the string on the screen, the second version is more direct. Choose the version that is better for your program.

One final point about the standard library may be obvious to some but not to others. If your program uses functions from the standard library, the actual code for those functions is supplied automatically by the compile-link process. (See Chapter 6.) In other words, the C compiler supplies the code necessary for the standard library functions used in your program so that you do not have to rewrite them explicitly.

A Simple Program

Now that you know something about the standard library, let's use some of its functions to write a simple program to display your name on the screen. (See program 5.1.)

```
#include <stdio. h>      /* read in the standard I/O file */

#define MAX 80         /* maximum length of name */
#define CLEAR "\014"  /* an ASCII 12 clears my screen */

main()
{
    char name[MAX], c;
    int i;


    printf(CLEAR);
    printf("Enter your name: ");

    for (i = 0; (c = getch()) != '\r' && i < MAX-1; ++i)
        name[i] = c;

    name[i] = '\0';

    printf("\n\nYour name is: %s\n", name);
}
```

Program 5.1.

#include

Because many C programs often use certain variables and symbolic constants repeatedly, most C compilers have a *header* file (for example, stdio. h) that contains these variables and constants. You may want to think of the header file as a file that contains *overhead* code. In program 5.1 the file that contains these functions is stdio. h. Because they are referred to as header files, the convention is to use a . h file extension for them so that they can be distinguished from program source files (. c).

The #include command is a *preprocessor* directive that instructs the C compiler to read the contents of a file into memory for use in the program. The contents of the header file become part of the source code when it is compiled (similar to the APPEND command in some BASICs). The general form of the #include directive is

```
#include <filename>
```

Note that the #include directive is not limited to a specific file. If you write a C program named color. h and want to include it as part of a new program, a #include <color. h> will have the same effect as rewriting color. h into the current program.

In most of the programs presented thus far, you have seen the #include used as

```
#include <stdio. h>
```

However, another use is

```
#include "stdio. h"
```

which uses double quotation marks rather than angle brackets. The two versions are not exactly the same. The #include version with double quotation marks instructs the preprocessor to search first for the file to be included in the same file directory where the program source code is found. If the file is not found in the source file directory, the operating system (or the compiler) may instruct other directories to be searched. On the other hand, the angle brackets work much the same, but they say *not* to search the directory that contains the program source file. Because most C programmers often have the compiler in one directory and the source file in another, we have used the angle brackets in our examples. You may use either form as you see fit.

As a general rule, header files do not include functions that are likely candidates for the library. Instead, header files contain global variables that are used repeatedly in many programs and symbolic constants that might be hardware-dependent.

#define

The #define command establishes the symbolic constants used in a program (as discussed in Chapter 2). If the symbolic constants pertain to only one program, there is little value in creating a separate header file for them because they won't be used again. Therefore, #defines that appear in the source code of a program usually reflect the unique needs for that program. If you have a large number of #defines that will be used in a number of source programs, you might combine them into a single header file and #include that file into each program.

In program 5.1 #define MAX 80 reserves 80 characters for the name and sets CLEAR to the ASCII code 12 (014 octal or 0C hexadecimal) that clears the terminal screen. Symbolic constants are used so that you can easily change these variables in the future. Otherwise, you would have to search through the entire program to find and change each occurrence of 80, "-014", and "-x0c".

Because "-014" and "-x0c" are between quotation marks, both are *string constants* that are stored in memory as ′-014′ or ′-x0c′ and ′-0′ ; the null is placed at the end of the string. A string constant is *not* the same as a character constant. A *character constant* appears between single quotation marks, such as ′-014′ or ′-x0c′ , and represents a *single* character; no null is added on. As expected, character constants cannot be printed out with printf(), using the "%s" conversion character. [You could try printing a character constant as a string. The printf() function will spin through memory until it finds a binary zero somewhere. An old saying: "Those who like to experiment learn much, but reboot often."]

String constants use the %s conversion character in printf(), whereas character constants use %c. A %c prints only one character at a time (and does not look for a null terminator), but %s prints whatever characters are present before the null character constant (′\0′) is read. (See the next section for details on the null character constant.)

If you have access to the source code for stdio. h, you should find a number of #defines there also. (Don't be concerned if you cannot fully understand what is in stdio. h. We haven't covered much of what will likely be found there.) Whenever the compiler finds MAX,

CLEAR, or any other #defines in the program, the compiler substitutes the defined constants in their places. A #define results in a global substitution of the constants throughout the program. The only exception is that substitution does not take place within quoted strings. That is,

```
printf("It really is a CLEAR day\n");
```

would not find CLEAR in printf() replaced with "\Ø14".

Although program 5.1 should look familiar to you by now, let's examine code fragment 5.2.

```
for (i = Ø; (c = getch()) != '\r' && i < MAX-1; ++i)
    name[i] = c;

name[i] = '\Ø';
```

Code fragment 5.2.

In the for loop, the initial value of i is set to zero, and the terminal value of the for loop is a combined test of i and c. (&& is the logical AND operator in C.) The test on i is straightforward; we don't want more than 79 characters entered, because MAX was set to 8Ø by #define. The 80th position (at most) must be saved for the null terminator.

The getch() function, which is part of the standard library, gets a single character from the standard input device (usually the keyboard). The getch() function then assigns the character you enter to c. The character is tested in the for loop to determine whether the character is (1) a carriage return character constant ('\r'), which corresponds to pressing the RETURN key; or (2) the 79th character (that is, MAX - 1). If neither condition is True, then the character is assigned to the proper element in the name[ ] array by the name[i] = c statement.

Note: The getch() function used in program 5.1 assumes that you do *not* have to press RETURN after each character is entered. Some compilers have a getchar() function that works in this manner, whereas others require pressing RETURN after each character. If you do not have a getch() function, check your documentation for an alternate function that doesn't require pressing RETURN after each character is entered. (Check your I/O routines for "unbuffered" I/O.) Some compilers may implement getch() as a direct call to the operating system. If you dig deep enough, you'll probably find a replacement.

Another potential problem may be the use of the carriage return character (' \r') to sense end of input. It is quite possible that your compiler will look for the newline (' \n') character instead. Use whichever character gets the job done.

We will use getch() and ' \r' in several subsequent programs; keep the caveats mentioned here in mind when you write your own versions of the sample programs.

The for loop continues executing until either MAX-1 characters are entered or the carriage return character (' \r') is detected. When either condition is sensed, the for loop is terminated.

The program line in code fragment 5.2 can be shortened, as shown in code fragment 5.3.

Code fragment 5.3.

```
for (i = 0; (name[i] = getch()) != '\r' && i < MAX-1; ++i)
   ;
name[i] = '\0' ;
```

Here the line serves the same purpose but fills the name[ ] array in the for loop construct itself. The characters returned from getch() are assigned directly into name[ ]; c is no longer used. Don't forget the lone semicolon; it's a do-nothing statement, but it's needed by the for loop so that it will function properly. Because this type of for loop is a common construct in C, you should familiarize your-self with it.

The Null Terminator

After the name is completed, the name[i] = ' \0' statement is exe-cuted. In the case of my name, the resulting string looks like

```
Jack Purdum\0
```

in memory. The' \0' character signals the end of the string and is called the null character. [The null character must be at the end of the string to tell strlen() that it has reached the end of the string and to inform printf() when to stop printing. Using this informa-tion, write your own version of strlen(), then compare it to the ver-sion in your library.]

The printf() function prints the string with the %s option. Because the null character has been added to the name, printf() properly displays the name as a string.

As previously stated, the null terminator is a single character with a value of zero. More formally, an ASCII null has a value of *machine zero* (that is, 00000000 in binary). We use the ' \0' as a notation to signal that it is *not* the same as the ASCII *character* for zero. The decimal value for the zero ASCII character is 48 (binary 00110000), which is not the same as the null terminator (machine zero). Knowing the difference between the null terminator and the decimal value for zero is quite important. For example, instead of

```
while (*s != ' \0' )
```

we can use

```
while (*s)
```

because a `while` statement terminates whenever the test criterion evaluates to logical False (that is, machine zero). We can leave out the explicit test for the null because the null character has a value of machine zero. This reason for omitting ' \0' may be difficult to grasp at first, but does make sense, and the omission occurs often in C programs. (Review the material in Appendix 2 if the concept seems unclear to you.)

If you tried to write your own `strlen()` function as previously suggested, you may have used the idea in finding the string length. One alternative is shown in code fragment 5.4.

In this case, we make use of the fact that the null character can terminate a `while` loop. Does your version use the same general approach? (There's nothing "etched in granite" or "right versus wrong" when writing your own functions. It is nice, however, when you can make things simple and still have them do their jobs.)

Accumulating Functions

We can use the previous routine in a more general way than just entering it in a program. To that end, let's write a simple function to input a string from the keyboard, as shown in code fragment 5.5.

The test in the `while` loop looks a bit busy but is no different than the test in the `for` loop shown in program 5.1. Note that we use a postincrement on variable `s` in the `while` loop. Convince yourself

```
/*******
          Function that determines the length of a string
     character array.

     Argument list:          char *s   the input character array
                                       (the lvalue)

     Return value:           int i     the number of characters
                                       before reading the null

*******/

int strlen(s)
char *s;
{
          int i;

          i = 0;
          while (*s++)
                    ++i;

          return (i);
}
```

Code fragment 5.4.

that, if a preincrement were used, the first character in s would
most likely be garbage. You should be able to decipher for yourself
the rest of the code in the function.

```
     /* a function that accepts a string from the keyboard */

void inputs(s)
char *s;
{
     int i;

     i = 0;
     while ((*s++ = getch()) != '\r' && i < MAX - 1)
          ++i;

     *s = '\0';
}
```

Code fragment 5.5.

After you have compiled the function, consult the documentation that came with your linker. It probably contains a utility program called a "librarian." The purpose of a librarian is to collect a group of unrelated (but useful) functions into a single module. This module becomes another library that you can use with your C programs.

Obviously, the more functions you have in your own private library, the easier it is to write C programs because most of the work is already done. [A more complete discussion of writing functions for a library is found in the *C Programmer's Library* (Que Corporation, 1984).]

Some Details on String Arrays

We learned in Chapter 4 that all variables in C must be placed somewhere in memory so that the compiler can find them later. For example, the definition

```
char name[20];
```

will be created by the compiler at some unique memory address. We also saw that this unique memory address is the lvalue for the variable. Furthermore, we saw that this lvalue corresponds to name[0] or, more simply, name; they are one and the same.

The lvalue that the compiler gives to a variable is constant and fixed by the compiler. Any attempt to change the lvalue will draw an error message. The example

```
++&name;
```

is an attempt to increment the lvalue of name, and the compiler won't allow it. Another common example is

```
char name[30];
```


```
name = 'A';
```

Here the programmer probably wants to place the letter A into the first element of the name[ ] array. Why is this wrong? Keep in mind that name without a subscript is the lvalue of the array. This code is another attempt to change the memory address (that is, name's lvalue) where the compiler placed `name[]`. What the programmer wanted to do is

```
name[0] = 'A';
```

The rule is simple: Never try to change the lvalue of a variable.

Getting Numeric Data into a Program

When we created the function to enter a string from the keyboard, we relied on the standard library function `getch()` to do most of the work for us. This function gets one character at a time from the keyboard. We can use the same concept, however, for numeric data. C doesn't provide an input statement for a number. (In other words, there is no equivalent to INPUT,A in C.) You must write your own function (unless your compiler has one in the standard library). Program 5.2 shows a crude version of the input function. [We have assumed that `inputs()` is now part of the standard library.]

```
#include <stdio.h>

#define MAXDIGIT 20        /* set max digits to 20 */

main()
{
    char s[MAX];
    int x;

    x = askint(s);
    printf("The number is: %d", x);
    printf("\nand its square is: %d\n", x * x);
}


/*******
        This routine requests and converts a string to a signed integer value.

    Argument list:        char s[]   character array that
                                     holds ASCII represen-
                                     tation of the number

    Return value:         int        integer value of the
                                     number
```

```
******/

int askint(s)
char s[];
{
    int i, sign, num;
    void inputs();

    printf("Enter an integer number: ");
    inputs(s);              /* get the character digits   */

    i = 0;
    sign = 1;

    if (s[i] == '-') { /* determine if negative       */
        sign = -1;     /* assume plus sign not entered */
        ++i;           /* (we said it was crude!)      */
    }

    for (num = 0; s[i] >= '0' && s[i] <= '9'; i++)
        num = 10 * num + s[i] - '0';

    return (num * sign);
}
```

Program 5.2.

The askint() function requests an integer number from the keyboard and relies on inputs(s) to create the string of digit characters. The function prints a prompt to the user, and inputs() gets the input from the user. [The standard library routine gets() could be used instead of inputs().] The character array s now holds the ASCII representation of the number.

Note that we declared inputs() to return a void data type. Any time a function returns a data type other than (the default) int, you should declare the return data type in the function that uses it. If you don't declare such functions, some compilers will issue an error message. In other cases, the program simply won't work properly.

How do you know which functions return something other than an int? In Chapter 3, you saw that every function has a type specifier which tells you what data type is returned from the function. Whenever you use a function that has a non-int type specifier, you should declare the function.

The sign is assumed to be positive for the number, but the if statement checks to see whether a negative sign were entered. If it was,
sign is set to -1, and i is incremented to look at the next digit in the
string. (You might want to improve the function at this point to look
for a plus sign, leading blank spaces, etc.)

In the for loop, num is initialized to zero, and the character is
checked to determine whether it falls between an ASCII zero and
nine. Notice that we are checking for ASCII zero, *not* the null terminator. If the character does fall between zero and nine, the appropriate value is assigned to num. The routine ends by returning
the product of num and its sign.

To illustrate how this program works, let's suppose that the character string contains "123\0" when it returns from inputs(s). On
the first pass through the loop, the ′1′ is translated as shown in
figure 5.1 (using decimal values for the ASCII equivalents).

```
num = 10 * num + s[i] - ′0′;    /* s[i] = ′1′ */
num = 10 * 0 + 49 - 48;
num = 10 * 0 + 1;
num = 1;
```

Figure 5.1.

Figure 5.2 shows subsequent passes through the loop.

```
num = 10 * num + s[i] - ′0′;    /* s[i] = ′2′ */
num = 10 * 1 + 50 - 48;
num = 10 * 1 + 2;
num = 10 + 2;
num = 12;
```

```
num = 10 * num + s[i] - ′0′;    /* s[i] = ′3′ */
num = 10 * 12 + 51 - 48;
num = 10 * 12 + 3;
num = 120 + 3;
num = 123;
```

Figure 5.2.

The loop then reads the fourth character, which is the null terminator for the string. Because the null character does not fall within
the required range of values (it has a value of machine zero, remember?), the loop ends. In short, the scan of the string ends on
the first nondigit, other than the minus sign. The returned value is
123 because the sign variable has a value of plus one.

The return to `main()` displays the number, then squares it to prove that we are dealing with numeric values, not strings.

Most compilers have numeric conversion functions as part of the standard library. The `askint()` function is similar to the `atoi()` function found in most libraries, except that we prompted for the string as part of the function. The `atoi()` (*ASCII to integer*) function usually requests a pointer to the location of the string, then returns the integer.

Most libraries include conversion functions for every data type that is supported by the compiler. (Subset compilers usually do not support floating-point numbers, however.) The function `atof()`, for example, converts an ASCII string to a floating-point number. Check your compiler's documentation for the conversion routines supplied in your standard library.

Output from a Program: printf( ) Options

Two other ways that information can be displayed on the screen are `putchar(c)`, which displays a single character on the screen, and `puts(s)`, which displays string data only. Of additional alternatives, `printf()` is preferred for its flexibility. However, `printf()` is a complex function that generates a larger amount of code than `putchar()` or `puts()`. If you do not need the features of `printf()`, then one of the alternatives should result in smaller program code size.

Many beginning C programmers often commit a minor oversight. Even when their programs contain `printf()`, the programmers still use either `putchar()` or `puts()`. Because `printf()` can do the job of the other two functions, using these functions places unnecessary code in the program. Some compilers provide integer-only versions of `printf()`, which can result in significantly smaller programs because the floating-point converters are left out. Check your documentation.

The following discussion of `printf()` and `scanf()` is based on the *System V Interface Definition*, D. E. Kevorkian, editor in chief (AT&T, 1985). Because of the newness of that publication, some of the features described for `printf()` and `scanf()` are not likely to be found on your compiler. Nevertheless, these features are presented here for completeness.

As we saw in Chapter 1, the format for `printf()` is

```
printf("control string", argument 1, argument 2,...);
```

The control string can contain the normal complement of ASCII characters plus the special characters, or *escape sequences*, shown in table 5.1.

Table 5.1

\n	newline (corresponds to a line feed)
\b	backspace
\t	tab
\r	carriage return
\f	form feed
\Ø	null
\'	single quote
\\	backslash
\nnn	octal bit pattern
\xnnn	hexadecimal bit pattern

The control string may also contain a percent sign (%), which is a conversion character with the available options listed in table 5.2.

The conversion character may be followed by a digit string (similar to that found in FORTRAN but not too different from PRINT USING). If the leading digit is a zero, any blank elements in the field are filled with zeros. Some examples are shown in table 5.4. The broken vertical line represents the left side of the CRT. Let's assume that a string variable named c exists and contains the word "computer\Ø".

Some compilers also support a special conversion character that lets the user set format fields at run time. This new conversion character is the asterisk. An example is

```
printf("%*.*f", width, precision, number);
```

Table 5.2

d   decimal

x   hexadecimal

o   octal (unsigned)

u   unsigned decimal

c   single character

s   string of characters (assumes \0 is the last character in
           the string)

e   decimal floating point in scientific notation (such as
           1.234E11)

f   decimal floating point

g   the shorter of e or f

printf( ) also permits all the options to be formatted as shown in table 5.3.

Table 5.3

-          left-justification of the argument right-justification of the
           argument by default

l   el for the long data type (data types are discussed in
           Chapter 6)

The pound sign indicates that whatever variable follows
           is to be converted into an alternate form. The pound
           sign has no effect when used with c, d, s, and u
           conversion characters. When used with the octal
           conversion character (that is, o), the pound sign forces
           the first digit to be zero by increasing the precision of
           the number. The pound sign has the same effect on
           hexadecimal conversions (that is, x). If the pound sign is
           used with any of the floating-point conversions, the
           printed result is always given with a decimal point even
           if the result does not call for one.

Table 5.4

Statement	Result
printf("123456789012345");	123456789012345
printf("My name is:");	My name is:
printf("%s", c);	computer
printf("%-15s", c);	computer
printf("%15s", c)	computer
printf("%4.2f", 123.456);	123.46
printf("%c", 'c');	c
printf("Answer is %d", 1234);	Answer is 1234
printf("x=%d and y=%d", 5, 8)	x=5 and y=8
printf("%05d", 17);	00017

If the value of width is 8 and precision is 4, the preceding line is equivalent to

```
printf("%8.4f", width, precision, number);
```

Thus, the first asterisk is replaced with the value of width, and the second asterisk is replaced with the value of precision. Obviously, width and precision are passed to printf() as part of the function call. This new conversion gives the programmer a little more flexibility than is provided with the fixed formats presented earlier.

Experiment with each option until you are sure of what effect it has on the resulting output. The printf() function is quite versatile, and you will find that it is capable of handling almost any output requirement.

scanf( ): The General Input Function

So far, we have concentrated on functions that display the output of a C program. The printf() function has been the workhorse in most of the sample programs. The input side of I/O operations, however, gives a program the flexibility needed to make it useful in a variety of circumstances. (After all, who wants to recode-recompile a program each time a new set of numbers is used?)

We have used the getch() function to get a character from the keyboard and do something with it in a program. This function, however, is a low-level means of entering data into a program. The inputs() function (in code fragment 5.5) used getch() to construct an integer number in the askint() function (in program 5.2). Despite these uses, a high-level input function that provides a more direct means of entering data would be very helpful. Such a function is scanf(), which is similar to printf() and has the same general format:

```
scanf("control string", argument 1, argument 2,...)
```

Because scanf() is used to enter data, the control string is used to specify the format in which the data is entered. The arguments to scanf() are supplied by the user.

The control string may contain the same type of data as printf(). The percent sign (%) is used for conversion purposes, and the asterisk (*) has a special meaning that is discussed later. Table 5.5 contains an interpretation for the control string.

Note that scanf() ignores leading white space in most cases. (The [] conversion character is an exception.) However, trailing white space, if not defined as part of the scanset, terminates the input for the field.

Whenever scanf() is used, the *arguments must be pointers* to the data type specified in the control string. The example

```
scanf("%d", &num);
```

says that we want a decimal number to be entered (the %d conversion) and the result placed in the variable named num. Because &num is used, the compiler places the number you enter at num's address. [You will recall from the discussion of pointers that the lvalue of num is passed to scanf().]

What happens if you enter a floating-point number instead of an integer? If the compiler does not support floating-point numbers, the decimal fraction is stripped away. You should check the behavior of your version of scanf() to see what happens. (It's a good idea to check all "standard" library functions to see what happens when unexpected data is entered.)

Some not-so-funny things can happen with scanf() if you don't plan carefully. Consider program 5.3.

Table 5.5

n   Return the number of characters scanned from the start of the scan

d   Input a decimal integer

u   Input an unsigned decimal integer

x   Input a hexadecimal integer

o   Input an octal integer

i   Input an integer number with conversion. That is, whether a hex, octal, or decimal number is input, all are converted to a decimal integer.

e, f, g   Input a floating-point number

c   Input a character

s   Input a character string

[Input a character string within a given range or scanset. For example, if you wish to input a digit and nothing else,

```
scanf("%[0123456789]", buff);
```
and
```
scanf("%[0-9]", buff);
```

produce the desired result in buff. Leading white space is significant. At least one input character must match a character between the brackets, or the scan fails.

^   Accept anything but the given scanset. For example,

```
scanf("%[^0-9]", buff);
```

will accept anything except a digit. The circumflex, therefore, works as a complement of the given scanset.

```
main()
{
    char adr[15];

    printf("Enter address: ");
    scanf("%s", adr);
    printf("Address is\n\n%s", adr);
}
```

Program 5.3.

Let's suppose that you want to enter "123 Main Street" for the address. Two problems arise. First, scanf() terminates its input on the first white space it finds. A white space includes blanks, tabs, carriage returns, form feeds, and newlines. Therefore, adr will contain "123" when you finish typing, because of the blank space between "123" and "Main". Yet even if scanf() behaved differently, a second problem still exists.

If the address with all 15 characters could be entered, everything would be okay, right? Wrong! Don't forget that all strings must be terminated with a null ('\0'). Because the address uses all 15 characters of the array, no room exists for the null. You must make sure that the character array (that is, adr[]) is large enough for the input *plus* the null terminator.

Another thing to keep in mind when you use scanf() is that array names are pointers; therefore, you should not use the ampersand (&) before such arrays in scanf(). In all other cases, the arguments must be pointers to the data type requested as input.

When an asterisk is used in the control string for scanf(), the asterisk becomes a special character that makes the program ignore the next data type you enter. Look at the lines in code fragment 5.6.

```
char name[15];
int num, new_num, old_num;

scanf(" %s %d %*d %d", name, &num, &new-num, &old_num);
```

Code fragment 5.6.

These lines receive

```
Fred 1111 2222 3333
```

from the keyboard; adr[] receives Fred, num equals 1111, new_num is ignored (because of the %*d in the control string), and old_num is 3333.

If the control string is

```
scanf("%3d", &num);
```

and the input entered is 11111, only the first three digits (111), at most, are assigned to num. In other words, if a number follows the conversion character (%) and precedes the data type (d), that number specifies the maximum width for the input field. The field width specification can be used with either numeric or string data. If a white space is detected before the maximum field width is reached, the input stream is still terminated at the white space. If a width specification is present, it should be interpreted as an "at most" limit from the input stream.

The scanf() function should cover most types of input you will need. However, you should verify that your "standard" library version of scanf() functions as it should.

One final point about scanf() should be made. It is a huge function and often represents an "H-bomb-to-kill-an-ant" approach to inputting data. On full C compilers, scanf() not only has to provide for getting the data into the right place, but also must have full conversion capability even if some conversions are not used (such as long and floating-point conversions). In many situations, code size will be smaller if discrete functions [such as gets() and atoi()] are used instead of scanf().

As an exercise, try writing C functions that duplicate the following BASIC input functions:

```
10 INPUT"Enter the address:", ADR
20 PRINT "Screen or Printer (S,P): ",
30 T$=INPUT$(1)\REM Get only one character
```

Input Functions with a Little Class

In the preceding BASIC functions, line 30 asks you to simulate the INPUT$ (or INCHAR$) command found in most dialects of BASIC. Both of these input commands request that a single character be entered from the keyboard. These commands are often used when you must select from a limited choice in which only a single keystroke is needed.

If you have ever used such commands, you know that they are usually preceded by some form of prompt to inform the user about what is being requested. A typical example in BASIC is the following:

100 PRINT "Output to Screen or Printer (S,P):",
110 T$=INPUT$(1)

C does not limit you to a predetermined set of input routines. Because the prompt is usually needed, let's write a function that allows us to include the prompt as part of the input function. (See program 5.4.)

```
#include <stdio.h>

main()
{
        char letter;

        letter = inchar("Enter a single letter");
        printf("\n\nThe letter is %c\n", letter);
}



/*******
        Function requests a single character input after
    printing a prompt on the screen.

        Argument list:      char *prompt    the prompt to be
                                            displayed

        Return value:       int             the single letter
                                            entered by user

*******/

int inchar(prompt)
char *prompt;
{

        puts("\n%s", prompt);
        return (getch());
}
```

Program 5.4.

The argument for the new inchar() function call is the prompt string that we want printed. This prompt string is passed to inchar() as a pointer to char. Recall that all string constants (that is, those within double quotation marks) are resolved to a pointer to char. Therefore, inchar() declares the prompt to be a pointer to char.

After being passed to inchar(), the prompt is displayed by puts() on the screen. The getch() function allows a single character to be entered without your pressing RETURN; the character is passed back to main() through the return (getch()) statement. The program then displays the character that was just entered.

[Because getch() does not echo the character entered to the screen, you will have to add your own code to display the key that is struck. The getch() function hides whatever letter was entered, which makes getch() perfect for entering passwords and other information that you don't want left on the screen after input.]

Note that we declared inchar() to return an int even though we know that the user only entered a char. The function description also says that we're sending an int back to main(). Why? The reason is that, when a char is either sent to or returned from a function, the character is automatically promoted to an int. When the character is returned back to main() and assigned into letter, the character is converted back to a char again. We will discuss the conversion issue in more detail in Chapter 6.

What would we do if we wanted a fixed number of characters to be entered, but not just one character? We would need to add two new arguments to the program to determine (1) the number of characters we want, and (2) a character array in which to store the input. (See program 5.5.)

The inchar() function in program 5.5 expands the argument list to include the number of characters wanted (repet) and a character array (answer) to hold the input.

Notice that the escape sequence for the backspace (\b) is used in the first printf(). Because a ZIP code has five digits (is it nine yet?), we printed five dots to represent the field width. These dots give the user some idea of what is expected on input. The backspaces simply move the cursor back five spaces to the first dot in the field.

Because we want to treat the result as a string, the null character (\Ø) must be appended at the end of the input in the function.

```
#include <stdio.h>

#define MAXLINE 80

main()
{
      char result[MAXLINE];
      void inchar();

      inchar("Enter Zip Code .....\b\b\b\b\b", 5, result);
      printf("\n\nThe Zip is %s\n", result);
}

void inchar(prompt, repet, answer)
char *prompt, *answer;
int repet;
{
      int j;

      printf("\n%s", prompt);

      for (j = 0; j < repet; ++j)
          *answer++ = getch();

      *answer = '\0';
}
```

Program 5.5.

We now have a generalized input function capable of printing various prompts and accepting any field width. The maximum length of the input string is limited to one less than the symbolic constant MAXLINE. (The length must be one less so that we can append the null at the end.)

To test your understanding, try modifying the inchar() function so that the letters are displayed on the screen as they are entered.

A Little More Class

Most screens let you position the cursor at any given row-column coordinates on the screen. We can do this positioning in C by using direct cursor control. Before you can use direct cursor control in a program, you must know the appropriate screen codes. The control codes for several popular screens are listed in table 5.6.

Table 5.6

Direct Cursor Control and Clear Screen Codes

CRT Screen	Cursor Codes	Clear
ADM-3	27, 61, -1, 31	26
ADDS, Intertec	27, 89, 31, 31	12
Advantage	27, 62, 31, 31	30, 15
Hazeltine	126, 17, -1, -1	126, 28
Heath, Zenith	27, 89, 31, 31	27, 69
IBM PC (ANSI)	"\033[%s;%sH"	"\033[2J"
Infoton	27, 102, 31, 32	12
OS1	27, 61, 32, 32	26
SOL	27, 2, -1, 27, 1, -1	11
Soroc, TeleVideo	27, 61, 31, 31	27, 42
SWTP	11, -1, 1	28, 18

The codes in table 5.6 are (ASCII) decimal values. Typically, such constants in a C program are written as an escape sequence in octal, or base 8, numbers. The escape sequence for decimal 27 is ′ \033′ . (The second digit times 8 plus the third digit = 8 times 3 plus 3 = 27.) For decimal 20, the escape sequence is ′ \024′ in octal. Conversion values are given for decimal, octal, hex, and binary in Appendix A.

If you look at the table, the cursor codes for the ADDS, Zenith, and Heath terminals are the same. Because the decimal number for 89 in the ASCII character set is ′ Y′ , we can write the sequence as "\033Y". Quotation marks are used because two characters are needed. (Single quotation marks are used for single characters, not for string constants.)

You cannot use a decimal 27 for the ASCII Escape code because decimal 27 is not a printing character in ASCII. (If you tried "27Y", that's exactly what would be printed on the screen. The Escape code 27 gives the CRT the information it needs to initiate special functions for the terminal.

If you look closely at table 5.6, you'll notice that both the cursor and the clear screen codes for the IBM PC appear a bit strange compared to the other codes in the table. The reason is that the IBM PC uses the ANSI standard codes for both cursor addressing and clearing the screen. Actually, many minicomputers and mainframe computers use these ANSI standard codes. The codes increase the portability of the programs that use them. If you use the IBM PC and the ANSI standard codes, make sure that the config.sys boot file has device=ansi.sys. At the end of this chapter, you will be shown how to use the ANSI codes to write the functions for cursor positioning and clearing the screen.

Because you may want to start the program with a clear screen, the clear screen codes are included in table 5.6 for each CRT. If your particular CRT is not on the list, you should be able to find the proper codes in your CRT manual. Try looking under "direct cursor addressing," "loading the cursor," "ANSI," and "clear screen-home cursor."

Program 5.6 illustrates one use of direct cursor control. Take a few minutes to study the program, then key it into your computer.

```
#include <stdio.h>

#define CLEARS  '\014'     /* clear screen for my CRT */
                           /*    and is a decimal 12   */
#define CURSPOS "\033Y"    /* cursor control lead in   */
                           /* 27 and then 89 = Y in    */
                           /*         ASCII            */
#define BELL    '\007'     /*    CRT ASCII bell code    */

main()
{

        char letter;
        int er;

        er = 0;
        putchar(CLEARS);
miss:   set_curs(5, 15, 0);
        letter = inchar("Enter a digit 0 through 9");
        if (letter < '0' || letter > '9') {
                er = set_curs (1, 50, 1);
                goto miss;
```

```
            } else
                    puts("\nEntry was a digit");

            if (er == 2)
                    set_curs(1, 50, 2);
}



/*******
            Function positions cursor at the row-column
       coordinates given by function call. If ring
       variable is 0, normal cursor control done. If
       ring is 1, bell sounded. Any other value, the
       previous error message is erased.

       Argument list: int row    row screen position
                      int col    column screen position
                      int ring   flag to determine whether
                                 to:
                                      1) do a simple return (0)
                                      2) ring bell and display
                                         error message (1)
                                      3) clear error message
                                         from screen (and other
                                         value)


       Return value:  int

*******/

int set_curs(row, col, ring)
int row, col, ring;
{
        printf("%s%c%c", CURSPOS, row + 31, col + 31);
        if (ring == 0)
                return;
        if (ring == 1) {
                ring = 2;
                puts("ERROR");
                putchar(BELL);
                return (ring);
        } else
                puts("                              ");
}
```

```
/*******
          Function requests a single character input after
printing a prompt on the screen.

      Argument list:       char *prompt    the prompt to be
                                           displayed


      Return value:        int             the single letter
                                           entered by user


*******/

int inchar(prompt)
char *prompt;
{
      printf("\n%s: ", prompt);
      return (getch());
}
```

Program 5.6.

This program uses the inchar() function discussed previously to enter a single digit from the keyboard. [A slight change was made in inchar() for you to consider.] Note the use of the words miss and goto miss in the program. The former is a label that references a specific statement in the program. The goto followed by a label reference transfers program control to the statement following the label-name-colon. The general form is

```
label name :
goto label name;
```

The colon must follow label name.

When we first reach miss, we set the cursor at row 5, column 15, and call the cursor-positioning function set_curs(). The row-column coordinates tell the function where to print the prompt on the screen.

The function call to set_curs() also passes a third argument to the function to detect an error condition. When the function is first called, the variable named ring is set to zero. When set_curs() receives its arguments, it positions the cursor at row 5, column 15. Because ring has a value of zero, the if statement causes a simple return to main().

The program then calls inchar() to get a character from the keyboard. The if statement in main() checks to see whether a digit was in fact entered. If it was not, then set_curs() is called again but with different arguments. Now the row-column coordinates are used to print an error message in an *error window* located at row one, column 50. Because ring equals 1 on entering the function, the if statement in set_curs() reassigns ring to equal 2, prints the error message in the window, and rings the CRT's bell.

Note that the variable er is assigned the value of ring when it is returned from set_curs(). If an error occurred, you should try to prove to yourself that er now equals 2.

When control returns to main(), the goto miss is executed. The goto statement causes control to be sent unconditionally to the location of the label name after the goto. In our example, control is sent to miss. Program execution resumes with the statement that follows the label name. The program then asks you to reenter the character.

This time, if a digit is entered in main(), the program will print a message to indicate that a digit was entered. If an error was made, the error message ("ERROR") is still on the screen in the error window. Because everything is okay now, we need to "erase" the error message. This is exactly what the final call to set_curs() does in main(). set_curs() prints 28 blank spaces in the error window, which erases the word ERROR from the screen. The if statement in main() assures that the final call to set_curs() will be performed only if an error message is on the screen.

In program 5.6 printf() and puts() were used to print information on the screen. The two functions do have similar uses. printf() is the formatted print function. puts() writes (puts) a string on the screen, as in

```
puts(string)
char *string;
```

There are two basic differences between printf() and puts(). First, printf() can use one or more arguments, the first of which is the control string; whereas puts() has only one argument: the string (character array) to be put to the screen. Thus, printf() will perform formatting functions (%6.2f, %s, %-6.d) when printing, but puts() does not perform any formatting conversions. If you need formatted printing, you must use printf(). However, both puts() and printf() recognize and properly translate all escape characters (\r for carriage return, \b for backspace, \t for tab, etc.).

The second difference varies among compilers, and you should check your compiler's documentation. puts() automatically prints a newline (\n) after the string is printed, but printf() does not. Therefore, the cursor automatically advances to the first position of the next line after printing the puts() string. With the printf() function, the newline character must be included in the control string, as in

```
printf("%s\n", "The cursor moves to the next line after the period");
```

puts() executes faster and is easier to use than printf(). The newline (\n) character is automatically printed at the end of the string. printf() is more versatile. To write a string of characters to the screen, you may use either puts() or printf(), but puts() is a much smaller function. If the cursor does not advance to the next line [as the cursor did for the inchar() function] or if formatted printing is required, use printf().

Structured Programming and goto's

Some people are obsessed about not using gotos in their code. Perhaps a more practical view is needed. If a goto rather than some form of convoluted logic makes it easier to decipher what a program is doing, use the goto. (That's one of the nice things about compiled code; it's pretty tough for someone to figure out whether you used a goto in the source code!)

For the student (and the purist) who would like to see how the program could be written without a goto, consider program 5.7.

In this variation, we force an infinite while loop by using TRUE for the while expression. As long as a nondigit is entered, the user spins around within the while loop. If a digit is entered, the break statement is executed, and we exit from the while loop. The rest of the program is the same as before.

The switch( ) Statement

Let's take another look at the set_curs() function. Once the cursor is positioned at the desired location, we have a series of if statements that depend on the value of ring. This series can be written in BASIC as

```
100 IF RING>1 THEN RING=2 ELSE RING=RING+1
110 ON RING GOTO 120,130,140
120 RETURN
130 RING=2:PRINT "ERROR" CHR$(7):RETURN
140 PRINT "                                    ":RETURN
```

C provides a similar alternative to the BASIC ON-GOTO, which is also used to replace a series of if statements. Let's rewrite this BASIC program in C. (See code program 5.7.)

```c
#include <stdio.h>
#define TRUE      1      /* to set up infinite while loop */
#define CLEARS  '\014'   /* clear screen for my terminal  */
                         /*   and is a decimal 12         */
#define CURSPOS "\033Y"  /* cursor control lead in        */
                         /* 27 and then 89 = Y in         */
                         /*          ASCII                */
#define BELL    '\007'   /*    ASCII bell code            */

main()
{

        char letter;
        int er;

        er = 0;
        putchar(CLEARS);

        while (TRUE) {
                set_curs(5, 15, 0);
                letter = inchar("Enter a digit 0 through 9");
                if (letter < '0' || letter > '9')
                        er = set_curs(1, 50, 1);
                else
                        break;
        }                                /* end while (TRUE) */

        puts("\nEntry was a digit");

        if (er == 2)
                set_curs(1, 50, 2);
}
```

```
set_curs(row, col, ring)
int row, col, ring;
{
        printf("%s%c%c", CURSPOS, row + 31, col + 31);
        switch (ring) {
          case 0:
                return;
          case 1:
                ring = 2;
                puts("ERROR");
                putc(BELL);
                return(ring);
          default:
                puts("                               ");
        }
}
```

Program 5.7.

The set_curs() function performs as before but uses the switch statement to decide which case to execute. The switch is followed by an integer expression that determines which case will be executed. In program 5.7, the value of ring is used, then compared to the expression that follows case. If a match is found (for example, ring = 0, and case = 0), then the program statements for that case are executed. Note that braces are not used for the statements associated with an individual case value. In other words, we would not use

```
  case 0: {              /* WRONG! */
        return (0);
  }                      /* WRONG! */
```

If there is no match between the switch expression and a case, the default is executed. If the default case is left out and there is no match, no case is executed.

If you are in a case in a switch and want to exit the switch when you are done, use a break statement. A break statement causes control to exit from a switch in much the same way as in a loop.

Note that each case must evaluate to a constant integer expression and be followed by a colon. Modify the program to include the form in program 5.7 and experiment with it. One possibility is to have different cases for different error messages and to use the value of ring to select the appropriate message. This way, you can get

get messages that are more informative than just "ERROR". Give it a try.

Using the ANSI Codes for Cursor Positioning and Clearing the Screen

If your computer uses the ANSI codes for screen control, the set_cur() function and CLEARS symbolic constant must be changed to perform properly. Usually, your compiler will already have these functions written for you [look for cursor() and clrscr()], but in case they are missing, the functions are presented here.

The ANSI code for clearing the screen is

```
ESC [ 2 J
```

where the ESC is the ASCII escape character (a decimal 27). Because the ANSI codes are always ASCII characters, everything used in the ANSI code must be an ASCII character. Therefore, the first thing you must do in program 5.6 is to change

```
#define CLEARS '\014'
```

to

```
#define CLEARS "\033[2J"
```

Note, however, that the original CLEARS was a single character, but we have replaced it with a string constant. Because of this change, we cannot use

```
putchar(CLEARS);
```

as we did in program 5.6, because putchar() prints only a single character, not a string. To use the ANSI clear screen codes, we must use

```
printf("%s", CLEARS);
```

Although it is possible to use puts(), keep in mind that many programs will already have the code for printf() included, but not for puts(). Using puts() in such programs increases code size unnecessarily. In addition, puts() appends a newline character to the end of the printed string; such a character may cause cursor-positioning problems in some instances.

The cursor-positioning changes are somewhat more complex. In this case, we shall write a separate function for cursor positioning. Refer to program 5.8.

Because the row-column positions are sent to cursor() as integer variables, but ANSI codes must be in ASCII, we use the itoa() from the standard library to convert from integer variables into the ASCII representation of the row and column variables. The call to printf() then prints the proper lead-in ANSI codes that must precede the ASCII representation of row. Because buff now contains the ASCII character values of row, a %s prints out the ASCII row position as it appears in buff. Note that a semicolon is part of the printf() control string.

A second call to itoa() converts the column value to ASCII, and a final call to printf() prints the ASCII representation of column as it appears in buff. Again, notice that a capital H is part of the control string. After this sequence is completed, the cursor will be positioned at the proper row-column coordinates on the screen.

To use the cursor() function in program 5.6, you simply replace the print() in set_cur() with a call to cursor(), using the proper row-column values. Don't forget to declare that cursor() is a void function. If your library supplies the clrscr() and cursor() functions, you might want to examine these functions to see how they were written for your compiler.

```
#include <stdio.h>
main()
{
        int row, col;

        clr();
        cursor(10, 15);
        printf("This is in the middle");
        cursor(21, 40);
        printf("At the bottom");
        getch();
}
```

```
/******

        Function that positions the cursor on an ANSI
    terminal.

    Argument list:          int r            row position
                            int c            column position


    Return value:           none

*****/

void cursor(r, c)
int r, c;
{
        char buff[4];

        itoa(buff, r);
        printf("-033[%s;", buff);
        itoa(buff, c);
        printf("%sH", buff);
}



/*****

            Function that clears the screen for an ANSI terminal
        and leaves the cursor in the home position.

        Argument list:          none

        Return value:           none

*****/

void clr()
{
        printf("-033[2J");
}
```

6

Other Data Types

Until now, we have used only character and integer variables. Most C compilers, even the most inexpensive, support these two data types. However, many applications require floating-point numbers (that is, numbers with a decimal fraction) or integers with values that exceed the limits of those used thus far.

If your compiler doesn't offer data types other than `int` and `char`, you should still read the rest of this text. The fact that you've made it this far suggests that you have more than a passing interest in C, and you may want to upgrade to a more complete C compiler. Appendix B can help you make a selection.

Fundamental Data Types

C has four basic data types:

```
char    int    float    double
```

We already know about the `char` and `int` data types, including their storage requirements and ranges. A `float` data type represents a single-precision, floating-point number (that is, a number with a decimal value like 3.14). A `float` typically is stored as a 32-bit number with 6 digits of precision.

A `double` data type represents a double-precision, floating-point number. Usually, a double has 14 (or more) digits of precision and is stored internally as a 64-bit number. `doubles` represent the same type of data that `floats` represent, but with greater precision.

Why settle for less than double? First of all, a double requires twice as much storage as that of a float. Second, a variable often doesn't need to be either a float or a double. A variable that controls a for loop is a common example. Because integer numbers contain fewer bits, they are processed faster than floats or doubles. The programmer must decide which data type is best for a given situation.

Keep in mind that the exact precision and internal bit requirements for each data type may vary among machines. Each C compiler can be written with different design goals and hardware restrictions. For example, many small computers use an 8-bit data bus, and data types tend to be even multiples of 8 bits. With the increased popularity of 16-bit machines, some data types may change bit requirements. (Some 16-bit C compilers have "large" and "small" models. The small model can address 64K of code and 64K of data; such models use 16-bit pointers. The large model can address a much larger amount of memory because 32-bit pointers are used.)

It's important not to jump to conclusions about precision and bit requirements. Even if the bit requirements are the same for each data type, the numeric precision may vary because of the way numbers are processed internally. Other things being equal, arithmetic processing in binary is faster than binary coded decimal (BCD). However, binary arithmetic is more prone to rounding errors for a given bit representation than BCD. Such differences may be unimportant in counting cell growth but are critical in accounting applications. Check your compiler's documentation for details about how the data types are processed.

Extensions of the Fundamental Data Types

Other data types can be derived from the four data types just mentioned. In C, the words long, short, and unsigned can be used as adjectives to create new data types. The following line illustrates how these new data types are formed:

```
short int   unsigned int   long int   long float
```

short

A `short int` is an integer number that can be positive or negative. Although the creators of C probably intended `short int` to be an integer that was smaller than an `int`, on many computers a `short int` is identical to an `int`. (An exception could be mainframe computer systems where an `int` is 32 bits and a `short int` is 16 bits.) Check your compiler's documentation to see whether any distinction is made.

unsigned

An `unsigned int` is an integer number that assumes only positive values. Because an `unsigned int` is not sign extended, it can assume larger values than an `int` can. For most micro- and minicomputers, an `unsigned int` uses 16 bits and has a value between 0 and 65,536 (that is, 2^{16}). Most minicomputers and mainframe computers use 32-bits, and `unsigned int` has a range from 0 to 4,294,967,295.

If you tried to print a pointer address with the `%d` conversion character in any of the sample programs, the pointer address was probably displayed as a negative number. This happened because data addresses are often stored in high memory—addresses that exceed the permitted range of an `int`. Because the most significant bit (that is, MSB, or the 16th or 32nd bit) is turned on, the number is interpreted as a negative number. If you use the `unsigned` conversion character (`%u`) in `printf()`, the address will be displayed correctly.

Apparently, the `unsigned` adjective will be extended to include `unsigned char`, `unsigned short int`, and `unsigned long int`. Because `unsigned` means that the MSB is no longer regarded as a sign bit, these new data types will extend the range of their signed counterparts.

long

The adjective `long` can be used with either integer (`long int`) or floating-point (`long float`) numbers. A `long` varies among systems, but its bit requirements are usually *twice* that of an `int`. For most micro- and minicomputers, a `long int` requires 32 bits and may assume positive or negative values. Permissible values for a `long int` range from -2,147,483,648 to 2,147,483,647—a fairly large range.

A long float has twice the bit requirement of a float, which makes a long float the same as a double. Therefore, no distinction is made between a long float and a double, and a long float is treated as a double by the compiler. Because a long float is the same as a double, the long float will no doubt eventually die of neglect.

Whenever an adjective (short, long, or unsigned) is used without a data type specifier, the compiler treats the data type as an int. For example,

```
unsigned address;
short steps;
long walk;
```

results in the compiler treating the variables as ints (that is, long int address, short int steps, and long int walk). If you use an adjective without a data type specifier, the variable will default to its int data type.

Mixing Data Types

With all the data type options available, you might think that confusion will reign supreme when arithmetic operations are performed. In fact, they are performed in an orderly manner, with the compiler taking care of most of the details. The rules for these operations are discussed in the next sections.

char and int

Rule 1: Any variable of data type char that is used in an arithmetic expression is converted to an int. For example, the atoi(string) function in C has the same purpose as the VAL(S$) statement in BASIC: the function converts an ASCII string of character digits to an integer. If you examine the code for atoi() in your library (or look at program 5.3 in Chapter 5), you will see one line of code in the function that looks similar to

```
number = 10 * number + string[i] - '0';
```

Remember that a character data type can be used in an arithmetic operation. To do this, the compiler first promotes (automatically) the character to an int. In this case, string[i] and the character constant '0' are both converted to an int before the arithmetic operations (multiply and add) are performed.

Conversion and Assignment

Rule 2. Whenever different data types are used in an assignment expression, the data type on the right side of the expression is converted to the one on the left side. Consider

```
number = string[1];
string[2] = number + 1;
```

In the first case, `string[1]` is converted to an integer, then assigned to `number`. Because a character data type needs fewer bits than an `int`, `string[1]` is normally zero-filled on the left during conversion. (The designer of the compiler has some latitude on this conversion.)

In the second case, where an integer is assigned to a character, any excess bits in `number` are thrown away before the assignment to `string[2]`. Because `char`s are typically 8 bits and integers are 16 bits, the "top" (that is, most significant) 8 bits of `number` are discarded. Again, the number of discarded bits may vary among compilers.

Type conversions are also performed on other data types during assignment. Refer to code fragment 6.1.

```
float big_num;
int little_num;
```

Code fragment 6.1.

```
little_num = big_num;
```

In this code fragment, `float big_num` is forced to an integer before the assignment to `little_num`. If `big_num` contains a decimal fraction, `big_num` is truncated to an integer before assignment. If the process involves moving from `double` to `float`, rounding is performed (not truncation).

Binary Operators and Mixed Data Types

Rule 3. A *binary* operator needs two operands. The term *operator* refers to the operation indicated by a symbol. The plus sign (+), for example, is the addition operator. Because an addition operation needs two numbers, the addition operator is called a binary operator. Each number is referred to as an operand. For example, when you multiply 2 times 3, the numbers 2 and 3 are the operands. Multiplication, therefore, is a binary operation because two operands (that is, numbers) are required. Likewise, subtraction and division are binary operations. A *unary* operator has one operand, and a *ternary* operator needs three operands.

If you perform a binary operation (requiring two operands) on two different data types, the compiler will convert the "smaller" operand to the "higher" data type. A "higher" data type can be thought of as the operand that requires the greater number of bits for internal storage. If an int and a double are multiplied, for example, the int will be forced to a double *before* multiplication because the double has a higher bit requirement. The result becomes the higher data type—a double in this example.

Floating-Point Arithmetic and Double Precision

Rule 4. If two floating-point numbers are used in an arithmetic expression, both will be promoted to double before the arithmetic operation is performed. If the result is assigned to a float, the result is *rounded* to fit the float. If the result is assigned to an integer, the result is *truncated* to fit the (smaller) int.

This rule means that all floating-point arithmetic is done in double precision even if both operands are floats. If you think about it, the rule also means that data conversions will be required for any arithmetic operation on a float data type.

Function Arguments and Promotion

Rule 5. If a char or short is passed to a function as part of an argument list, both will be promoted to an int. Likewise, a float is promoted to a double. However, is_letr may be used as type char, and is_flot may be used as a float in the function. An example is shown in code fragment 6.2.

```
main()
{
    char is_letr;
    float is_flot;
          .
          .
          .
    dummy(is_letr, is_flot);
          .
}

dummy(let, flot)
char let;
float flot;
{
          .
          .
          .
}
```

Code fragment 6.2.

The char and float in main() are promoted to an int and a double when passed to dummy(). However, they are declared as char and float in the argument declarations, and each may therefore be used as its declared data type in the function.

Promoting the Unpromoted

Despite the preceding five rules, in some operations the data types are not changed automatically. What do you do when you want to change a data type, but the compiler won't do it automatically for you? For example, let's suppose that you have two variables: one an int and the other a double. Normally, both numbers would be promoted to a double before an arithmetic operation (see rule 3). But let's suppose that you want the result to be an int. In this case, you would use a *cast*.

A cast in C *lets you convert one data type into another.* Thus, you can force a conversion of data types and "unpromote" a data type that normally is promoted by the compiler. A cast has the form

(data type) expression

in which the data type to cast is the data type you want. If you want to divide dbl_num by int_num, then the result will normally be a double. By using a cast, however, you can unpromote the double to an int after division. The syntax is shown in figure 6.1.

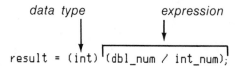

```
result = (int) (dbl_num / int_num);
```

Figure 6.1.

By using a cast, you force the result of the division of dbl_num by int_num to an int after the division is performed. The answer assigned to result is an int. If you do not use a cast, the result will be a double.

The cast is also commonly used with pointers. You probably have a function in your library called calloc(). The general form for calloc() is

```
char *calloc(count, size)
```

which returns a pointer to sufficient storage for count items, each of size size. Notice, however, that the function is designed to return a pointer to char; the pointer returned from calloc() has a scalar of 1.

Now suppose that you need enough storage for x integers, but x is determined by the user when the program is run. In other words, you have no way of anticipating what x will be. Therefore, you need to allocate enough storage for the ints "on the fly." One way to do this is

```
int x, *ptr;
char *calloc();



ptr = (int *) calloc(x, sizeof(int));

```

First, notice that we declared what calloc() returns from the function call (that is, a pointer to char). If we didn't make this declaration, the program would think calloc() returned an int (the default data type).

Now examine the call to calloc(). First, sizeof is an operator in C. It is *not* a function even though it may look like one. It determines the number of bytes required to store the data type that is the operand for sizeof. In our example,

```
sizeof(int)
```

will produce 2 as the result of the `sizeof()` expression because that is the number of units of storage required for an `int` with my compiler.

You might say, "Since I know that an integer takes two bytes of storage on my system, why can't I simply write the call to `calloc()` as the following":

```
ptr = (int *) calloc(x, 2);    /* bad idea */
```

Well, this solution will work, but it is not very portable. If you upgrade your computer to a larger machine or give the program to a friend whose compiler requires more than 2 bytes of storage for an `int`, the program won't work correctly. The `sizeof` operator will determine the proper storage requirements for the system being used; thus, the use of `sizeof` makes the code more portable. Always use `sizeof` when working with data-specific requirements.

If x has a value of 50 (that is, we want enough storage for 50 integers), the line resolves to

```
ptr = (int *) calloc(50, 2);
```

The arguments to `calloc()` are therefore interpreted as: "I need enough memory to hold 50 data items, each of which needs two units of storage."

The call to `calloc()` can respond in one of two ways. If it cannot find enough storage for the request, `calloc()` returns a NULL (that is, zero) pointer. Recall that a pointer with a value of zero does not point to anything useful. Therefore, if the pointer returned from `calloc()` is NULL, enough free memory wasn't available to satisfy your request. Therefore, you will often see code similar to

```
ptr = (int *) calloc(x, sizeof(int));
if (!ptr) {
     printf("Out of memory. \n");
     exit(1);
}
```

If `calloc()` returns a NULL pointer, we are out of memory. The `if` test says that if the pointer is NULL (that is, logical False), then "not pointer" (`!ptr`) is logical True, and the error message is printed. The call to `exit()` then returns control to the operating system, thus ending the program. (You should convince yourself that a valid pointer would not terminate the program.)

Any nonzero value returned from calloc() means that we now have a pointer to a place in memory that can satisfy the request for storage. However, since calloc() returns "pointer to char" and you want a "pointer to int", the scalars for the pointers are different. The cast is used to force the pointer returned from calloc() to be scaled to a pointer to int. Therefore, the expression

(int *) *expression*;

may be verbalized as: "Take whatever is in *expression* and cast it to be a 'pointer to int'." Once the cast is completed, the scalar will have been adjusted to that of an int.

Because we did use a cast, any operations on ptr (such as incrementing or decrementing) will be scaled correctly for the data type being pointed to.

Using Other Data Types

We can use this information to write a square root function for your library. We shall assume that the number is entered from the keyboard and stored internally as a string. Therefore, we will need first a function to convert the string of character digits to a floating-point number, then a function to determine the square root of the number. Let's examine the function to convert ASCII characters to a floating-point number.

Converting ASCII Characters to a Floating-Point Number

Consider code fragment 6.3.

```
/*******
        Function converts character string to floating-
   point number.

   Argument list:      char s[]  character array with
                                 character representation
                                 of f-p number


   Return value        double    the f-p number
```

```
*******/

double atof(s)
char s[];
{
    double val, power;
    int i, sign;

    i = 0;
    sign = 1;

    if (s[i] == '+' || s[i] == '-')          /* sign ? */
        sign = (s[i++] == '+') ? 1 : -1;

    for (val = 0; s[i] >= '0' && s[i] <= '9'; i++)
        val = 10 * val + s[i] - '0';

    if (s[i] == '.')                          /* fraction ? */
        i++;

    for (power = 1; s[i] >= '0' && s[i] <= '9'; i++) {
        val = 10 * val + s[i] - '0';
        power *= 10;
    }
    return (sign * val / power);
}
```

Code fragment 6.3.

The function begins with a type specifier which states that the function named atof() returns a double from the function. The argument supplied to the function is declared to be a character array. It holds the character digits to be converted.

The body of the function sets up some temporary variables, then checks to see whether the first digit in the array is a plus or minus sign. If a plus or minus sign is present, the line

```
sign = (s[i++] == '+') ? 1 : -1;
```

is executed. This line is an example of a *ternary operator* with the general form

$$expression\ 1\ \ ?\ \ expression\ 2\ :\ \ expression\ 3;$$

The ternary operator agrees with what was previously stated: it requires three operands. If *expression 1* evaluates to logical True, then *expression 2* is evaluated. If *expression 1* is logical False, then *expression 3* is evaluated. This process is illustrated in figure 6.2.

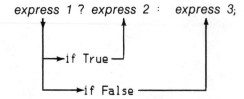

Figure 6.2.

The ternary operator is similar to IF-THEN-ELSE in BASIC. The BASIC and C equivalents of this process are shown in figure 6.3.

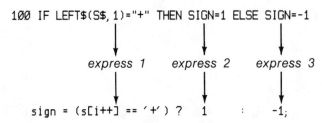

Figure 6.3.

The ternary operator in C replaces the simple IF-THEN-ELSE conditional expression in the BASIC program line. This line could be rewritten in C without the ternary operator, as shown in code fragment 6.4.

```
if (s[1] == '+' )
      sign = 1;
else
      sign = -1;
```

Code fragment 6.4.

Once you become accustomed to seeing the ternary operator, it provides a more concise and readable way of stating simple `if-else` statements.

After the sign is determined, the function uses the digits in the string to construct the number. Notice that we have used rule 3 to construct the number. Each digit is a `char` in the array but is promoted to a `double` because of rule 3: Operands in arithmetic functions are elevated to the highest operand used in the expression. Because we are using the variable `val` as a `double`, all operands in the expression become a `double`. In other words, the result of `s[i]-'0'` is promoted to a `double` before it is added to `val`.

If the character string contains a decimal point, i is incremented to pass over it and read the decimal fraction. Each character read after the decimal point causes power to be multiplied by ten, which is necessary because of the way val is calculated. For example, if the character string entered is 4. 12, val equals 412 just before the return is executed. Because power equals 100, however, the return statement becomes

```
return(1 * 412 / 100);
```

and returns the proper value of 4. 12 from the function. Bear in mind that the value returned is a double. (Rule 5: The function is also explicitly declared to return a double.)

The atof() function in code fragment 6.3 is fairly crude (for example, scientific notation fails, and an extraneous decimal point will have an unpredictable result), but the function will serve the purpose here. [Indeed, why not try writing an atof() to handle these errors properly? Also, you might try using pointers for variable s instead of treating it as an array. Having done that, you can time the array and pointer versions by calling atof() several thousand times in a for loop. Is there any speed difference?]

Finding the Square Root of a Number

Now that we have converted the character string to a double-precision, floating-point number, we can write the square root function, as shown in program 6.1. It is assumed that the atof() and gets() functions are in your library.

```
/* program to get number from user and find its square root */

    #include <stdio. h>

    #define CLEARS 12

    main()
    {
```

```
        double num, x, atof(), srt();
        int i;
        char s[12], *gets();
        void fpabs();

        putchar(CLEARS);
        printf("\nEnter a number: ");
        gets(s);
        num = atof(s);

        x = srt(num);
        printf("The square root of %f is %f", num, x);
}
```

```
/*******
        Function to return absolute value of a floating
point number. Note that it changes a negative f-p
number to positive via a unary minus on the pointer.

        Argument list:          double *num      pointer to f-p
                                                 number


        Return value:           none



*******/

void fpabs(num)
double *num;
{
        *num = *num < 0.0 ? -(*num)  :  *num;
}

/*******
        Function to return square root by Newton's
approximation accurate to about 5 decimal places.

        Argument list:          double num       the f-p number to
                                                 find square root

        Return value:           double           the square root of
                                                 num
```

```
******/

double srt(num)
double num;
{
    void fpabs();
    double a1, b1;

    if (num <= 0){
            printf("-nUndefined square root-n");
            return(0);
    }

    b1 = num / 2;
    a1 = num;

    while (a1 > .00001 * b1) {
            a1 = (num / b1) - b1;
            fpabs(&a1);
            b1 = ((num / b1) + b1) / 2;
    }
    return (b1);
}
```

Program 6.1.

This program may seem ambitious at first, but taken piece by piece, it's not too complex. The first thing that you should notice is the declaration of atof() and srt() as data type double, gets() as a pointer to char, and fpabs() as a void function in main(). *Unless explicitly stated otherwise, all functions return an int to the calling function after a function call.* Because all the programs in earlier chapters used only chars and ints, we never had to declare them explicitly (rules 1 and 5) unless they were void. Now that we are using pointers and floating-point numbers, however, we must declare explicitly all functions that return data types other than int. Forgetting to declare such functions in the calling function is a common mistake.

The program asks you to enter a number, which is placed in the s[] array by the call to gets(). The program then calls atof() to convert the string to a double-precision, floating-point number. After the number is returned from the function call, it is assigned to num.

The program then calls the srt() function, using num as its argument. A pointer was not used to pass the value to srt() because, with a pointer, num would be replaced by its square root, and the original num would be lost. With the previous program, a copy of num is passed to srt(), and num is preserved in main().

Remember that a pointer is used as an argument in a function call when we want to alter the variable pointed to by the argument from within the called function. (Arrays are an exception because they are not copied during a function call; the function receives the lvalue of the array.)

The srt() function declares num to be a double; then overhead variables are declared. The srt() function checks whether num is zero, or negative. If it is, then num is returned as zero. A smarter program would use this fact to signal an error condition. You should change your version of program 6.1 to signal this condition. [Hint: A simple if with a printf() ought to do it.]

We won't discuss Newton's approximation for square root in detail here. However, the while loop tests (relative) convergence on the square root and uses the absolute value of intermediate results. The fpabs() function gives us the absolute value of variable a1 when needed. Because the value of a1 must be altered permanently when fpabs() is called, we have passed the address of a1 (its lvalue) to fpabs() by using a pointer to reference it within fpabs().

Within fpabs(), the ternary operator is used to determine whether the number (num) is positive or negative. If the number is negative, the unary minus is used to convert the number to a positive value. Notice that the test uses 0.0 rather than just 0 in order to suggest a test on a floating-point number, not an integer. The use of 0.0 is necessary so that the compiler can generate a floating-point 0, not an integer 0.

Is a return statement in fpabs() necessary? No. Because a pointer was passed, we will permanently change the value of num in the function. There is no return value from fpabs(). To be consistent, however, we have declared it to return a void in the srt() function.

Eventually, the test in the while loop becomes False, and the square root (to about five decimal places) is returned to main() as a double. The program then prints out the original number and its square root. Type in program 6.1 and add the error handling discussed previously. You might also change the precision constant and see what effect it has on processing time and the result.

Using an unsigned Data Type

As discussed earlier, an unsigned int data type is an integer without sign extension. When we were limited to ints and chars, a meaningful memory address could not be printed out because the variable would probably be stored at an address that exceeded the range of valid numbers for an int.

Because this problem does not exist with an unsigned int, let's use this extended range to reinforce our understanding of pointers. Program 6.2 uses the unsigned data type to print out memory addresses in connection with the printf() function. (TheΔs represent blank spaces in the program lines.)

```
/* a simple program to use the unsigned date type  */
/* to print out lvalues and rvalues for an integer */
/* pointer and integer                             */


#include <stdio.h>

main()
{
    int num, *ptr_num;

    num = 5;
    ptr_num = &num;

    printf("\n");
    printf("\t\tptr_num\t\t\t\tnum\n");
    printf("\t\t|ΔΔΔΔΔ|\t\t\t\t|ΔΔ\\\n");
    printf("\tΔΔΔlvalueΔΔΔΔΔrvalue\t\t\tΔΔΔlvalueΔΔΔΔrvalue\n");
    printf("\t\t|ΔΔΔΔΔ|\t\t\t\t|ΔΔΔΔ\\\n");
    printf("\tΔΔΔΔΔ%uΔΔΔΔΔ%u\t\t\tΔΔΔΔ%uΔΔΔΔΔΔΔ%d\n",
           &ptr_num, ptr_num, &num, num);
    printf("\t\t\t|------------------|\n");
    printf("\t\t\tΔΔΔΔΔ*ptr_num = %d", *ptr_num);
```

Program 6.2.   }

The program is little more than a bunch of printf() function calls with tab (\t) statements. We have declared two variables: an int named num, and a pointer to an int named ptr_num. The program assigns num to equal 5, and ptr_num to point to num. The rest of the program prints out the lvalue and rvalue for each variable. The last printf() displays the rvalue of what ptr_num is pointing to. (If your compiler uses the large memory model, you may have to alter the tabs to get things aligned properly. The results, however, should be correct.)

Because it may be difficult for you to visualize how the program looks when it is run, the output of an actual run of the program is shown in figure 6.4. If you still feel uncomfortable with pointers, try keying in the program, running it, and studying its output.

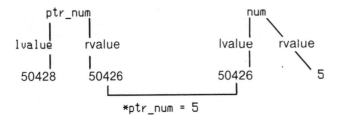

Figure 6.4.

Figure 6.4 tells us that ptr_num itself is stored at memory address 50428. This number is greater than the permissible range for an int; therefore, the unsigned int conversion character was used in printf(). Because the rvalue of a pointer is the address of what the pointer is pointing to, the rvalue of ptr_num should be the lvalue of num, and it is.

The lvalue of the variable num is the location where it is stored in memory (50426), and num's rvalue is its assigned value (5). Finally, *ptr_num tells us what the pointer is pointing to (5 in this example).

Notice that the lvalues for ptr_num and num are two "memory addresses" apart (that is, 2 bytes). The lvalues have to be separated by at least that much because each integer number requires 16 bits (2 bytes) on my compiler. However, you cannot always rely on variables being separated from one another by the length of an int. (More often than not, they won't be.) It just happened to work out that way for this program.

As a suggestion, if you ever have trouble figuring out what a pointer variable is pointing to, code similar to that in program 6.2 may be helpful in debugging.

Using a long Data Type

Earlier in this chapter, we saw that the long data type can be used to describe either an integer (long int) or a float (long float). Generally, the rules applying to a double also apply to a long float because a long float is treated as a double by the compiler.

The advantage of a long int (compared to an int) is its extended range of values. The long int is also used in several disk file library functions. If the long data type is supported by your compiler, any constant that exceeds the range for an int will be promoted to a long int.

Given that a long int requires as much storage as a float, which one should you use for an integer number that is larger than the range of an int, but within that of a long int? Usually, a long int is processed faster than a float and generates less code. Other things being equal (does that ever really happen?), the long int is the better choice.

The assignment of a long constant is written as

```
long big_num;        /* declare a long int */

big_num = 5000L;
```

The trailing letter L (or l) signifies that you are using a long constant even though the constant is within the range of an int. The L should be used when declaring any long integer constant, regardless of whether the constant could be represented by an int. This assignment increases program readability and eliminates any interpretation error by the compiler.

To gain some practice with the long data type, try rewriting the cube() function (discussed in Chapter 3) to work with long ints. Having done that, you might ask yourself what changes would be necessary to make the cube() function work with floats and doubles. Which would be more useful?

Right-Left Rule

As you gain experience with C, you will find yourself using more complex data structures. C lets you carry complexity about as far as you want to go. For example, what does the following line actually declare?

```
int (*p_array[MAX])();
```

To decipher this line, first look for the identifier (name of the variable) in parentheses, ignoring the asterisk (that is, pointer to something). In this example, p_array is the identifier. Once you've found the identifier (p_array) as the innermost term, look first to the right to see whether it is an array. In our example, we now know that the variable named p_array is an array variable of size MAX.

Now look left to see what's in the array. Because the identifier is preceded by an asterisk, the array must be an array of pointers. So far, we know that we have an array of *pointers* named p_array.

To determine what the pointers point to, look to the right of the array pointer. In this case, the () tell us that we are pointing to functions.

We then look to the left to find out what these functions return. In the example, each function returns an int data type. Now look to the right for any further terms in the declaration. Because there are none, we know what the declaration is. In this example, we are declaring "an array of pointers to functions returning ints."

Let's examine the procedure we followed earlier. First, we must find the identifier (ignoring any asterisks). In complex declarations, we must go to the innermost level of parentheses. Second, we begin a right-left-right-left scan of the declaration to work our way out of the parentheses. The scanning steps for the previous declaration are shown in figure 6.5.

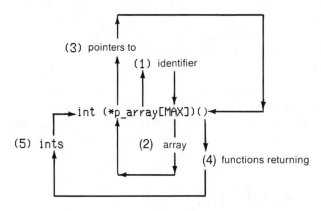

Figure 6.5.

Notice how the right-left-right-left scan (or parse) of the declaration was used. This *right-left* rule can be applied to any complex declaration and will define what you are looking at as you work your way out of the declaration.

A Shorthand for Data Types

Let's suppose that we need three such arrays in a program. We could use three declarations like the preceding one, or we could use the typedef command C provides. *A typedef lets us consolidate a complex declaration into a single new word.* If we use the previous example, then

```
typedef int (*P_ARRAY[])();
P_ARRAY growth[MAX], yield[MAX], heat[MAX];
```

establishes a complex data "adjective" called P_ARRAY for variables that are an "array of pointers to functions returning ints." A typedef, therefore, is a shorthand form for complex data declarations. A typedef does not "create" a new data type but merely collects one or more existing types into a single word. Uppercase letters emphasize that a typedef is being used for the declaration.

Proper use of a typedef can makes things clearer. For example,

```
typedef char *CHAR_PTR;
CHAR_PTR message, prompt;
```

declares message and prompt to be pointers to characters. For some people, this declaration is easier to understand than the more direct char *message declaration. Use whichever one you think is better.

Multidimensioned Arrays

Although arrays are useful in presenting lists of data, multidimensioned arrays are used for tabular data. Those accustomed to programming in BASIC are familiar with the following syntax:

```
100   FOR    J=1 TO 3
110            FOR K=1 TO 5
120               Y(J,K)=X(J,K)
130            NEXT K
140   NEXT   J
```

The variables X and Y are both two-dimensional arrays. At some point in the program, there is probably a dimension statement

```
50 DIM  X(3,5), Y(3,5)
```

In C, the declaration for similar arrays is

```
int x[3][5], y[3][5];
```

which declares two variables, each with three rows and five columns. What is the scalar for these declarations? When two-dimensional arrays are declared, the second subscript (for example, 5) is the scalar for the variable. This distinction is important because of the way increment and decrement operators work. For example, if we start at x[0][0] (the lvalue of x) and perform

```
++x;
```

the statement would mean that we are now looking at x[1][0], not x[0][1]. The increment operator does what we expect: it looks at the next element in the array, not the next integer in a given element. (The impact of this behavior on function calls is discussed next.)

To initialize the x[][] array with integer values, use a declaration like that shown in code fragment 6.5.

```
int x[3] [5] = {
     {0,  1,  2,  3,  4},
     {0,  1,  4,  9,  16},
     {0,  1,  8,  27,  64}       /* note: no comma here */
};
```

Code fragment 6.5.

The declaration creates a two-dimensional array in which the first row contains integer values, and the second and third rows are the square and cube of the first row. You might try to write a short program that increments the array in code fragment 6.5 and print out the values as you work through the array.

Note carefully that the last element initialized in code fragment 6.5 is *not* followed by a comma. This practice is consistent for all initializers in C, regardless of data type.

The compiler, of course, stores the x[][] array as a single vector in memory and partitions it according to the declaration. In other words, the second dimension of the array determines where the vector is "folded." It follows that the second dimension is also the scalar for the variable x.

Because the declaration of the array tells what kind of data type is being used, all the compiler really needs to know is how many columns are in the array. Therefore, if you need to pass a two-dimensional array to a function, you must explicitly declare the column count. With single-dimensioned arrays, we could get away with what we see in code fragment 6.6.

```
func(x)
int x[];
{



}
```

Code fragment 6.6.

With multidimensioned arrays, however, all we can get away with is shown in code fragment 6.7.

```
func(x)
int x[][5];          /* must have column count */
{


}
```

Code fragment 6.7.

The compiler must have the column count to set the scalar so that it can partition the array (vector) properly. In all other respects, arrays behave as you would expect.

As an exercise, try writing a program that calls a function to compute the square and cube of some integer values and stores the results in a two-dimensional array. Then use printf() to display the results with nested for loops (that is, a for loop within a for loop). To verify what's been said here, you should also test to see what impact an increment or decrement operator has on the array.

7

Structures and Unions

If you have worked with BASIC, you probably have had occasion to handle a group of data that you wanted to "keep together." One common example is a group of names, addresses, and telephone numbers. Because BASIC doesn't provide a convenient means of working with a group of dissimilar data items, you probably selected similar variable names so that you could at least keep track of the data.

C has a better way of handling these problems: using a structure. A structure *organizes* different data types so that they can be *referenced as a single unit*. It usually consists of two or more variables (although nothing prevents you from using a structure with only one variable). BASIC does not have a corresponding statement for a structure. (The FIELD statement is the closest.)

Before a structure can be used in a program, the structure must be declared with the keyword struct. As an example, let's suppose that you want to organize the attributes of your screen for subsequent use in a program. To keep things simple, let's assume that you want to use the clear screen function, indicate the number of characters that can appear on one line, and determine the number of lines to be displayed. The structure declaration is shown in code fragment 7.1.

```
struct terminal {
        char clear;     /* clear screen */
        int  width;     /* characters per line */
        int  lines;     /* number of lines */
    };
```

Code fragment 7.1.

In this declaration the word `terminal` is the *structure tag*. The tag allows us to give this structure a name for future reference. It is *not* a variable name. Indeed, no variable yet exists that can use this structure. All we have at this point is a template for the structure; we have declared a "mold" from which variables can be formed.

The structure declaration in code fragment 7.1 creates a template in memory, as represented in figure 7.1. (We'll assume 16-bit addresses and integers and that the template for the structure starts at memory location 20000.)

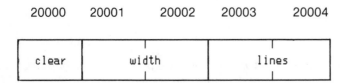

Figure 7.1.

A single `char` (8 bits) is declared for the clear screen code, and two `int`s (16 bits each) are declared for `width` and `lines`. The three data types in the structure declaration are the *members* that make up the structure. A member, therefore, is one of the data items that is declared within the structure.

As things stand now, there are still no variables that can use this structure. To define such a variable, you use the following definition:

```
struct terminal crt;
```

This definition tells the compiler to create, or reserve storage for, a variable named `crt` by using the structure "mold" named `terminal`. The structure tag `terminal` tells the compiler which structure (or mold) is to be applied to the variable named `crt`. We now have a variable (`crt`) that consists of three members: (1) `clear`, (2) `width`, and (3) `lines`.

We could create the same variable with the structure definition shown in code fragment 7.2.

```
struct {
     char clear;
     int width;
     int lines;
} crt;
```

Code fragment 7.2.

This definition both *declares* and then *defines* a variable named `crt`, which is a structure of the same type as that shown in code fragment 7.1.

Note that the structure tag is missing in code fragment 7.2. A structure tag is optional and is used only when you want multiple variables of the same structure type. For example, if we wanted two variables of the `terminal` structure, we might follow the structure definition with

```
struct terminal crt, crt1;
```

This line uses the structure-template named `terminal` to define two variables (`crt` and `crt1`), each of which uses the same structure definition. The actual makeup of variables `crt` and `crt1` is identical because they are "molded" from the same structure (that is, the `terminal` structure).

Note: A structure tag is used only when two or more variables of the same structure content are needed. The `terminal` structure tag would probably not be used because the program would be used with a particular CRT. In other words, the structure declaration in code fragment 7.2 would be used in this instance.

Initializing a Structure

Once a variable is defined as being of a certain structure type, the members of the structure are empty (that is, they contain nothing useful). Each member contains whatever happens to be in memory at the time that the compiler established the variables. Now we need to initialize the members of the structure.

We can use the information in table 5.1 (see Chapter 5) to initialize the variable named `crt` in one of two ways. If we use a structure tag in the structure declaration, the structure is initialized as

```
struct terminal crt = {
    '\014',             /* clear screen code */
    80,                 /* number of columns */
    24                  /* number of rows    */
};
```

which sets the structure member named `clear` to the decimal value 12, the member named `width` to equal 80, and the member named `lines` to equal 24.

If no tag were used in the declaration of the structure, the structure would be initialized as part of the definition, as shown in code fragment 7.3.

```
struct {
     char clear;
     int width;
     int lines;
} crt = { '\014', 80, 24};
```

Code fragment 7.3.

Initialization, therefore, depends on the way the structure is defined. If no structure tag is used, the structure is initialized properly as part of the structure definition.

Regardless of whether a structure tag is used or not, the initialization of the structure produces the same result. If the variable crt existed in memory at location 50000, the variable would look like that in figure 7.2.

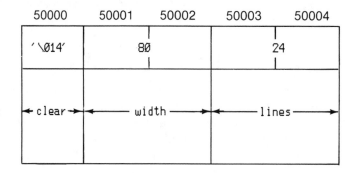

Structure variable named crt (ADDS)

Figure 7.2.

If your terminal uses two or more codes to clear the screen, you will have to use a different structure definition. For example, the SOROC CRT uses an ASCII ESC (decimal 27) followed by an asterisk. Because two ASCII codes cannot be combined in a single character, we need a character array for the clear member. The structure definition and initialization, in this case, might appear as shown in code fragment 7.4.

Why reserve three elements in clear[]? Because clear[] will be used as a string, you will need enough room for two ASCII codes

Code fragment 7.4.

```
struct {
      char clear[3];
      int width;
      int lines;
} crt = { "\033*", 80, 24};
```

(Escape plus the asterisk) followed by the null terminator (' \0'), for a total of three elements. The structure would now look like that shown in figure 7.3.

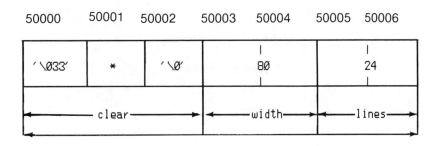

Figure 7.3.   Structure variable named crt (SOROC)

The nature of the structure is the same except that the member named clear was changed to accommodate two ASCII characters and the null terminator. Now you can use it as a string.

Using a Structure

Because we have our structure, we need to learn how to access it for use in a program. Program 7.1 illustrates one use of a structure.

In program 7.1 the structure variable crt is defined without a structure tag and initialized as part of the structure definition. Because the structure is defined outside a function, crt is treated as an external variable.

This program uses the function puts() to print a message on the screen. [puts() is usually part of the standard library.] All puts() does is "put a string" on the screen. We could have used printf() instead, but puts() is a much simpler function that generates less code.

The program then waits for you to press a key before continuing with a function call to getch(). After a key is pressed, the program

```
#include <stdio.h>

struct {
    char clear;
    int width;
    int lines;
} crt = { '\014', 80, 24};

main()
{

    puts("This is a test of the clear screen. ");
    puts("Press any key to continue: ");
    getch();
    putchar(crt.clear);          /* use puts() for string */

    puts("The screen should have been cleared. ");
}
```

Program 7.1.

calls the putchar() function by using the clear member of the crt structure as its argument. The putchar() function (also from the library) "puts a single character" on the screen. If your terminal uses more than one code to clear the screen, you will have to use the puts() function.

Notice how we referenced the member clear of the crt structure. Its general form is

  structure_name. member

or

  crt.clear

in our example. The "dot" operator that follows the structure name specifies which *member* of the structure is to be referenced. In effect, the dot operator says: "Give me the structure member named clear from the crt structure." From the compiler's point of view, this makes sense; it needs to know first which structure, then which member within that structure.

The program then clears the screen and displays a message to that effect. If you needed either of the other members of the structure, it would be referenced in similar fashion (that is, crt.width and crt.lines).

Structures do not let us do anything that we could not do already with the (discrete) data types discussed previously. The advantage of a structure is that it references various data types as a single, cohesive unit. In this sense, programs can be better understood.

Using Structures with Functions

Often a structure is created so that its members can be used as arguments in a function call. Many C compilers currently on the market, especially those for personal computers, do not allow you to pass a structure to a function, or return a structure from a function. (Although some compilers do permit the passing of structures to functions, we shall proceed as if this is not the case. All compilers that support structures do allow you to pass members of the structure to a function.)

All you can do in a function call is give the function the address of the structure (using &) or reference a member of the structure. Let's see how a member of a structure is referenced in a function call.

Let's suppose that you want a function that uses our crt structure to pause in printing a list of data when the screen is filled, as illustrated in program 7.2.

To let you view the data, the pause() function stops the display when the screen is filled. After you have finished reading the data, you press any key to reset the line counter to 1. The function returns the letter pressed if the screen was filled. Otherwise, nothing useful is returned from the function.

If you press the # key, the if statement after the function call to pause() is True, and the break statement is executed. This action breaks us out of the infinite for loop and ends the program.

If any key other than the # key is pressed, then num_lines equals one after the function call to pause(). This causes the screen to clear in main() before displaying the next screenful of data. A pause() is therefore a practical function for a long list of data being displayed on the screen. (This function is quite useful for those who cannot read at 9600 baud.)

Notice how only the line counter is passed to pause() on each pass through the loop. The argument passed is a pointer to the line

```
#include <stdio.h>

struct {                     /* define crt attributes */
     char clear;
     int width;
     int lines;
} crt = { '\014', 80, 24};

main()
{
     char c;
     int num_lines;

     num_lines = 1;

     for (;;) {
          if (num_lines == 1)
                putchar(crt.clear);
          puts("Print something on the screen.");
          num_lines += 1;
          c = pause(&num_lines);
          if (c == '#')
                break;.
     }
}



/*******
         Function pauses the screen after crt.lines - 2
lines of output are displayed. The line counter is
reset to 1 when screen is filled.

     Argument list:        int *so_far      pointer to the line
                                            counter

     Return value          int              0 if < crt.line - 2
                                            lines are displayed
                                            otherwise the character
                                            entered by the user

*******/
```

```
int pause(so_far)
int *so_far;
{
    char c;

    if (*so_far != crt.lines - 2)
        return (0);
    printf("\n\t\tPress any key to continue or # to end: ");
    c = getch();
    *so_far = 1;
    return (c);
}
```

Program 7.2.

counter variable (num_lines), which keeps a count of the number of lines displayed so far. A pointer is used because we must be able to reset the line counter if the screen is filled with data.

Why don't we pass the structure member crt.lines to the pause() function as part of the argument list? As you will recall from Chapter 3, if a definition occurs outside a function, whatever has been so declared has an external storage class. This is the case for the crt structure. As a result, the crt structure is available to any function in the same file without explicit definition within the function.

Structures and Privacy

What if we want to make the structure private to a function? In this case, consider program 7.3.

In this program, we have defined the crt structure within main(), thereby removing crt from the external storage class. Structures defined within a function cannot be initialized in the same manner as external structures. Inside a function, structures are initialized by simple assignment.

As a general rule, arrays and structures with the auto storage class (that is, those defined within a function) cannot be initialized. (Is there a way to initialize structures within a function as though they were external? Hint: Think about the static storage class.)

Because pause() needs to know how many lines can be displayed at one time, but crt.lines is private to main(), we must pass this information to pause() in the argument list. In this instance, we don't need to alter the contents of the crt.lines structure member. Therefore, no pointer to it is needed in pause(); crt.lines behaves like any other function argument.

```
#include <stdio.h>

main()
{
        char c;
        int num_lines;

        struct {    /* structure declared within main() */
                char clear;
                int width;
                int lines;
        } crt;
                    /* and initialized within main() */
        crt.clear = '\014';
        crt.width = 80;
        crt.lines = 24;

        num_lines = 1;

        for (;;) {
                if (num_lines == 1)
                        putchar(crt.clear);
                puts("Print something on the screen.");
                num_lines += 1;
                c = pause(&num_lines, crt.lines);
                if (c == '#')
                        break;
        }
}

/*******
        Function pauses the screen after crt.lines - 2
    lines of output are displayed.  The line counter is
    reset to 1 when screen is filled.

    Argument list:          int *so_far    pointer to the line
                                           counter
                            int max        maximum lines for a
                                           full screen
```

```
      Return value              int              0 if < crt.line - 2
                                                 lines are displayed
                                                 otherwise the character
                                                 entered by the user


*******/

int pause(so_far, max)
int *so_far, max;
{
        char c;

        if (*so_far != max - 2)
                return(0);
        printf("\n\t\tPress any key to continue: ");
        c = getch();
        *so_far = 1;
        return (c);
}
```

Program 7.3.

Whereas copies of structures are typically not supported in function calls, individual members can be copied, as shown in program 7.3. If you try this program, you will find that it functions exactly as before. (See program 7.2.)

Altering a Structure Member in a Function Call

At times, you will want a function call to alter the contents of a structure member. To alter member crt.lines in the pause() function call, try the modifications in code fragment 7.5. (This is a skeleton taken from program 7.3.)

The function call to pause() in this case passes the *address* (the lvalue) of structure member crt.lines to pause(). By treating the variable max as a pointer in pause(), we can alter the contents of crt.lines through indirection. Structure members are passed to functions in the same manner as any other variable.

```
main()
{
                            /* pass the address... */
        .
        c = pause(&num_lines, &crt.lines);
        .
        .
}


int pause(so_far, max)
int *so_far, *max;         /* ...and use a pointer */
{
        .
        .
}
```

Code fragment 7.5.

Passing the Entire Structure to a Function

If the situation arises in which you want a function to alter every member in the structure, you must use pointers. Because structures typically are not copied during a function call, the address (again, the lvalue) of a structure must be passed to the called function. Look at the previous example and notice the subtle differences between it and program 7.4.

In this case, the entire terminal structure is available to pause() because we have declared the structure outside any function; pause() has access to the template of the structure. The structure tag must have an external storage class so that the compiler can decipher the contents of the structure when it generates code for pause().

The crt structure created from the template is private, however, because crt is defined within main(). The pause() function knows nothing of what is contained in any structure that has been defined with the terminal structure tag inside the main() function, unless we pass pause() the address of the crt structure (that is, &crt) during the function call to pause().

```
#include <stdio.h>

struct terminal {
        char clear;
        int width;
        int lines;
};

main()
{
        char c;
        int num_lines;
        struct terminal crt;

        crt.clear = '\014';
        crt.width = 80;
        crt.lines = 24;
        num_lines = 1;

        for (;;) {
                if (num_lines == 1)
                        putchar(crt.clear);
                puts("Print something on the screen.");
                num_lines += 1;
                c = pause(&num_lines, &crt);
                if (c == '#')
                        break;
        }
}


/*******
        Function pauses the screen after crt.lines - 2
lines of output are displayed. The line counter is
reset to 1 when screen is filled.

Argument list:  int *so_far     pointer to the line
                                counter
                struct terminal *max    pointer to structure
                                        of type max
```

```
     Return value          int          Ø if < crt.line - 2
                                        lines are displayed
                                        otherwise the character
                                        entered by the user


*******/

int pause(so_far, max)
int *so_far;
struct terminal *max;            /* note the difference */
{
        char c;

        if (*so_far != max->lines - 2)
                return (Ø);
        printf("\n\t\tPress any key to continue: ");
        c = getch();
        *so_far = 1;
        return (c);
}
```

Program 7.4.

When pause() receives the address of a structure, the function needs to know what type of data is found at that address. For this reason, we use the argument declaration

    struct terminal *max;

This declaration tells the compiler to use a structure of type terminal and the variable named max as a pointer to that structure. The variable max, therefore, becomes a pointer to the crt structure declared in main(). Because pointers always pass an lvalue, max has the starting address for the crt structure as its rvalue.

Because we are referencing the crt structure through a pointer (that is, through indirection), the syntax for getting the contents of the structure must reflect that fact. We could use

    (*max).lines;

to access the desired member (crt.lines) of the crt structure. The parentheses around *max are necessary because the "dot" (structure member) operator *has higher precedence* than *—the "contents of" operator. (The precedence of operators is at the end of this chapter.)

Referencing structure members with a pointer is such a frequent task in C, however, that a special operator is used, as in

```
max->lines;
```

The "arrow operator" causes the structure pointer variable named max to access the specified member of the structure—the member named lines in this example. The arrow operator accesses the structure member crt.lines in program 7.4 and is equivalent to the (*max).lines presented earlier.

If you have a compiler that does allow you to pass the entire structure to a function, you would alter program 7.4, as shown in code fragment 7.6 (a skeleton of program 7.4).

```
main()
{
        .
        c = pause(&num_lines, crt);        /* send it all */
        .

}


int pause(so_far, max)
int *so_far;
struct terminal max;          /* note no pointer */
{
        .
        if (*so_far != max.lines - 2)
                return (0);
        .
        .

}
```

Code fragment 7.6.

The ability to pass the entire structure means that you do not have to use max as a pointer to the structure. Because the function has direct access to the entire structure, the dot operator can be used again.

Structures and Arrays

The example that we've been building in this chapter is simpler than what you might use in an actual program. Indeed, it would be easier to declare the variables in the `crt` structure as constants instead. A simple example, however, often is a better learning tool. Now that we have a basic understanding of structures, let's move on to something more practical.

Let's suppose that your firm pays its employees in cash and uses a "pay envelope" for that purpose. A certain number of 20's, 10's, 5's, and so on, will be required to make up the contents of the pay envelope. Each envelope's contents are different but must be the correct amount. The question is, Given the pay of each employee, how much of each currency denomination is needed to pay all the employees?

The information needed to pay each employee is (1) the employee's name, (2) the employee's wage, and (3) a count of the denominations that make up the wage—to the penny. Consider the structure definition and the initialization of the `denom[]` array in code fragment 7.7.

```
struct bill_count {
      char name[NAMSIZ];
      int wage;
      int curncy[8];
} totals[MAXSIZ];

int denom[8] = {2000, 1000, 500, 100, 25, 10, 5, 1};
```

Code fragment 7.7.

We have assumed that the structure is defined outside any function and, therefore, that it has an external storage class. The structure contains a character array member (`name[]`) capable of holding `NAMSIZ` characters. Let's assume that the character constant `NAMSIZ` has been `#defined` elsewhere in the program.

The structure also contains an integer to hold the employee's wage. It might seem more logical to use a `float` here to cover any "change" in the pay envelope. If you look at the initialized content of the `denom[]` array, you may be able to guess why an `int` was chosen instead. (Those of you who have really made it big might need a `long` instead of an `int`. Alas, such is not my situation.)

We will use the penny (the smallest unit of currency) as our basis of counting. The cash value is, therefore, the denomination (an integer) divided by 100. For example, element denom[0] is initialized to 2000. If we divide by 100, we see that this element determines the number of twenty-dollar bills needed to pay an individual. Similarly, element denom[7] holds the pennies (denom[7] = 1/100 = $.01).

The last member of the structure is an integer array named curncy[] that stores the proper denomination count for each individual. Because the twenty-dollar bill is the largest unit of currency we are using, we need eight elements in this array. (Look at denom[]'s initialization if this isn't clear.) The template for the structure declaration is shown in figure 7.4.

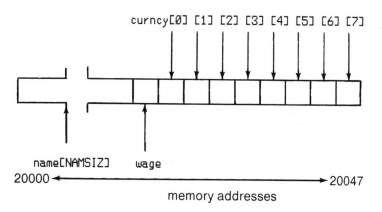

Figure 7.4.

If we assume that NAMSIZ is 30 characters, then the template uses 48 bytes of memory.

After the structure declaration, an array named totals[MAXSIZ] is defined as being of the structure type bill_count. If MAXSIZ is 50, for example, we are defining a 50-element array named totals[], where *each* element in the array is of this structure type. If this array began at memory location 50000, it might look like that shown in figure 7.5.

You can see that this figure represents an array of structures. Each structure can hold a name, wage, and the amount of each denomination required to pay the employee.

50000   50047

totals[0] [|]

totals[1] [|]

.   .
.   .
.   .

totals[49] [|]

52352   52400   *Figure 7.5.*

Once the array is established, the rest of the program fills in each
element of the array with the necessary data. Program 7.5 shows
how this is done.

The program starts by defining the totals[] array of structures.
The members of the structure should be clear from the definition.
The curncy[] member is an integer array that holds the amount of
each currency denomination needed to make up the appropriate
pay envelope.

The denom[] array holds the different types of currency that will be
used to pay the employee, starting with a twenty-dollar bill (in other
words, 2,000 pennies) and ending with a penny. This array has
been initialized outside a function so that the array is an external.
It could be made internal to main() because main() is the only
function that uses the array. However, the program is clearer when
denom[] is placed near the structure definition for totals[]. In addition, if the array were internal to main(), we would have to initialize it differently (by assignment) or declare it with the static
storage class.

After the definitions in main(), the program calls the getfld() function to fill the first member of the first structure in the totals[] array.
Because a for loop controls most of main(), the call to getfld()
passes the address of totals[0].name on the first pass through the
loop. The address of totals[0].name is the address of the name
member of the structure.

The getfld() function fills in the name member of totals[] with
the employee's name. The last statement in the function appends
a null to the name so that it can be printed as a string. There is no
need to return the member from getfld() because we are placing
the name in the structure itself.

```c
#include <stdio.h>

#define MAXSIZ 50          /* sets maximum number of employees */
#define NAMSIZ 30          /* sets max characters in name      */

struct bill_count{
        char name[NAMSIZ];
        int wage;
        int curncy[8];
} totals[MAXSIZ];

int denom[8] = {2000, 1000, 500, 100, 25, 10, 5, 1};

main()
{
        char string[NAMSIZ], c;
        int x, i, j, part;
        float sum;
        void getfld();

        for (i = 0; i < MAXSIZ; i++) {
                getfld("\n\nName (30 chars max, #=END): ",
                    NAMSIZ-1, totals[i].name);

                if (totals[i].name[0] == '#')
                        break;
                totals[i].wage = part = getsum("\nEnter wage: ");


                for (j = 0; j < 8; ++j) {
                        sum = part;
                        totals[i].curncy[j] = sum / denom[j];
                        part %= denom[j];
                }
        }
        printf("\n\tWage\t$20\t$10\t$5\t$1\t.25\t.10\t.05\t.01");
        for (j = 0; j < 8; j++)
                denom[j] = 0;
        for (j = 0; j < i; j++) {
                printf("\n%s\t%d\n\t      ",
                    totals[j].name, totals[j].wage);
```

```
                    for (x = 0; x < 8; x++) {
                         printf("%7d ", totals[j].curncy[x]);
                         denom[x] += totals[j].curncy[x];
                    }
          }
     printf("\n\n");
     for (j = 1; j < 78; j++)
          printf("-");

     printf("\n\nTotals:       ");

     for (j = 0; j < 8; j++)
          printf("%7d ", denom[j]);
     printf("\n");

}


/*******

          Function to fill in the name of the employees.

     Argument list: char individ[]        character array to hold
                                          names

                    char *prompt          pointer to prompt from
                                          main()

                    int biggest           maximum characters that
                                          can be in a name


     Return value   none

*******/

void getfld(prompt, biggest, individ)
char individ[]; *prompt;
int biggest;
{
     char c;
     int i;
```

```
        printf("%s", prompt);
        i = 0;
        while ((c = getch()) != '\r' && i < biggest) {
                individ[i] = c;
                i++;
        }
        individ[i] = '\0';
}


/*******

        Function to enter the wage rate as a string and then
    convert it to an integer number.

    Argument list:        char *prompt    screen prompt for data
                                          entry


    Return value:         int             the wage that was entered
                                          as an integer

*******/

int getsum(prompt)
char *prompt;
{
    char wage[NAMSIZ], c;
    int i;

    printf("%s", prompt);
    i = 0;
    while ((c = getch()) != '\r' && i < NAMSIZ-1) {
            if (c != '.') {
                    wage[i] = c;
                    i++;
            }
    }
    wage[i] = '\0';
    return (atoi(wage));
}
```

Program 7.5.

The program returns to main() and checks to see whether the first character in the name member is a pound sign (#). If the character is, then this signals the end of data input; the program breaks out of the controlling for loop and displays the results.

If the first character in the name member of the structure array is not a pound sign, then the program asks that the wage be entered. Note that any decimal points are ignored, because a penny is our base unit and the wage is treated as an integer even when coins are to be included in the pay envelope.

When the RETURN key is pressed, a null is appended to the (string) representation of the wage. The function returns the wage as an integer by a function call to atoi() in the return statement. You will recall that atoi() converts an ASCII string to an integer number. [Rich people will have to use atol() which converts an ASCII string to a long. Don't forget to change the type specifier of get-sum() to return a long and tell getsum() that atol() returns a long, too. Having done that, you'd better let main() know that getsum() returns a long rather than an int.]

After the wage is returned from getsum(), the wage is assigned to the wage member of the totals[] structure array, as well as to the integer variable named part. *C permits multiple assignments in one statement*, as you can see in the statement

```
totals[i].wage = part = getsum("\nEnter wage: ");
```

which is equivalent to

```
part = getsum("\nEnter wage: ");
totals[i].wage = part;
```

For most compilers, there is no limit to the number of assignments that can be made in a single statement.

The nested for loop (a for loop within a for loop) does the real work of the program. The loop is repeated in code fragment 7.8 for easy reference.

```
for (j = 0;  j < 8;  ++j) {
      sum = part;
      totals[i].curncy[j] = sum / denom[j];
      part %= denom[j];
}
```

Code fragment 7.8.

The loop calculates the currency and coins needed to pay the employee and fills the curncy[] member of the totals[] structure array.

The first thing the for loop does is assign sum as equal to part. However, because sum is a variable of data type float and part is an integer, the wage for the employee is forced (that is, promoted) to a float before being assigned to sum. sum is then divided by the jth element of the denom[] array. (For example, on the first pass, the wage is divided by 2,000.) The number of each denomination is assigned to its respective array member in totals[].

The next statement in the loop uses the modulo divide (%) operation for integer numbers. The statement

```
part %= denom[j];
```

is the same as

```
part = part % denom[j];
```

The result of modulo division gives the remainder after division. For example, if the wage is $44, part equals 4400. If denom[j] equals 2,000, a modulo divide yields 400 as the remainder. Think of it as subtraction to the point where a negative number would result. (See figure 7.6.)

```
  4400
 -2000
 ─────
  2400    (The result is greater than 2,000,
 -2000      so we do it again.)
 ─────
   400    (Any further subtraction is negative.)
```

Figure 7.6.

The variable part, therefore, would be assigned 400 in the example.

On the next pass through the loop, part is assigned to sum again, but this time sum equals the modulo divide done previously. Using the $44 wage, sum now equals 400. Because the next element in denom[] is 1000, no ten-dollar bill would be needed. Make sure that you understand why we need only four one-dollar bills.

After eight passes through the j loop, the program falls through to the next iteration of the i loop and starts over again with the next employee's name.

Because this program is longer than most, let's look at the sample run shown in table 7.1.

	Wage	$20	$10	$5	$1	.25	.10	.05	.01
Katie	3333	1	1	0	3	1	0	1	3
John	9999	4	1	1	4	3	2	0	4
Totals		5	2	1	7	4	2	1	7

Table 7.1

The bottom row in table 7.1 indicates how much of each denomination is needed to pay all the employees the exact amount due. As an exercise, try to print the wage as $33.33 rather than as the 3333 it is now. You can do this without using floating-point numbers.

unions

A union *is a small segment of memory that can hold different data types.* It allows a variable to hold more than one type of data. The syntax for using a union is very close to that used for structures. For example, let's suppose that we need a variable that is capable of holding a char, an int, a float, and a double. Furthermore, suppose that we want to call the variable all_type. The syntax for the union appears in code fragment 7.9.

```
union {
      char t_char;
      int  t_int;
      float t_float;
      double t_double;
} all_type;
```

Code fragment 7.9.

If we anticipated using more than one such union, we could supply a name after union as an *optional union tag*, as shown in code fragment 7.10.

Code fragment 7.10.

```
union opt_tag {
     char t_char;
     int  t_int;
     float t_float;
     double t_double;
} all_type;
```

Here opt_tag is the optional union tag for this union definition.

Remember that a union provides us with a place to keep different data types. In this respect, a union behaves as though it is a small storage buffer capable of holding several different types of data. In our example, we want to create a place where a char, int, float, or double can reside. The compiler, seeing the keyword union, knows that it must reserve enough storage to hold the *largest* item in the union declaration. The compiler will scan the list of data types in the declaration and find the one that requires the most storage (a double in our example, which typically has 64 bits).

Once the compiler knows the largest data size the union must hold, it allocates enough storage to hold that (largest) data type. For our example, the storage area might look like that shown in figure 7.7.

50000   50007

Figure 7.7.

The compiler establishes a union variable named all_type and creates storage for it at memory locations 50000 through 50007. Eight bytes (64 bits) are allocated because that is the storage requirement for a double.

Let's suppose that a function call returns a character to main() but that we don't want to use it until later in the program. If we later assign the character to a type char variable named letter, the syntax is

```
letter all_type.t_char;
```

The compiler will then move a type char variable out of the union named all_type and assign it to letter. The syntax is the same as that for a structure; we use the dot operator to reference the desired data in the union.

This assignment illustrates the kind of mischief you can cause when you think that the union holds a char when, in fact, the last thing you placed in the union was some other data type. The compiler will pull out of the union exactly what you request.

However, if you request a char when, in fact, an int is currently in the union, the compiler will give you "half an int." Making an improper request produces uncertain results. Usually, such a mistake produces recognizable garbage. In some cases, however, such mistakes will appear to work one time, only to fail badly on a program run that uses different data. *Caution: It is your responsibility to keep track of what actually resides in the* union.

Like structures, unions can have pointers to them. The syntax for referencing is the same. For example, if u_ptr is a pointer variable to the union all_type, a double can be assigned to variable d_answer, as shown in code fragment 7.11.

```
double d_answer;
    .
    .
d_answer = u_ptr->t_double;
```

Code fragment 7.11.

This assumes, of course, that a double is in the union at the time that the union is accessed and the assignment is made.

Generally, a union is a useful holding place for different data types that are being returned from function calls and needed in later parts of the program. With a union, you can use a single variable to hold the different data types throughout the program rather than to define different variables for each data type.

Often, because you are not separately defining all the required data types the union will hold, code size is less than it would be without a union. For example, if the members of all_type were defined separately, 15 bytes of storage would be needed. With a union, only 8 bytes are used.

sizeof Operator

The `sizeof` operator returns an integer value that is equal to the number of bytes required for the object specified. Its general form is

```
sizeof(unknown)
```

where unknown is the object whose size we want to determine. One typical use is

```
x = sizeof(y);
```

which assigns to x the number of bytes required for variable y, whatever its data type.

You should experiment with `sizeof` to learn what it actually does. It should return the scalar of a data type. For example, what gets assigned into sz in the following?

```
int i[4][20], sz;
```

```
sz = sizeof(i);
```

Write a little program to execute the previous code fragment and print out the value for sz. What do you conclude about `sizeof`? Why?

The use of `sizeof` should not be limited to those situations in which you are unsure of the size of a data item. Instead, `sizeof` gives you a portable means of using machine-dependent constants in a program. We saw an example of this in Chapter 4 when we called the `calloc()` function for a storage request. If you need enough storage for MAX ints (assuming each takes 2 bytes), you could say

```
i_ptr = calloc(MAX, 2);                    /* not portable */
```

Now what happens when you try to run your program on a CRAY 2, where ints are 32-bit (4-byte) values? It won't work properly. You should use

```
i_ptr = calloc(MAX, sizeof(int));         /* portable */
```

instead. This way, you can move the statement to any machine, and the call to `calloc()` will give you the proper amount of storage. The `sizeof` operator lets you determine scalar sizes for all data types without having to know their bit requirements explicitly. Use `sizeof` whenever applicable, rather than constants.

Hierarchy of Operators and Some Loose Ends

You may be happy to know that you have now been introduced to all the operators that C has to offer. The complete list of assignment operators is shown in table 7.2.

Table 7.2

Operator	Example	Comment
=	x = y;	Simple assignment
+=	x += 1;	Same as x = x + 1;
-=	x -= 1;	Same as x = x - 1;
*=	x *= 2;	Same as x = x * 2;
/=	x /= 2;	Same as x = x / 2;
%=	x %= 2;	Same as x = x % a2; modulo divide
>>=	x >>= 1;	Same as x = x >> 1; shift right
<<=	x <<= 1;	Same as x = x << 1; shift left
&=	x &= Øx7f	Same as x = x & Øx7f; bitwise AND
|=	x |= Øx7f	Same as x = x | Øx7f; bitwise OR
^=	x ^= Øx7f	Same as x = x ^ Øx7f; bitwise EOR

The order in which complex expressions are evaluated is determined by the hierarchy of the operators being used. In table 7.3 the various operators are ranked in *descending* order.

You may want to place a paper clip on this page to mark it for future reference. When you use a complex equation with pointers, you may need to refer to the hierarchy of the operators to make sure that you are doing the operations in the correct sequence. For example, does the line

```
x = *p++;
```

fetch the contents of what p points to and then increment it, or does the line increment and then fetch? What will x contain? Write a short program that initializes an int to some value (such as 5). Initialize p to point to the int and print out the contents of x. Does x equal what you thought it would? Check table 7.3 if you were wrong.

Table 7.3

Rank	Operator
1	`->  .  () function call  []`

2	`(cast) sizeof ! ++ -- ~`
	`*            /* indirection for pointers */`
	`-            /* unary minus */`

3	`/  %` `*            /* multiply */`
4	`+` `-            /* subtraction */`
5	`<<  >>`
6	`>   >=  <=  <`
7	`==  !=`
8	`&            /* bitwise AND */`
9	`^`
10	`|`
11	`&&`
12	`||`
13	`?:           /* ternary */`
14	All operators presented in Table 7.2
15	`,`

Bit Fields and enum

As shown in the previous section, C provides operators (for example, AND, OR, EOR, and shifts) to perform manipulation of bits. In fact, C was born from a desire to have a high-level language that could perform "bit fiddling." So strong was that desire that the creators of C developed a means by which bit manipulations could be performed in an easier way.

The general form of a bit field is

type specifier   identifier : constant expression

where: (1) the *type specifier* refers to some data type, (2) the *identifier* is the variable name (or the field name), and (3) the *constant expression* is the number of bits being designated. For example,

```
unsigned  flag : 1;
```

declares flag as a variable that uses 1 bit. Therefore, the only values flag can assume would be Ø or 1. On the other hand,

```
unsigned nibble : 4;
```

creates a variable named nibble with 4 bits, Thus, nibble can assume a value of Ø through 15. (Check Appendix 2 and Appendix A if you're not sure why 4 bits yield this range of values.)

One of the primary reasons for bit fields is to be able to pack information into a limited space. For example, binary coded decimal (BCD) numbers are stored using only 4 bits for each digit in a number. As you will recall from Appendix 2, 4 binary digits can represent the values Ø through 15. Because a decimal digit can assume only the values Ø through 9, we can store 2 decimal numbers in a single byte provided that we keep the bits separated.

A convenient way to use the bit fields is to place them in a structure, as shown in code fragment 7.12.

```
struct bcd_num {
      unsigned int digit1 : 4;
      unsigned int digit2 : 4;
};
```

```
struct bcd_num val;
```

Code fragment 7.12.

This code fragment creates a variable named val that can have two BCD numbers stored in it. If we assume that the variable val is stored in memory at 50000, the display might look like that shown in figure 7.8.

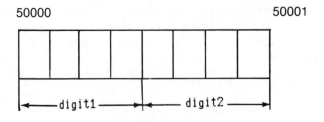

Figure 7.8.

Note an important difference. Both fields are declared as an unsigned int, but only one byte is actually used because only one byte is required to store the bit fields. The remaining byte associated with the unsigned int is unused (or could be used to hold two more BCD digits).

Once the fields are declared, we can use them as we would any other data type. If, for example, we want to assign the digit 5 to digit1, as in

```
val.digit1 = 5;
```

the memory representation would appear as shown in figure 7.9.

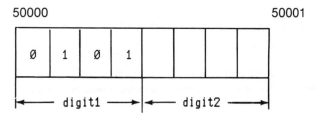

Figure 7.9.

We can, of course, work the assignment in the other direction, too:

```
x = val.digit1;
```

Here the value 5 is assigned into x.

Remember that bit fields can only appear within a structure. They also give you nothing that cannot be done with ordinary bitwise operators. However, bit fields offer a more convenient means of manipulating bit values.

enum Data Type

The enumerated (enum) data type is relatively new to C, but some compilers do support the enum data type. This data type evolved because of a desire for stronger type-checking in C.

Consider the following example of an enumerated data type:

```
enum sex {female, male};              /* define */

enum sex school_age, college, adult;  /* declare */
```

The first statement defines an enum type called sex. In this example, sex is much like a structure or union tag; it says to create a data type called `sex`, of which the only legitimate values that can be used with variables of this type are `female` and `male`.

So what are the values of `female` and `male`? When the enum data type is defined, the compiler assigns values to the list enclosed within the braces, starting with 0 and counting up by 1 for each variable in the list. To the compiler, the list would appear as

```
num sex {female, male};          /* as written */

num sex {  0 ,  1 };             /* to compiler */
```

The declaration of the variables `school_age`, `college`, and `adult` creates three enum data type variables, each of which can assume only the values 0 or 1.

An example of the use of an enum variable is

```
college = female;
```

which assigns the value of 0 into `college`. If you try to assign a value other than 0 or 1 into `college`, the compiler should issue an error message. The idea is that it should not be possible to assign a "non-enumerated" value into an enum data type.

What if you need an enumerated data type that starts with the value of 55? Do you have to define 55 "bogus" identifiers before the one you actually need? Fortunately, the answer is no. The following is an example:

```
enum speed {usa = 55, canada = 60} arrest;
```

In this example, we have set the usa variable to the value of 55 and canada to 60 and declared a speed enum data type called `arrest`. If we had left out the assignment of canada, as in

```
enum speed {usa = 55, canada} arrest;
```

the canada speed limit would be assumed to be 56 (that is, the usa value incremented by 1). You should convince yourself that, using this second example, the only legal values for `arrest` would be 55 and 56.

C versus C

Some confusion exists as to what constitutes a "full" C compiler. It would appear that, if the compiler does not support `longs`, `floats`, and `doubles`, the compiler should properly be called a "subset" compiler. But many compilers, particularly on the smaller 8-bit machines, support all the features of C except bit fields and the enum data type. Should these compilers be classed as "full" C compilers? The question poses a true dilemma (with two alternatives, both bad). On the one hand, bit fields offer nothing that cannot be done with bitwise operators, although bit fields are more convenient. On the other hand, the enum data type is not yet a formal part of the C language but represents part of the evolution of the language.

Since society needs someone to throw rocks at, I volunteer by suggesting that a compiler is a "full" C compiler if it supports all data types and operators except bit fields and the enum data type. (Other factors, such as passing structures to functions, also cloud the issue.) At the time this book was being written, the American National Standards Institute had the X3-J11 committee working on an ANSI standard definition of the C language. Until the work by that committee is finished, the definition of "full" C versus "subset" C will continue to be somewhat foggy.

8

Disk File Operations

Any useful programming language must be able to communicate with disk data files. The link for this communication depends on the disk operating system (or DOS) under which the language is run. Several popular operating systems for C are available, including Bell Laboratories' UNIX, Microsoft's MS-DOS, and Digital Research's CP/M. Because UNIX is the DOS under which C was developed, much of the file input-output (I/O) in C reflects the disk I/O facilities that are "built into" UNIX.

Other operating systems, however, may not provide the same I/O facilities as those of UNIX. As a result, C compilers developed for the other environments must emulate some of the disk I/O functions that are native to UNIX. Fortunately, most C compilers do this in a fairly consistent manner. Still, there may be differences in the way your compiler does file I/O and in the functions provided. Review your compiler's documentation on file I/O after you read this chapter.

Low-Level versus High-Level Disk I/O

Reading and writing data stored on disk can be accomplished at two levels in C. *Low-level* disk I/O under UNIX is accomplished through calls to the operating system. Because other operating systems may not provide the same calls as those in UNIX, these calls are "built up" from the I/O facilities that do exist. Most C compilers provide both levels of disk I/O and use (more or less) standard C syntax regardless of the operating system.

Low-level disk I/O provides the means for getting data from disk and making the data available to the program. At this level, the data is read from the disk in a size that is convenient for the operating system (for example, 512 bytes for UNIX and 128 bytes for CP/M).

On the other hand, the program might be designed to work with the data in a more manageable (smaller) form, such as one byte at a time. The *high-level* disk I/O functions provide the data in a form that is convenient to the program. As a result, they typically are built up from the low-level functions. Usually, we can accomplish what is needed by using the high-level disk functions.

Opening a File

A file must be opened before anything can be done with it. To open the file, the operating system needs to know certain things about the file. Specific overhead information on each file must be available before the program can access the file. This overhead information is stored in a structure.

The structure is defined in the file that contains the standard I/O function definitions. (Typically, this file is named stdio.h.) If you look at the contents of the stdio.h file, you will probably find a structure definition similar to that in code fragment 8.1.

```
#define _MAXFILE    10    /* number of available files */

typedef struct _buffer{
        int _fd;           /* file descriptor              */
        int _cleft;        /* characters left in buffer  */
        int _mode;         /* how we will work with file */
        char *_nextc;      /* next character location     */
        char *_buff;       /* location of file buffer     */
} FILE;

extern FILE _efile[_MAXFILE];
```

Code fragment 8.1.

The overhead information for a particular file is available through the structure named FILE. Because each file needs the same information, we have declared an array of such structures, called _efile[] (in other words, one structure for each *file*). This array of structures is defined with the external storage class, thereby making them available to all functions that need the information.

The symbolic constant _MAXFILE determines the maximum number of files that can be open at one time. The actual value for _MAXFILE depends on the compiler's design considerations and any related constraints of the operating system. The documentation provided with your compiler should tell you how many files can be open at one time. If the documentation does not supply this information, you should list the stdio. h file to see what value has been set for _MAXFILE (or its equivalent).

The contents of the structure provide the information necessary for using the file in a C program. Fortunately, most of these details don't need to concern us. (Additional information about file structures is provided in Appendix 8.) Our immediate concern is to determine what function gives us access to a file. In other words, how do we open a file so that we can work with it? We can use the function named fopen().

The fopen() function (1) fills in the FILE structure with the information needed by both the operating system and the program so that they can communicate with each other, and (2) returns to us a pointer to the location where the structure that contains the information is stored. The declaration might be

    FILE *f1;

FILE is a typedef that refers to the structure defined in stdio. h. (See code fragment 8.1.) The pointer variable *f1 is a "pointer to a structure of type FILE."

Each file has its own structure of type FILE associated with it. You can access a given file through the file pointer (for example, *f1) to its own FILE structure. One pointer is needed for each file that may be open at the same time in the program. If you expect to have two files open at the same time, you may find

    FILE *f1, *f2;

If you expect to work with several files, but only one will be open at a time, you can "reuse" the pointer for a second file after you have finished with (that is, closed) the first one. As a general rule, you should declare enough file pointers to equal the number of files that may be open at the same time.

You are now ready to open a file. The compiler needs to know three things: (1) the name of the file you want to access, (2) what you want to do with the file, and (3) where to find the relevant information about the file. The statement

```
f1 = fopen(filename, mode);
```

gives the compiler the following information: (1) filename resolves to a pointer to the name of the file as it exists on the disk; (2) mode specifies what you want to do with the file; and (3) f1 is a pointer to the FILE structure for the specified file. This pointer becomes your communication link to the structure and tells the program what it needs to know about the file.

The filename is the name of the file (such as TEXT.TXT) as it appears on the disk. The mode options available are (1) r for reading a disk file, (2) w for writing to a disk file, and (3) a for appending data to an existing disk file. These are the minimal options available. Other options may permit reading *and* writing to the file (for example, "r+"). Consult your documentation to see whether such options are available on your compiler.

If, for writing or appending, you fopen() a file that doesn't already exist, a file will be created at the time of the fopen() function call. Note: If the w mode is used for a file that already exists, it will be deleted, and a new file will be created; the previous contents of the file will be lost. Plan accordingly!

Errors (such as a disk full condition or defective disk) can occur during a fopen() function call. If such an error occurs, fopen() returns an error condition indicator. The error condition is usually #defined in stdio.h as a symbolic constant. The most common symbolic constant used is NULL, but ERROR, ERR, or EOF may also be used. Because the error condition is treated as a symbolic constant, you don't have to worry about the specifics of the code itself, but only that an error occurred. (We shall find out later what to do about it.)

Now that the file is open, you can either read or write data to it (depending on the mode under which the file was opened). Program 8.1 writes a series of ASCII characters to a file, using high-level file I/O.

This program begins with the #include preprocessor directive to include the standard I/O library (such as stdio.h) in the program. The I/O library establishes the overhead information required to work with the data file(s). This information is required for all programs that use disk files.

```
/* simple program to write ASCII text to a disk file */

#include <stdio.h>

#define CLEARS 12          /* clear screen character */
#define TRUE   1           /* may already be defined in stdio.h */

main()
{
        char fname[80], c;
        int i, c_count;
        FILE *f1, *fopen();
        void get_f();

        putchar(CLEARS);
        get_f(fname);

        if ((f1 = fopen(fname, "w")) == NULL) {
                printf("I can't create %s\n", fname);
                exit(1);
        }

        putchar(CLEARS);
        puts("Enter text (# to end):");

        while ((c = getch()) != '#')
                putc(c, f1);

        fclose(f1);
}

/******
        Function to get the name of the file to write to.
    The file name has been limited to 12 characters,
    including file extension; an example is PPPPPPPP.SSS.

    Argument list:  char name[]    pointer to character array
                                   to hold file name

    Return value:         none

******/
```

```
#define _MAXNAME     12          /* max chars in filename */

void get_f(name)
char name[];
{
        int i, c_count;
        char c, *gets();

        puts("\nThe file name cannot have a primary name of");
        puts("more than: 8 characters, a period, and a file");
        puts("extension of three characters. XXXXXXXX.YYY.\n");

        while (TRUE) {
                puts("\nEnter the name of the output file: ");
                gets(name);
                c_count = strlen(name);

                if (c_count > _MAXNAME)
                    puts("Filename too long.\n");
                else
                    if (c_count == _MAXNAME && name[8] != '.') {
                            puts("Too many characters in Filename")
                            puts(" and extent.\n");
                    }
                else
                        break;
        }
}

#undef _MAXNAME
```

Program 8.1.

We have also #defined TRUE with a value of 1. Some compilers may already have TRUE defined in stdio.h. If this is the case, simply remove the #define from the program. (Chapter 9 shows an alternative way of handling this problem.) The program then declares several variables, including a character array for the file name and a pointer to the FILE structure (*f1).

Notice that the function fopen() is declared to return a pointer to a structure of type FILE. Why do we need to do this? The reason is that, if we didn't have this declaration, main() would think that FILE returns an int data type. Since pointers and ints are not the same (even though they may require the same amount of storage), *all* functions that do not return an int must explicitly declare what they do return. [Why is gets() declared in get_f()?]

Next, the screen is cleared, and the filename is requested by a function call to get_f(). Entering the filename is fairly straightforward. The filename is checked to see that it does not exceed 12 characters. (The fname[] array is much larger than needed to minimize the chance of your writing data into some unknown area of memory. The operating system used to test the program sets a maximum of 8 characters for the primary file name and 3 for the secondary file name. The two names are separated by a "." for a maximum of 12 characters.)

A #define is used to set the limit of filename to 12 characters. Notice that we have used a #undef at the end of the get_f() function definition. The purpose of a #undef is to "undefine" a symbolic constant. In other words, _MAXNAME is defined only for the code that defines get_f(). This prevents _MAXNAME from colliding with another _MAXNAME that might be used by the programmer.

After the filename is entered, fopen() is called with the file name (or fname in program 8.1) and w as the function's arguments. Because the write mode is used, the call to fopen() creates filename if it doesn't already exist, or opens filename for writing (and destroys whatever filename contains).

If anything goes wrong, such as a disk full condition, an error message is given. Note that we opened the file and tested against NULL to see whether all went well. Both operations (opening the file and testing against NULL) were done within the if expression. This is a common C construct, and you will see it often.

If something did go wrong while opening the file, the exit() function aborts program execution. Usually, an argument of zero [such as exit(0)] means that everything is okay, and nonzero means something is wrong. In either event, all files are closed, and program execution stops. In program 8.1 the exit() function signals an abort because something prevented us from opening the file.

If we assume that the file was opened successfully, a while loop is used to enter text for subsequent writing to the data file. Each character of text is assigned to variable c after the call to putchar().

The while loop controls the putc() function call, which is called whenever a character is entered with the character and the file pointer as the argument. The file pointer (f1) points to a FILE structure. A pointer in that structure points to a buffer where each character is stored. (A *buffer* is a small amount of memory that is set aside to hold some type of data—characters in this example.) Other members of the structure keep track of the details about this file (for example, how much room is left in the buffer, the mode of operation, etc.).

Each time the buffer is filled with characters, its contents are written to the disk. The process of emptying the buffer by writing its contents to the disk is called "flushing the buffer." After the buffer is flushed, the variables in the FILE structure are updated, and the process can be repeated.

Program 8.1 continues placing characters into the buffer until you enter a pound sign (#) to signal that you are through entering text to the file. The program then does a function call to fclose() and uses pointer f1 as the argument. The call to fclose() flushes the buffer, closes the file, and the program ends.

Although you may never have thought about it, when you press the RETURN key on your terminal, the cursor moves to the extreme left side of the screen (a carriage return or CR), then down to the next line (a line feed or LF). In other words, a single keystroke (RETURN) generates two ASCII characters—a CR-LF pair. (See Appendix A if this discussion seems strange.) However, only an LF is placed in the file buffer when RETURN is pressed and putc() is being used.

Some operating systems store only the line feed of a CR-LF pair. The putc() function supplies the missing CR automatically when ASCII text is being entered. As a result, when you read the text file, it will look the same as it did when you entered it. What do you do if you only want a LF stored in the file? Most compilers also provide for a binary write operation. This is often signified with the mode wb for "write binary." As an experiment, try substituting the wb mode in program 8.1. If the text looks the same in both cases, then your system supplies the missing CR automatically. Some C libraries have a special putc() function to supply the CR. Check your documentation to see which is the case for your compiler and whether the binary mode is supported.

Finally, don't confuse the function of putc() with putchar(). The putc() function typically places a character in a file buffer and uses a file pointer and a character as the function's arguments. The putchar() function, on the other hand, has a single argument: the character to be displayed on the screen. putchar() does not directly relate to the FILE structure. If your compiler allows output to be redirected, you can use either `putc()` or `putchar()`. (We shall discuss I/O redirection later in the chapter.)

Reading a File

Program 8.1 wrote an ASCII text file to the disk—or did it? The fact that you may have heard the disk drives activate during the program doesn't necessarily mean that the data was written to the disk. What we need now is a simple program to read the contents of the file and display them on the screen. Look at program 8.2.

```
/* read an ASCII data file */


#include <stdio.h>

#define CLEARS 12

main(argc, argv)
int argc;
char **argv;
{

        int c;
        FILE *f1, *fopen();

        putchar(CLEARS);
        if (argc != 2){
            puts("\n Usage: programname filename");
            exit(1);
        }

        if ((f1 = fopen(argv[1], "r")) == NULL) {
                printf("I can't open %s\n", argv[1]);
                exit(1);
        }

        while ((c = getc(f1)) != EOF)
                putchar(c);

        fclose(f1);
}
```

Program 8.2.

Command Line Arguments: argc and argv

The first thing you probably noticed about program 8.2 was that the main() function had two arguments to it: argc and argv. This may be confusing when you remember that main() marks the beginning of the program. Therefore, you might think that main() can't have an argument because it *is* the first function in the program. So where do the arguments to main() come from?

Actually, the arguments to main() are given *before* the program starts executing. The variable argc, which counts the *number* of command line arguments supplied to main(), is an *argument counter*. The variable argv, a pointer variable that *points* to the command line arguments, is an *argument vector*.

What is a *command line argument*? It is a parameter supplied to main() when the program is invoked. For example, let's suppose that the file name you used when you tested the program in program 8.1 was TEST. TXT. Let's further suppose that you have already typed in program 8.2. If you study that program, you will see that it does not ask you for the file to be read. Where does the program get the TEST. TXT file name? From the command line argument.

If we assume that you've compiled program 8.2 and that it is stored on the disk as READFILE, you can examine the contents of your text file by using the operating system command

```
A>READFILE TEST. TXT        /* A> is a DOS prompt */
```

and pressing the RETURN key. READFILE and TEST. TXT are the command line arguments to main() in program 8.2. The program name (READFILE) is always argv[0]. The text file (TEST. TXT) is argv[1]. Therefore, in this example, the argument in argc equals 2. If the argument count is 1 (argc = 1), the program is invoked without any other command line arguments. Program 8.2 checks for two arguments and aborts if they are not present. The variable argc is simply an integer variable that keeps track of the argument declarations for main(). For argc to do its job, a space must be entered between each command line argument.

What does argv[0] contain? Actually, it is a pointer to a location in memory where the characters READFILE are stored; argv[0] is a pointer to a string of characters. If argv[0] points to memory location 50000 (that is, the rvalue of argv[0]), then you would see the display in figure 8.1.

50000   50008

R	E	A	D	F	I	L	E	\0

Figure 8.1.

Therefore, argv[0] is a pointer that points to the file name of the program. Because argv[0] is null terminated, you can treat it as a string in the program if you like. (You should be aware, however, that some operating systems may alter argv[0] so that its contents are unreliable.)

Similarly, argv[1] is a pointer that points to the second command line argument, which is TEST. TXT in our example. If the rvalue of argv[1] is 50009, then you would see the display in figure 8.2.

50009   50017

T	E	S	T	.	T	X	T	\0

Figure 8.2.

In summary, argc contains the number of arguments given when the program was invoked, and argv[] gives us a pointer to where the arguments have been stored in memory. Together, the command line arguments allow us to pass information, or parameters, to main() for use in the program before execution.

Given the use of argc and argv[], what does the argument declaration **argv mean? Using the right-left rule from Chapter 7 and looking to the right of argv, we find nothing. Looking left, we see *pointer*. Looking right, we see nothing again, so we look back and find a second *pointer*. Because there is nothing left to parse, argv must return chars. Therefore, **argv is a "pointer to a pointer to characters."

Often, you will see argv declared as

    char *argv[];

which is "an array of pointers to characters." If you think about it, the two argument declarations are the same. If we increment the argument vector (*argv++), we are requesting the second argument in the vector. This is the same as changing an array of pointers from `argv[0]` to `argv[1]`; pointer arithmetic is consistent. If you feel more comfortable with one form rather than the other, by all means use the one you prefer. Both are commonly used, and either will work.

The program establishes a file pointer to the FILE structure and initializes it with the call to `fopen()`. Note how we used `argv[1]` to replace the file name. (Recall that `argv[1]` points to the file name entered as a command line argument. Could we have used `*++argv` instead of `argv[1]`?) The mode for `fopen()` is r for reading. If the call to `fopen()` fails, an error message is given, and the program aborts.

Notice that we always check the FILE pointer against NULL after the call to `fopen()`. Why? Recall our discussion in Chapter 4 that a pointer value of 0 is guaranteed not to point to anything useful. Looking in `stdio.h`, we find that NULL is `#defined` to equal 0. Therefore, if `fopen()` returns a 0, it will be assigned into f1. Checking f1 against NULL (that is, 0) tells us whether we opened the file successfully.

If we assume that the file is open, the call to function `getc()` retrieves the data from the f1 FILE structure's buffer one character at a time and assigns it to variable c. A call to `putchar()` displays the data on the screen.

Why is `getc()` declared to be an integer variable rather than a `char`? After all, we are reading one character at a time. This is a little bit of defensive coding. Again, if you look at how EOF is defined in `stdio.h`, EOF probably has a value of -1. However, a `char` data type is used to represent ASCII data, of which only seven of the eight bits are meaningful. If the manufacturer of the compiler does not do sign expansion on a `char` (that is, pay attention to the eighth bit), there is no way to sense a -1 in a `char` data type. By making c an `int`, we know that we are able to detect a negative value. The conversion from the `int` to a `char` will be done for us automatically, as discussed in the previous chapter.

Once again, note that the function `getc()` is not the same as `getch()`. The `getc()` function retrieves data from the buffer maintained in the FILE structure. Typically, the `getch()` function works directly through the operating system to get a character from the keyboard. Because `getch()` doesn't go through the file buffers, it is referred to as "unbuffered" I/O. The `getc()` (see Appendix 8) and `getchar()` functions, on the other hand, usually go through the file buffers and, therefore, are referred to as "buffered" I/O. [Recall that getch() does not require pressing RETURN after each keystroke, but getchar() does.]

The while loop keeps executing until getc() finds an end-of-file (EOF). At that time, the call to fclose() function closes the file, and the program ends.

Before you continue with this chapter, type programs 8.1 and 8.2 and experiment with them. Review your documentation for any special functions in your library that might make life a little easier for you (for example, functions that can search directory paths, delete files, etc.) and try some of these functions in your programs.

Simple Data Plotting

Now that you know how to read and write ASCII data files, let's try writing a program that does more than read a data file. Although a considerable body of literature exists on data protection (encryption) schemes, less has been written about data decryption.

The first step in breaking an encryption code is to examine the frequency of characters in the text. Because the letter E is one of the more frequently used letters in standard text, a plot of the characters in the file gives us a starting place for data decryption.

Program 8.3 gives a frequency distribution of the ASCII letters in a text file. The real purpose of this program, however, is to use file I/O and show how data might be plotted, using direct cursor control. Although the plot is only ASCII characters in this example, the plot routine can be generalized to any form of numeric-alphanumeric data.

There is really nothing new in this program even though it may seem longer than others we've examined. The program begins by including the standard I/O library file and defining a number of symbolic constants. Some of these constants will have to be changed for your particular terminal, and others may be changed to make a more aesthetic presentation (for example, graphics for BAR and DASH).

The main() function has two command line arguments: the program name and the name of the text file you want to plot. We then declare a file pointer (*f1) and several functions that return a pointer to the FILE structure.

```
/* program to plot read ASCII text file */
/* and plot frequency of letters */

#include <stdio.h>

#define CLEARS      12              /* control codes for ADDS   */
#define CURSOR      "\033Y"         /* Viewpoint terminal       */
#define BACK        '\010'          /* backspace                */
#define BAR         '|'             /* vertical axis char       */
#define DASH        '-'             /* horizontal axis char     */
#define ALPHA       26              /* chars in alphabet        */
#define ROWS        24              /* rows on screen           */
#define WIDE        80              /* columns on screen        */

int let[ALPHA + 1];

main(argc, argv)
int argc;
char **argv;
{
        FILE *f1, *fopen(), *look();
        void axis(), count_let(), fill_in();

        putchar(CLEARS);

        f1 = look(argc, argv);    /* open the file               */

        axis();                   /* draw axis                   */

        count_let(f1);            /* count the number of chars   */

        fclose(f1);               /* close the file              */

        fill_in();                /* fill in histogram           */
}
```

```
/*******
        Function to see if two command line arguments are
present and then open the file.

        Argument list:        int count        argument count from com-
                                                mand line
                              char *ptr[]       pointer to argument vec-
                                                tor from command line

        Return value:         FILE *            pointer to fp of open
                                                file

*******/

FILE *look(count, ptr)
int count;
char *ptr[];
{
        FILE *fp, *fopen();

        if (count != 2) {
                printf("usage: programname filename\n");
                exit(1);
        }

        if ((fp = fopen(ptr[1], "r")) == NULL) {
                printf("Cannot open %s\n", ptr[1]);
                exit(1);
        }

        return (fp);
}
```

```
/*******
          Function to draw axis for graph.  If terminal supports
    special graphics characters,  change BAR and DASH.

    Argument list:        none

    Return value:         none

*******/

void axis()
{
        int j;
                                        /* draw the axes */
        for (j = 1;  j < ROWS - 2;  ++j)
             set_cur(j, 1, BAR);

        set_cur(ROWS - 2, 1, DASH);
        for (j = 0;  j < WIDE - 2;  ++j)
              putchar(DASH);

}

/*******
          Function to count each letter of the input file.  The
    array is indexed according to its relationship to the letter
    'A'.  All input letters are converted to uppercase.

    Argument list:        FILE *ptr    FILE pointer to input file

    Return value:         none

*******/

void count_let(ptr)
FILE *ptr;
{
        int c;
```

```
        while ((c = getc(ptr)) != EOF) {
                c = toupper(c);
                if (c >= 'A' && c <= 'Z')
                        let[c - 'A'] += 1;
        }
}


/*******
        Function to scale the data to fit on the screen and
   then print the histogram.

   Argument list:      none

   Return value:       none

*******/

void fill_in()
{
        int colcnt, i, j, k, did, unit, max;
        char dit;
        void set_cur();

        j = ALPHA + 1;
        max = f_max(j);             /* find biggest... */

        if (max < ROWS - 3)
                max = ROWS - 3;


        set_cur(1, 2, BACK);
        printf("%d", max);          /* and print it */

        unit = max / 20;            /* scale to biggest */
        if (unit < 1)
                unit = 1;

                                    /* do histogram of */
                                    /* the count */
        for (j = colcnt = 0; j < ALPHA + 1; ++i, ++j) {
                colcnt += 3;
                k = 22 - (let[j] / unit);
                dit = (let[j] == 0) ? ' ' : '*';
                for (i = k; i < ROWS - 2; ++i)
                        set_cur(i, colcnt, dit);
        }
```

```
        set_cur(23, 2, ' ');        /* print axis label */
        for (j = 'A'; j <= 'Z'; ++j)
                printf("%c  ", j);

        set_cur(22, 1, BACK);       /* prevent scroll */

}

/*******
        Function that uses row-column to position the letter
    to be printed.

        Argument list:        int row         row screen position
                              int col         column screen position
                              int let         letter to print


        Return value          none

*******/

void set_cur(row, col, let)
int row, col, let;
{
    printf("%s%c%c%c", CURSOR, row+31, col+31, let);
}

/*******
        Function to find the largest count.

        Argument list:        int el     number of elements in array

        Return value          int        array element with largest
                                          value

*******/
```

```
int f_max(el)
int el;
{
    int biggest, i;

    for (i = 0, biggest = 0; i < el; ++i)
        if (let[i] >= biggest)
            biggest = let[i];

    return (biggest);
}
```

Program 8.3.

The program then calls look() with the argument count and vectors that we entered on the command line. look() checks to see that both the program name and an input file name were given on the command line (that is, argc = 2). If not, an error message is given and the program aborts. If all goes well, look() tries to open the input file and complains if it cannot be opened.

The program does a function call to axis() to draw the axes with direct cursor control. Within axis(), a call to set_cur() requires the row-column coordinates and the character to be printed as function arguments. set_cur() prints the axes on the screen, using these function arguments.

Next, the program does a call to count_let(), using the FILE pointer as the function's argument. Calls to getc() assign to c each character read from the text file. Assignment continues until an end-of-file (EOF) is sensed and the while loop terminates. The function call to toupper() converts each character read to an uppercase letter. The library supplied with your compiler should include this function. The if statement checks to see whether the current character is a letter and, if it is, increments the appropriate count in the let[] array.

By the way, why is c declared as an int in count_let()? (Hint: Can a char necessarily detect -1 if sign expansion is not done?)

The call to fclose() simply closes the input text file.

The real work of the program is done by fill_in(). The function begins by declaring a number of auto variables that are needed in the function. Next, a call to f_max() determines which character in the let[] array has the largest count. After program control is returned from f_max(), the count of the most prevalent letter is assigned to the variable max.

The value of max is used to scale the data so that it will fit on 20 lines of the screen. For example, if max equals 2000, each unit on the plot represents 100 occurrences of the letter (unit = 2000 / 20 = 100). If unit is less than 1, it is set to ROWS - 3 (or 21) so that the plot will function if max is less than 21. A for loop is used to plot the data. The statement

```
k = 22 - (let[j] / unit);
```

does most of the work. The variable k places the cursor at its starting row position on the screen. For example, if max equals 2000 and also happens to be the letter in the let[] array, you will find that k equals

```
k = 21 - (2000 / 100);
```

```
k = 21 - 20
```

```
k = 1
```

The value of k is used to initialize the variable i in the for loop and becomes the row position for the call to set_cur(). The variable colcnt is the column position for set_cur(). The character to be printed is determined by the results of the ternary operation. If there is no count for a given letter (let[j] = 0), the variable dit is assigned to be a space. If a count is present, dit becomes an asterisk.

Now let's examine what the for loop and the set_cur() function call accomplish:

```
for (i = k; i < ROWS - 2; ++i)
    set_cur(i, colcnt, dit);
```

Because i equals 1 and colcnt equals 3, the first iteration of the for loop prints an asterisk at row 1, column 3. The second pass through the loop increments i by one, and the asterisk is printed in row 2, column 3. The for loop continues through i equal to 21 rows. In other words, a vertical line of asterisks is drawn. (You could substitute a graphics character for the asterisk if your terminal supports graphics.) Make sure that you understand why the first asterisk appears in row 11 when let[] equals 1000. The column position is determined by variable colcnt and the number of passes through the j loop.

After the plot is completed, the letters of the alphabet are printed below the horizontal axis. The last set_cur() function call places the cursor in row 22 to prevent the screen from scrolling when the program ends and the DOS prompt appears.

A number of improvements might be made in the program. The fill_in() function, for example, is a bit "busy" and might benefit from being broken into several smaller functions. If you have a graphics terminal, color and special characters can add an impressive "gee whiz" factor. Try experimenting with the skeleton program 8.3. You may be able to generalize things to the point where the functions are worth placing into your library.

Low-Level File I/O

Thus far, we have worked with disk files through the high-level file provisions of C. The high-level file operations used in the previous examples, however, are built up from the low-level file I/O operations. Now let's examine how low-level file I/O commands are used.

Low-level file I/O puts us one step closer to the underlying disk operating system (UNIX, CP/M, MS-DOS, etc.). In fact, low-level file I/O under UNIX is done through direct calls to the operating system. CP/M, on the other hand, doesn't provide directly for the same calls to the operating system. Therefore, the designer of a CP/M C compiler must "build" these calls from the disk primitives (BDOS calls) that do exist for CP/M. In either case, low-level file I/O is done in a way that is most "convenient" for the operating system.

Fortunately, you don't have to worry about the details of the operating system in most cases. Low-level file I/O is accomplished through four file commands: (1) open, (2) read, (3) write, and (4) close. In some cases, a "create" command may also exist, but new files may be created as part of the write command.

open( )

The open command has the general form

    file descriptor = open(filename, mode);

in which the *file descriptor* is an integer variable that is assigned when the file is opened. [The file descriptor is not the same as the *f1 pointer variable to the FILE structure associated with the high-level fopen() function call.] The filename is the name of the file that you are attempting to open. It can be a command line argument (such as argv[]) or a file name specified during program execution.

Three possible modes can be used with open(): (1) 0 for reading from a file, (2) 1 for writing to a file, and (3) 2 for both reading and writing to the file. If the file is opened for writing (mode = 1) and the file does not exist, it is created at that time. If the file already exists and it is opened for writing using mode 1, the file is re-created and the previous contents of the file are lost.

If something goes wrong during an open(), such as a disk full condition, an error code is returned. The value is usually a -1, but it may vary among compilers. The standard I/O library may have a symbolic constant (such as ERR) to indicate the error and free you from needing to know the specific value returned.

The open() function might appear in a program, as shown in code fragment 8.2.

```
if ((fd1 = open(argv[1], 0)) == ERR){
        printf("\nCan't open %s", argv[1]);
        exit(1);
}
```
Code fragment 8.2.

In this example, if the file cannot be opened, an error message is printed and the program aborts through the exit() function call. If things are okay, the variable fd1 is assigned an integer value that can be used later in the program to access the file just opened. The file descriptor is similar to the number (X) in the OPEN #X statement common in most dialects of BASIC and, therefore, is a shorthand notation for referencing filename in the open() function call.

read( )

Once the file has been opened, you can read or write to it according to the mode you used when open() was called. The general form of the read() function call is

```
num_byte = read(file_descriptor, buffer, count);
```

where: (1) file_descriptor is the integer number associated with the file and obtained from the open() call; (2) buffer is some storage, or "holding place," reserved for sliding data between the disk and the program; and (3) the variable count is the number of bytes to be read from the disk during the call to read(). The variable num_byte equals the number of bytes actually read during the call to read() and may differ from count.

Notice that read() cannot be used until a file descriptor has been obtained from a previous call to open(). The file name is not used after open() is called. All subsequent references are through the file descriptor.

The variable count often reflects "chunks" of data that are convenient for the operating system. One common value is the number of bytes per *sector* on the disk, typically 512 for UNIX and MS-DOS, but 128 for CP/M. (A sector is a hardware-dependent allocation of disk space.) Another common value for count is 1, in which case the file is read one byte at a time. Sector sizes for count are typically used to improve I/O speed.

The size of the variable buffer is related to the number of bytes you want to read from the disk during each call to read(). Clearly, if you plan to read from the disk one sector at a time, the buffer must be large enough to hold that many bytes of data. Anything can happen, however, if more bytes than the buffer can hold are read into the buffer.

The read() function can return three possible values for assignment to num_byte. The *first* possible value is the number of bytes that were read during the function call, which is the "normal" state of affairs during a read. The *second* value is the symbolic constant ERR (for example, -1 or as defined in stdio. h), which indicates that something went wrong during the read. The *final* value is zero, which indicates an end-of-file (EOF) and that there is no information left to read in the file.

The fact that zero is returned at an end-of-file makes the code for reading the file quite simple. Consider the skeletal example in code fragment 8.3.

```
while (num_byte = read(fd1, buffer, count)){
            .
            .
        /* read and do something with the data */
            .
```

Code fragment 8.3.   }

You will recall that a while loop continues to execute the statements within the loop as long as the expression is logical True (that is, nonzero). When the while expression becomes False (that is, zero), the statement(s) controlled by the while are no longer executed. Because read()ing an EOF evaluates to zero, num_byte is assigned the value of zero when num_byte encounters EOF and terminates the while loop. The while loop should contain a test for read errors because negative values do not terminate the while loop, and read errors (for example, ERR = -1) can occur.

write( )

The write() function call is similar to read(), except that the data goes to the disk. The general form is

```
write(fd1, buffer, count);
```

which says, "Take count bytes of data from buffer and write them to the fd1 data file." The interpretation of the fd1, buffer, and count variables is the same as that in the call to read().

The value returned from the write() function call is the number of bytes written during the call. As you might guess, any difference between count and the value returned by write() indicates that something went wrong (such as a disk full condition) during the write operation. To take advantage of this relationship, a common C construct for writing data is presented in code fragment 8.4.

```
if (write(fd1, buffer, count) != count){
     printf("Error occurred during write to %s", argv[1]);
     exit(1);
}
```

Code fragment 8.4.

In this case, if the number of bytes you want to write to the disk is not equal to the number of bytes actually written, an error message is displayed, and the program aborts. Although many variations are possible, you should provide a check for possible write errors.

close( )

When you have finished using a file, you should close it before you end the program. The general form for a close file statement is

```
close(file descriptor);
```

After the file is closed, the file descriptor can be reused for a new file through another open() function call.

The call to close() does more than it appears to on the surface. For example, when you write to a file, if close() is called before the buffer is filled, the call to close() *may* flush the contents of the partially filled buffer to the disk. In other cases, the contents of the buffer may not be written to the disk. Your compiler may have a flush() function to cover these situations.

If an exit() function call is executed (usually in response to an error condition), the call closes any files that may be open at that time. The argument to exit() [usually exit(-1) when something is wrong] determines what actually takes place during the call.

Review your documentation to see how your close() and exit() function calls work.

Using Low-Level File I/O

Program 8.4 uses low-level file I/O to copy the contents of an existing file to a new file. The constructs of this program closely follow those in the previous discussion.

This program is quite simple. Preprocessor directives cause the standard I/O library to be included in the program and define certain constants used in the program. (In some cases, ERR would be defined in stdio. h although, more likely, EOF is defined. Note that EOF and ERR often have the same value, too. We defined ERR explicitly in program 8.4 so that you can easily follow the logic in the program.)

We have also used symbolic constants to read (READF) and write (WRITEF) the data. It is easier to understand these symbolic constants, and they also improve the portability of the code. Note: Because differences exist among compilers as to the actual functioning of file I/O, some compilers may furnish a header file that contains certain #defines which should be used with disk files. The common name for this header file is fcntl. h. If such a file is supplied with your compiler, you should inspect its contents and #include the header file in your programs that use file I/O.

```
/* program to copy existing file to new file           */
/*       the program is invoked as:                     */
/* programname new-filename existing-filename

#include <stdio.h>

#define CLEARS  12              /* clear screen code     */

#define READF   0              /* mode for reading      */
#define WRITEF  1              /* mode for writing      */

#define BUFF    512            /* common sector size    */
#define BELL    '\007'         /* ASCII bell code       */
#define ERR     -1             /* something went wrong  */

char buffer[BUFF];             /* pass data through here */
int fd1, fd2;

main(argc, argv)
int argc;
char **argv;
{
        int num_byte;                    /* checks on data passed */
        void prelude(), copy(), postlude();

        putchar(CLEARS);

        prelude(argc, argv);             /* commands ok?  */
        copy(argv);                      /* copy 'em      */
        postlude(argv);                  /* close 'em out */
}

/*******

        Function to check for proper number of arguments and
        try to open the files.

        Argument list:     int count      command line count
                           char *ptr[]     command line vector

        Return value:      none

*******/
```

```
void prelude(count, ptr)
int count;
char *ptr[];
{

                                    /* enough command line args? */
        if (count != 3) {
                puts("Usage:program outfilename infilename\n");
                exit(ERR);
        }
                                    /* try opening source file */

        if ((fd2 = open(ptr[2], READF)) == ERR) {
                printf("Can't open %s\n", ptr[2]);
                exit(ERR);
        }
                                    /* try creating destination file */

        if ((fd1 = open(ptr[1], WRITEF)) == ERR)
                if ((fd1 = creat(ptr[1], WRITEF)) == ERR) {
                        printf("Can't open or create %s\n", ptr[1]);
                        exit(ERR);
                }
}

/*******

        Function to copy a file using low-level file I/O.

    Argument list:      char *argv[]    pointer to file names

    Return value:       none

*******/

void copy(argv)
char *argv[];
{
        int num_byte;
                                    /* do the copy */

        puts("\nStarting the copy. Variable num_byte is:\n");
```

```
        while (num_byte = read(fd2, buffer, BUFF)) {
                printf(" %d", num_byte);
                if (num_byte == ERR) {
                        printf("Trouble reading %s\n", argv[2]);
                        exit(ERR);
                }
                if (write(fd1, buffer, num_byte) != num_byte) {
                        printf("Trouble writing %s\n", argv[1]);
                        exit(ERR);
                }
        }
}


/*******

        Function to close the input and output files, or
complain if we can't close them. The fd's are globals.

        Argument list:      char *argv[]    pointer to file names

        Return value:       none

*******/

void postlude(argv)
char *argv[];
{
        void cerror();

                              /* wind it up */
        if (close(fd1) == EOF)
                cerror(argv[1]);

        if (close(fd2) == EOF)
                cerror(argv[2]);

        printf("%c", BELL);
        printf("\nAll done...\n");
}
```

```
/*******

          Function to print error message when closing a file.

     Argument list:        char **s        pointer to the file name
                                            that can't be closed


     Return value:         none

*******/

void cerror(s)
char **s;
{
     printf("Can't close file %s\n", s);
     exit(ERR);
}
```

Program 8.4.

The program then defines the size of the buffer and the file descriptors. Before the copy actually begins, we call prelude() to check that (1) three command line arguments were given; (2) we can open the source file; and (3) we can create the destination file. If any one of these three conditions is not met, an error message is given, and the program aborts through a function call to exit(ERR). The call to exit() closes any open files and terminates the program.

Note how we have tried to work around the open-create problem:

```
if ((fd1 = open(ptr[1], WRITEF)) == ERR)
     if ((fd1 = creat(ptr[1], WRITEF)) == ERR) {
          printf("Can't open or create %s\n", ptr[1]);
          exit(ERR);
     }
```

If we cannot open the file, we assume that it does not exist. Although some compilers have open() written to create the file if it doesn't exist, not all compilers act this way. The code assumes that, if we can't open the file, we must create it. If we can't create it, an error must exist, and the program then acts accordingly. Try to convince yourself that this approach improves portability by attempting to get around the differences that may exist in the open() functions.

If all went well, the program calls copy() to start copying the file. The while loop grabs BUFF bytes of data from the file associated with fd2 and shoves them into buffer[]. [The printf() shows how many bytes were read during the pass through the while loop, but printf() isn't really necessary for the program to function.]

We have declared both file descriptors (fd1 and fd2) and buffer[] to have the external storage class. This storage class makes them available to any function that needs them without having to pass them as an argument. We could have made them local to copy() but simply decided not to.

If the read() of fd2 returns an ERR, a "trouble reading" error message is displayed, and the program aborts through the call to exit(ERR). If the call to write() returns a value that is not equal to num_byte (that is, the number of bytes read), a "trouble writing" message is displayed. The program then aborts through the call to exit(ERR).

If both error checks are passed, the data is written to the disk. The while loop continues in this manner until the read() of fd2 finds an end-of-file. Eventually, num_byte will evaluate to zero because no more data is available to read and the while loop terminates.

The call to postlude() simply closes the files. This function is necessary because an unclosed file may not have the buffer contents written to disk. A check on the call to close(fd1) for the new file is made to make sure all went well. A call to close(fd2) frees up the file descriptor and closes the source file. A bell sounds, a message appears, and the program ends.

Try running program 8.4 for a given file and time how long it takes. Then try to copy the same file with the copy utility provided with your operating system, again recording the time. Having done that, change BUFF to a single character variable and copy the same file again. What happened to the copy time? How does the C program compare to the system copy utility time (which is usually written in assembler)?

Other Alternatives

All the examples we have seen in this chapter relied on reading and writing data in a sequential manner. That is, the file was opened, and then we began reading/writing the data from the beginning of the file to its end. The process is like that of a tape recording where all activity is referenced from the beginning of the tape.

As anyone who has ever worked with such storage devices knows, finding a given piece of data by a sequential read can be a very slow process. For example, let's suppose that you need a piece of information that is located 500 bytes from the beginning of the file. Sequential files force you to start at the beginning of a file and read through it until you reach the data you want. As a result, you waste time reading 499 bytes of "unwanted" data.

Random-access files, on the other hand, allow you to move about within a file as you see fit; you can go immediately to the desired information without reading the intervening data. Access time is substantially improved.

C provides for random-access techniques with data files. It assumes, however, that you know where you want to be in the file. The lseek() function places us at a given location in a file and has the following general form

```
lseek(file_descriptor, offset, base);
```

in which (1) file_descriptor is the integer number obtained from the call to open(); (2) offset is a long integer variable that contains the number of bytes to be positioned from the base; and (3) base is an integer variable that specifies the position in the file to be used as the base position.

There are three possible values for base. If base equals Ø, the beginning of the file becomes the reference point. If base equals 1, the current position in the file becomes the reference point. If base equals 2, the end of the file is the reference point. Let's look at some examples:

lseek(fd1, -1L, 1)	places us one byte toward the beginning of the file. It "ungets" a byte. A negative offset moves us toward the beginning of the file.
lseek(fd1, ØL, Ø)	places us at the beginning of the file.
lseek(fd1, ØL, 2)	places us at the end of the file.

We can make some generalizations from these examples. First, a negative value for offset when base is Ø is an error. A base of Ø suggests an attempt to place ourselves "in front of" the beginning of the file. Similarly, a base of 2 with a positive offset suggests that we're trying to go beyond the end-of-file, which is also an error. Therefore, offset cannot be negative when base is Ø, and offset cannot be positive when base is 2. Depending on the current position in the file, positive and negative values for offset are valid when base equals 1.

The lseek() function returns a value of zero if all is well and a negative value if an error occurred. Variations do exist, so you should check your documentation to see what is returned.

After the call to lseek() has positioned the pointer in the file, a read or write can be performed in the standard manner.

Some programmers prefer to use #defines to make a particular lseek() call more clear. Therefore, you might see

```
#define    START      Ø
#define    CURRENT    1
#define    END        2
```

used in a program that uses random-access files with lseek(). An example of subsequent code would be

```
lseek(fd1, ØL, START);
```

which appears at the beginning of the file. Once again, check the fcntl.h header file for predefined constants.

Those libraries that provide an lseek() function probably also provide a tell() function. The general form is

```
tell(fd1);
```

which returns a long int that is the current byte position in the file. If you get lost in a file, tell() "tells" you where you are, relative to the beginning of the file. A negative value indicates an error.

Check your documentation (and fnctl.h) for deviations. If the source code for your library is available, examine the code to see how the high-level file I/O functions are implemented. You can learn a great deal by taking the time to study it.

When Files Aren't Files

Chances are that you have already listed the contents of the stdio.h header file. Somewhere in there will be something like the following:

```
#define       stdin          &_iob[0]
#define       stdout         &_iob[1]
#define       stderr         &_iob[2]
#define       stdlst         &_iob[3]
```

For the moment, we won't be concerned about what iobs are. (Appendix 8 discusses them in detail). What we are interested in is what stdin, stdout, and the others actually are.

Simply stated, these are standard I/O definitions that can be used in C programs. As you probably guessed, stdin stands for the standard input device: the keyboard of the CRT. The standard output device is stdout—again the CRT. The standard error device is one that normally displays errors, once again the CRT. Finally, the standard list device (stdlst), which is nonstandard and not supplied on all compilers, is often the printer. However, since stdlst may not exist on all compilers, two examples of directing output to the printer are presented here. In program 8.5, we assume the MS-DOS operating system, which reserves the word "prn" as the name for the printer output device. In program 8.6, we use stdlst for the printer. You should check your compiler and operating system documentation to see the appropriate device name for your system.

We can use these (more or less) standard I/O devices to send output to almost any device we want. Consider the example presented in program 8.5.

This program contains no surprises. The stdio. h header must be included because we need the standard I/O definitions contained there. The #ifndef TRUE says that if TRUE has not yet been defined, define it at this time. If we did a simple #define for TRUE and stdio. h also defined TRUE, we would get a multiply-defined error message from the preprocessor. The FILE pointer (fp) is declared as a global (external storage class) just to simplify making it available to the functions that need it.

```
#include <stdio. h>

#ifndef TRUE
       #define TRUE          1
#endif

#ifndef ERR
       #define ERR          -1
#endif
```

```
FILE *fp;

main()
{
        char str[50];
        int device;
        void showit();

        device = choice();              /* output to where   */

        setfp(device);                  /* set the proper fd */

        strcpy(str, "\nOld saying: Wherever you go, there you are.\n\n");

        showit(str);                    /* send it out        */
        if (fp != stdout)
                fclose(fp);
}


/*****

        Function to determine whether the user wishes to direct
    output to the screen or the printer.

  Argument list:                none

  Return value:                 int i       the output device selected
                                            1 = screen, 2 = printer

*****/

int choice()
{
        char buf[3], *gets();
        int i;
```

```
        while (TRUE) {
                printf("\n\nDo you wish the output to go to:\n\n");
                printf("1. CRT    2. Printer   3. Disk File\n");
                printf("\n        Enter Option: ");
                i = atoi( gets(buf) );

                if (i > 0 && i < 4)
                        break;
        }

        return (i);
}



/*****

        Function to determine the fd associated with stdout or
    stdlst.

    Argument list:        int out        an integer that reflects
                                         whether output goes to the
                                         screen (1) or printer (2)

    Return value:         void           (assumes FILE *fp is global)

        Caution:          If the print device is selected, this function
                          shows how the printer is opened using MS-DOS. The
                          name given to the print device is op-system and
                          compiler specific.

*****/
```

```
int setfp(out)
int out;
{
        FILE *fopen();

        switch(out) {
                case 1:
                        fp = stdout;
                        break;
                case 2:        /*        WARNING!!                    */
                               /*                                     */
                               /*              +--- MS-DOS specific   */
                               /*              |                      */
                               /*              v                      */
                        if ((fp = fopen("prn", "w")) == ERR) {
                                printf("\nCannot write to printer\n");
                                exit(ERR);
                        }
                        break;
                case 3:
                        if ((fp = fopen("TEST.TXT", "w")) == ERR) {
                                printf("\nCan't open file\n");
                                exit(ERR);
                        }
                        break;
                default:
                        fp = NULL;
        }
}


/*****

        Function that writes a message to the output device
    determined by the fp.

    Argument list:            char *s        pointer to message to be
                                             written to fp

    Return value:             void

*****/
```

```
void showit(s)
char *s;
{
        fprintf(fp, s);
}
```

Program 8.5. Using standard I/O.

The program then asks the user where the output is to be sent by the call to choice(). The while loop forces the choice to be one of the three responses listed. The choice selected is returned from the function and assigned into device.

Next, the program calls setfp() with device as its argument. A switch is used to set the FILE pointer fp to the appropriate value for the output device selected. If the CRT is selected, fp is set to stdout (CRT). If the printer is selected, we fopen() the device named "prn". prn has a special meaning for MS-DOS because it is the reserved name for the printer device. Because of the way the MS-DOS operating system works, however, we can treat prn as we would any other file. If we cannot "open" the printer, an error message is given, and the program aborts. Note how this process is virtually the same for writing to a disk file (that is, in case 3 in program 8.5).

Next, we copy a string constant into the str[] character array for subsequent use. If you have a subset compiler that does not support initializers, this is the "poor man's" way of initializing a string array.

Finally, we call the showit() function with the string array (str[]) as the argument. All that the showit() function does is write the string to the output device selected, as determined by fp. The fprintf() function does exactly what printf() does but allows output to be sent to devices other than just the CRT. In other words, the printf() equivalent is

```
printf(s);
```

which would display the output on the CRT only. The FILE pointer fp allows the output to be sent to whatever I/O device is associated with fp.

After showit() is finished, the program checks to see whether output was sent to stdout. If output was not sent to stdout, we fclose() the output device associated with the fp, and the program ends.

The advantage of fprintf() is that we do not have to duplicate I/O device statements if we want to direct output to different devices.

CRT Output and Smaller Code

A situation may arise in which either code size or execution speed is critical. As mentioned several times in this text, printf() is a large function and contains features that may not always be needed (such as the floating-point routines). Speed may be important in some applications (for example, fast cursor addressing). If the need arises, we can often get by with the write() function rather than printf().

For example, if we just want to write a string to either the printer or the CRT, program 8.6 suggests one method without using printf().

```c
#include <stdio.h>

#ifndef TRUE
        #define TRUE          1
#endif


main()
{
        char str[50];
        int device, fd;
        void showit();

        device = choice();              /* output to where   */

        fd = setfd(device);             /* set the proper fd */

        strcpy(str, "\nOld saying: Wherever you go, there you are.\n");

        showit(str, fd);                /* send it out        */
}
```

```
/*****

        Function to determine whether the user wishes to direct
    output to the screen or the printer.

    Argument list:          none

    Return value:           int i             the output device selected
                                              1 = screen, 2 = printer

*****/

int choice()
{
        char buf[3], *gets();
        int i;

        while (TRUE) {
                printf("\n\nDo you wish the output to go to:\n\n");
                printf("1. CRT     2. Printer\n");
                printf("\n         Enter Option: ");
                i = atoi( gets(buf) );

                if (i == 1 || i ==2)
                        break;
        }

        return (i);
}



/*****

        Function to determine the fd associated with stdout or
    stdlst.

    Argument list:          int out           an integer that reflects
                                              whether output goes to the
                                              screen (1) or printer (2)

    Return value:           int i             the fd of the output device

*****/
```

```
int setfd(out)
int out;
{                                   /*                WARNING!!            */
                                    /*                  +-- compiler specific */
                                    /*                  |                  */
                                    /*                  v                  */
    return (out == 1) ? fileno(stdout) : fileno(stdlst);
}


/*****

        Function that writes a message to the output device
    determined by the fd. Because printf() is not used, code
    size should be smaller with this version of showit().

    Argument list:      int fd          fd for selected output device
                        char *s         pointer to message to be written
                                        to fd

      Return value:     void

*****/

void showit(s, fd)
int fd;
char *s;
{
        write(fd, s, strlen(s) + 1);
}
```

Program 8.6. String output with write( ).

Because this program parallels program 8.5, much of the detail doesn't need to be discussed here. However, note the difference between setfd() in program 8.6 and setfp() in program 8.5. In program 8.6, we use the fileno() function to return the fd associated with stdout and stdlst. Why do we need to do this? The reason is that write() expects an fd, not a FILE pointer (an fp). The purpose of the fileno() function, therefore, is to convert the FILE pointer associated with either stdout or stdlst (or any other FILE pointer) and to convert that pointer into the appropriate fd. The fd can then be used with write().

The write() function behaves as we discussed earlier. The only difference is that we used a call to strlen() to decide how many bytes to write. The + 1 after the strlen() call is necessary because strlen() does not include the null terminator in its calculations. Because we want to use *s as a string, we add 1 to the byte count from strlen() so that the null is included in the bytes written.

As an experiment, try writing a simple program that does nothing but print a string, using printf(). Then write the same string, using the write() function. What is the difference in code size? Next, try putting the printf() in a loop (for example, for 1,000 iterations) and note the time. Perform the same test using write(). How does the execution speed compare?

Disk files are the backbone of serious C programming applications. Spend enough time with the ideas in this chapter to feel comfortable with both low- and high-level I/O. You may find the appendix to this chapter useful in understanding how the standard I/O devices work with the underlying operating system.

Appendix 8
A Closer Look at File I/O

This Appendix provides details about file I/O that were not covered in Chapter 8. An understanding of the CP/M operating system is assumed in those areas where specifics about the DOS are needed. With UNIX, much of the "clutter" of the operating system disappears because direct calls to the operating system are possible. MS-DOS falls somewhere between CP/M and UNIX, but edges toward the UNIX end of the scale.

The FILE Structure

The form used for the FILE structure declaration is frequently similar to the one shown in code fragment 8A.1.

```
#define _MAXFILE    10    /* Max number of open files    */

typedef struct _buffer {
     int _fd;                /* file descriptor            */
     int _cleft;             /* characters left in buffer  */
     int _mode;              /* how you will work with file */
     char *_nextc;           /* location of next character */
     char *_buff;            /* buffer for characters      */
} FILE;

     extern FILE _efile[_MAXFILE]
```

Code fragment 8A.1.

If _MAXFILE equals 10, then we have an array of 10 structures like the array defined in code fragment 8A.1. Therefore, the elements of the array _efile[0] through _efile[9] are available to the programmer.

When the high-level disk I/O functions were used in Chapter 8, each program had a declaration similar to

```
FILE *f1, *fopen();
```

which declares the pointer variable f1 to point to a structure of type FILE. We also declare the fopen() to return a pointer of type FILE so that the compiler doesn't mistakenly think its receiving an int. As with any other pointer variable, f1 points to "garbage" until the pointer variable is initialized. To initialize f1 to point to something meaningful, we can use a statement similar to that shown in code fragment 8A.2.

```
if ((f1 = fopen(fname, "w")) == NULL) {
         .
         .
         .
}
```

Code fragment 8A.2.

This statement initializes f1 to point to a previously unused element of _efile[]. The call to fopen() checks for an unused element in _efile[]. If an unused element is available, fopen() returns a pointer of type FILE to that element. That is, after a successful fopen(), f1 has an rvalue that points to an element of _efile[] and maintains the "overhead" information about the file and its status.

What is less obvious is that the high-level fopen() call actually goes through a low-level open() call to open a file. An example is shown in figure 8A.1.

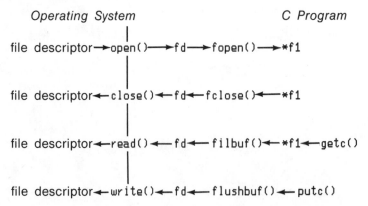

Figure 8A.1.

Every disk operating system must provide the four disk I/O functions shown in figure 8A.1 (open, close, read, and write). Some operating systems may also provide a creat() function if it is not part of the fopen() call.

Only a certain number of open files are allowed at one time. When you use an fopen() call, the program calls open() and causes the operating system to check whether it has any unused file descriptors available. (Under CP/M, for example, it looks for a file control block.)

The operating system looks for the first "unused" element in the array, then assigns to this unused element the file you are trying to open. A file descriptor is passed back to your program and used to keep track of which file belongs to what element in the operating system's array. Think of the file descriptor as the element position in the "available and used" array maintained by the operating system.

After the file descriptor is returned from the operating system, the descriptor is placed in the _fd member of the FILE structure. The fopen() function then passes back a pointer (for example, *f1) to the element in the _efile[] array; the element is used to keep track of the file you just opened. Note how fopen() actually "passes through" open() to get the file pointer. In the process, the program receives a file descriptor (fd), which is given to fopen(). Then fopen() gives you a file pointer (f1) after returning from the operating system. In reality, therefore, *the operating system uses only fd to communicate with your program.*

Figure 8A.2 illustrates this process. In this example, we have assumed that the operating system has an array of 10 available files (_fcb[]) and that the operating system selects the sixth one (actually _fcb[5]) to assign to the file you are trying to open. The operating system is on the left side of the figure, and your program is on the right.

Your program attempts to open a file, which causes the operating system to look for an "unused" file. If the operating system finds _fcb[5] available, the system passes back to your program the number 5 as the file descriptor. *This file descriptor becomes the communications link between your program and the operating system.* What fopen() actually receives is a pointer to fd. From now on, your program will "talk" with the operating system about this file by using the file descriptor 5. However, when you use the fopen(), fclose(), putc(), and getc() functions in your programs, the statements must use a FILE pointer (for example, an fp).

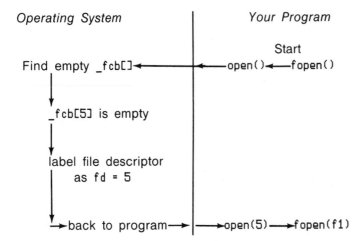

Figure 8A.2.

Communications with Files

Refer back to figure 8A.1 for a moment and note how getc() works. When you ask for a character from a file, getc() uses fd as its argument and looks at the _cleft member of FILE to see whether another character is in the buffer. If another character is found there, it is returned. If not, a function named filbuf() goes to the operating system to "refill" the buffer (and updates the _cleft and _nextc members of FILE). The putc() function works in much the same manner but reverses the direction of flow.

stdin, stdout, and stderr

The functions getchar() and putchar() work in much the same way. Let's consider getchar() first. You already know that this function gets a character from the keyboard. If getchar() works through the mechanism described in figure 8A.2 (and the function does), how does getchar() get a character from the keyboard rather than from a file?

Somewhere (often in stdio.h) you will find several #defines similar to those shown in code fragment 8A.3.

When getchar() is called, it calls getc() with stdin (standard input) as getc()'s argument. The operating system uses this element in the _efile[] array to access the keyboard because of the way _efile[0] was initialized. Similarly, putchar() calls putc() with the

```
#define stdin      (&_efile[0])
#define stdout     (&_efile[1])
#define stderr     (&_efile[2])
        .
        .
#define getchar()  getc(stdin)
#define putchar()  putc(c, stdout)
```

Code fragment 8A.3.

character c and stdout (standard output) as putc()'s arguments. Because of the way _efile[1] was initialized, output normally goes to the screen. If an error occurs, stderr (standard error) normally directs output to the screen.

If you dig around deep enough, you should find the initialization of stdin, stdout, and stderr. Look at code fragment 8A.4.

```
FILE _efile[_MAXFILE] = {
    ( 0, 0, _CONIN, NULL, NULL),  /* standard input  */
    ( 1, 0, _CONOUT, NULL, NULL), /* standard output */
    ( 2, 0, _CONOUT, NULL, NULL), /* standard error  */
};
```

Code fragment 8A.4.

Referring back to the declaration of the FILE structure, you can see how each member is initialized. In terms of the CP/M environment, _CONIN (character in) and _CONOUT (character out) are standard references to the CP/M "jump table." Other operating systems behave in a similar way. You can change these initialized assignments to "redirect" the inputs and outputs to other devices (such as a printer).

Finally, code fragment 8A.4 also suggests that the first three "files" provided by the operating system are "dedicated" to stdin, stdout, and stderr. (stdlst may also be included.) Therefore, if your operating system has a limit on the maximum number of files that can be used at one time, the actual number available to you is three less than the maximum because of the requirements of stdin, stdout, and stderr.

9

Common Mistakes
and Debugging

C is not an easy language to learn, but it is easier than some other languages (such as assembler). Let's examine some of the common mistakes that beginning C programmers make and point out what probably went wrong. We'll also look at some techniques you can use to debug your programs.

Common Mistakes

As with any language, the first level of program errors stems from not obeying the syntax rules of the language. Fortunately, these errors are the easiest to find. The compiler does most of the work.

Missing or Misplaced Semicolon

It may take you a while to get used to the idea of placing a semicolon at the end of a program statement. For example,

```
printf("This is a mistake\n")
```

obviously needs a semicolon after the closing parentheses of the printf() function call. The compiler should catch this error.

Some compilers, however, generate "misleading" error messages in such cases. While scanning (or "parsing") the input line, the compiler must check the syntax to see whether a valid C construct has been used. If a semicolon is left out, the compiler will parse the next line as though it were part of the line with the missing semicolon. Depending on what is contained in the offending line as well as in the following line, the compiler may generate misleading error messages.

If the compiler says that an error occurred in a given line and subsequent inspection of that line shows no errors, check the preceding line for a missing semicolon. With some compilers a missing semicolon in one line causes the compiler to "get lost" in the code. As a result, a series of error messages is given. In one case, a program had 46 errors. Once a single missing semicolon was found and corrected, the program compiled with no further errors.

Another common mistake is to place a semicolon where you really don't want one. For example, consider the following code:

```
for (i = Ø; i < MAX; ++i);          /* trouble! */
     x += 3;
```

This code was probably intended to add 3 to variable x MAX times. However, as the code is written, x is incremented by three only one time. The way this line executes becomes clearer when it is written as

```
for (i = Ø; i < MAX; ++i)
     ;
x += 3;
```

Obviously, this code is a "do nothing" loop. The statement controlled by the for loop is a null statement (that is, a lone semicolon). Such errors are worse than syntax errors because the code will compile and execute; it just doesn't execute properly. Similar mistakes can creep into other loops and conditional statements (for example, do-while, while, and if).

Missing Braces

Forgetting to supply an opening or closing brace is another common mistake. The brace is normally used to group two or more statements together so that they can be treated as a single statement. (Using braces for structures, unions, and initializing variables is less common.) If you forget to use braces when multiple statements are to be treated together, only the first program statement will be executed as planned. Refer, for example, to code fragment 9.1.

Wrong!	Intended
``	```

```
             Wrong!                          Intended
    while (i < MAX)                  while (i < MAX) {
        x[i] = func1();                  x[i] = func1();
        ++i;                             ++i;
                                     }
```

Code fragment 9.1.

The fragment is probably meant to stuff the x[] array with some value returned from the call to func1(). Because braces are not used, however, only one element of x[] is assigned. In addition, if only one brace is supplied, mysterious things can happen, depending on the subsequent code. Although the compiler should catch this error, some compilers may not.

Typically, a programmer may forget to supply matching braces when a loop construct is used with complex if statements. The compiler will catch this error but may not tell you whether an opening or closing brace is the problem. You are more likely to forget the closing brace, although this statement may be a dangerous generality.

Program 9.1, which performs a simple brace count, looks for a match between opening and closing braces. Although this program cannot tell you where the extra or missing brace is, the program is useful as a "precompile" step in checking complex code where you think you may have a missing brace. Such a program will probably execute faster than a compiler pass.

This program is fairly simple, but a few comments are warranted. The variable last_char lets us check for program comments, quoted strings, and single characters that may contain a brace. When the compiler senses a /* character pair, a single quotation mark, or double quotation marks, the program will "waste" characters until a matching */, ', or " is read.

The rest of the program keeps track of opening and closing braces. If the brace counts don't match, the user is informed. Given the higher probability of forgetting a closing brace, the brace counts can help you find the missing or extra brace.

```
/* program to check opening and closing braces */
/* assumes that file name to be checked */
/* is a command line argument */

#include <stdio.h>
#define CLEARS 12                    /* control codes for ADDS */
#define CURSOR "\033Y"               /* Viewpoint terminal */

main(argc, argv)
int argc;
char **argv;
{
        char last_char;
        int o_count, c_count, c;
        FILE *f1;
        void set_cur();

        putchar(CLEARS);
        if ((f1 = fopen(argv[1], "r")) == NULL){
                printf("Can't open %s\n", argv[1]);
                exit(1);
        }

        last_char = ' ';
        o_count = c_count = 0;
        puts("Opening Braces      Closing Braces\n");
        while ((c = getc(f1)) != EOF) {
                if (last_char == '/' && c == '*') {
                        while (c != '/' && last_char != '*')
                                c = getc(f1);
                }
                if (c == '\'') {
                        last_char = c;
                        c = getc(f1);
                        if (c == '\\') {
                                while (c != '\'')
                                        c = getc(f1);
                        }
                        if (c == '{' || c == '}')
                                c = getc(f1);
                }
```

```
                                 if (c == '"' && last_char != '\'') {
                                         c = getc(f1);
                                         while (c != '"')
                                                 c = getc(f1);
                                 }
                                 if (c == '{') {
                                         o_count += 1;
                                         set_cur(2, 7, o_count);
                                 }
                                 if (c == '}') {
                                         c_count += 1;
                                         set_cur(2, 30, c_count);
                                 }
                                 last_char = c;
                         }
                         fclose(f1);
                         printf("\n\nBrace count is ");
                         if ((o_count - c_count) == 0)
                                 printf("okay!!!\n");
                         else
                                 printf("incorrect. \n");
                 }
```

Program 9.1.

Assignment versus Relational Test

It is easy to forget a double-equal sign when you perform a relational test. Consider the error shown in code fragment 9.2.

Wrong!	Intended
(i = 0; i = MAX; ++i)	for (i = 0; i == MAX; ++i)

Code fragment 9.2.

The middle expression in a for loop usually involves some form of relational test between two variables. In code fragment 9.2, we have tried to *assign* i to equal MAX. Unless MAX happens to be #defined as 0, the loop will execute forever. The reason why is that a logical test is expected instead of an assignment. Because the value is nonzero, the test is viewed as logical True and produces an infinite loop.

Other assignment errors can be more subtle, however. The valid assignment

```
flag = start = end = x = Ø;
```

sets each variable to equal zero. Now consider

```
flag = arrayCi] == 'x';
```

which is also a valid statement but with an entirely different meaning. This statement says: If the character found at arrayCi] equals the character x, then the relation arrayCi] == 'x' is logical True, so *assign* flag to equal 1 (that is, True). This statement works this way because the precedence of the relational operator (==) is higher than that of assignment (=).

The same results can be obtained with the more conventional

```
flag = (arrayCi] == 'x') ? 1 : Ø;
```

Although the ternary operator makes this statement clearer, the other form is also valid. Experiment with the relational and assignment operators to verify the preceding discussion.

Program Comments

The /* and */ characters introduce comments into a program. Because the compiler strips away everything between these characters, you can make liberal use of comments in a program. They have no effect on the size or speed of the compiled program. Be sure to use them carefully, however.

A friend of mine was compiling a very complex program that involved a large number of functions which were not part of the common library. He painstakingly documented each function, including a heading that looked something like this:

```
/*********************************************************/
/*                    func1(*x, *y, *z)                 */
/* (Herein began a rather lengthy description of what the */
/*    function was designed to do. ...)                 */
/*********************************************************
```

When he tried to link everything together, several of the functions would not link properly. After much head scratching, we noticed that the trailing slash was missing in one of the headings, just as it is in the preceding heading.

In this particular case, several functions that immediately followed func1() had no comments. Because the compiler "throws away" everything between the opening /* and the companion */, it kept reading the missing functions as comments until it finally found a closing */. If there had been no further comments in the file, the compiler would probably have given us an "unexpected end-of-file" message. This would have made it easier to find the error.

You may want to reproduce this error on your compiler to see what error message, if any, is given. It's easier to figure out what went wrong when you see the error message under "controlled" conditions.

The first four types of errors are fairly common, and you should expect your fair share; making errors is a part of learning C. Errors, however, have a way of growing right along with you. As you gain experience, the errors you make also gain a level of sophistication. Generally, these errors are not caught by the compiler. The program compiles and links properly, but the results aren't correct.

It's at this point that raw perseverance comes into play. Let's proceed to level two.

Arguments to Functions Are Copies

Whenever you pass a variable to a function, a copy of the variable is made. So that the integrity of variables is preserved between functions, the function does *not* receive the actual variable. If you make variables local, or private, to the function, you reduce the chance of interaction between functions. (For a review, see Chapter 4 on using pointers.)

Array and pointer variables are exceptions to this rule. You can change the original value of a variable only if you purposely pass the address of the variable to the function. When an array is passed to a function, it receives the address of the array. (Specifically, the function receives the address of element zero in the array.)

One common mistake is to use an argument in the manner shown in program 9.2.

```
main()
{
    int x;

    .

    .

    cube(x);
    printf("\nThe cube is %d", x);

    .

}

cube(x)
int x;
{
    x = x * x * x;
    return (x);
}
```
                                                    Program 9.2.

In this example, the programmer passed a copy of x to cube() and
expected x to reflect the new value after the function call. However,
because the variable x in cube() is a copy that "dies" when you
leave the function, it has no way of changing x in main(). Only by
using a pointer can this program function properly. In other words,
we would have to pass the *address* of x to the function by using
cube(&x). We would also have to modify the cube() function as
shown in code fragment 9.3.

```
cube(x)
int *x;
{
    *x = *x * *x * *x;
}
```
                                                    Code fragment 9.3.

As a general rule, you should use a pointer only when you want a
function call to alter the original value of the argument to the function. If the function can do its job by using a copy of the argument,
don't use a pointer. If you don't use a pointer, don't expect the function to alter the value of an argument that is passed to it.

Keep in mind that arrays passed as arguments to a function do
pass the address (lvalue) of the array. Passing the name of an array
variable is the same as using a pointer. Passing a string with
double quotation marks as a function argument is also the same
as passing a pointer.

Forgetting To Declare Arguments in a Function Call

Consider the skeletal program 9.3.

```
main()
{
    char let[MAX];



    func1(let);

}

func1(s)
{


```

Program 9.3.

```
}
```

In this example, we want to pass the character array let[] to func1() to alter the contents of the array in some way. However, because the array is received as variable s in func1() and is not explicitly declared, s defaults to an int. Undeclared arguments in a function call are ints by default.

The actual code in func1() plays a large part in determining how tough such an error is to find and how much help the compiler is in locating the error. Make sure that you declare all arguments in a function call, including integer variables.

Forgetting To Declare Functions in main( )

Just as undeclared arguments to a function default to an int, so does whatever is returned from a function. Now consider the code fragment 9.4.

```
main()
{
     double bignum;

     bignum = func1(bignam);
     printf("\nThe answer is %e\n", bignum);
          .

}

func1(dbl)
double dbl;
{

          .

     return (dbl);
}
```

Code fragment 9.4.

So what's the problem? When the `return (dbl)` is executed, the value returned is an `int` because `func1()` is a function that returns an `int` by default. An `int` is returned because no type specifier was given in the function definition. A step in the right direction is to declare `func1()` to return a `double`. The function appears as shown in code fragment 9.5.

```
double func1(dbl)
double dbl;
{

          .

     return(dbl);
}
```

Code fragment 9.5.

Now the function is set up to return a double to `main()`. Unfortunately, we've solved only half the problem.

Function Calls Return Integers to main( )

As you know, the default data type passed to a function is an `int`. Any arguments other than integers must state their data types in the argument declarations. (Play it safe: Declare all arguments whether or not they are `int`s.) The same logic applies in the other direction: Anything returned from a function defaults to an `int`.

Although we corrected func1() to return a double to main() through the double func1() function declaration, main() still thinks that it is getting an integer back from func1(). To let main() in on func1()'s secret, you must declare the function name to return a double in main(). The proper form is shown in program 9.4.

```
main()
{
        double bignum, func1();   /* now main() knows */
        .
        .
        .
}

double func1(dbl)
double dbl;
{
        .
        .
        .
}
```

Program 9.4.

Now both func1() and main() are declared to handle the double properly. If a function will return something other than an int, two rules must be followed. First, the data type must precede the function name (that is, the type specifier) in the function definition. Second, the function name must be declared with the appropriate data type in the calling function [main() or any other function].

Another solution is to declare or define func1() before main() because function names are globally available to the rest of the program. The main() will then know that the function returns a double. Some programmers prefer to write (hence, define) all their functions before main(). This way, all other functions defined in the file "know" about them and their return data types. In many respects, however, this approach seems to be a crutch. Furthermore, it is not a practical solution because so many noninteger functions must be drawn from the standard library.

As of this writing, void will most certainly become a keyword in C. void is a valid data type in UNIX C. Note that void is interpreted as a new data type in C. Because void and int are different, functions that return void should be declared in the calling function. Although many compilers currently treat void and int the same, this treatment is likely to change in the near future. The programs in this book have been written as if this change were in effect now. In your own programs, you should acknowledge the difference between void and int. Then when compilers do implement the new meaning of void, you will not have to change your source code to correct for the new meaning.

Of all the calls I have received about programs not working, one of the most frequent causes of problems is forgetting to declare the return value of a function.

On a related topic, remember that chars are promoted to ints during a function call and that floats are promoted to doubles. If you plan to do a lot of number-crunching calls to functions using floats, it may be faster to do everything with doubles. If you use doubles, you can bypass the conversion of the float to double before the function call.

The same is true of math operations on floats. Because math operations are done in double precision, to use floats, you must convert to double, do the math operation, then convert back to float. When you use a double instead of a float, you skip two conversion steps.

However, if you must store a very large number of floating-point numbers in an array, a float can result in a substantial savings of memory. The same is true for such data stored on disk. The programmer must decide whether the memory and disk space savings are worth the conversion time.

A Pointer Contains Garbage until It Is Initialized

If you try to use a pointer before you assign it to a variable address, the pointer will undoubtedly *not* point to anything useful. This is the most frequent problem of programs that don't work properly. The rule is simple: Always initialize a pointer before you use it.

Another thing to remember about pointers is that, when an array variable is passed to a function, the array variable behaves like a pointer in that the function receives a pointer to the array. The reverse does not work, however. If you define an array in a function (that is, auto storage class), you cannot pass that pointer back to main() for subsequent work on the array created in the function. All variables defined in a function have an auto storage class and disappear when the function is exited. Their contents are lost outside the function. Only the static storage class preserves an array defined in a function.

Numeric Constants in Programs

Another common problem is to assume that the compiler is smarter than it actually is. For example,

```
double num;
    .
    .
    .
num = 3;
```

should assign num with a floating-point representation of the constant 3. However, when the preprocessor sees the 3, it assumes that 3 is an integer value. The preprocessor normally does not check the symbol table to see what num is. Therefore, two bytes are allocated for the constant 3, but num expects to get enough storage for a double (for example, eight bytes). The resulting garbage will probably make discovery of the error fairly easy.

The solution to the problem is to let the preprocessor know what you intend to do. If the statement is written

```
num = 3.0;
```

the preprocessor will know that a floating-point value is being used.

The long data type can cause the same problem, as in

```
long big;
    .
    .
    .
big = 3;
```

An error will occur for reasons that are similar to those of the floating-point problem: the preprocessor thinks that the constant 3 is an int rather than a long. To overcome the problem, use

```
big = 3L;
```

where the 'L' tells the preprocessor that the constant is a long data type.

Hierarchy of Operators

You can easily forget which operators are evaluated first in a complex expression. The expression

```
if (x = func1() == NULL)
```

suggests that the programmer probably wanted x to be assigned the value returned from func1() and then wanted to test x against NULL. However, because the test for equality (==) has higher precedence than does assignment (=), the code behaves in quite a different manner.

The call to func1() returns some value, which is then compared to NULL. Assuming that NULL is defined to be zero, if a zero is returned from the call to func1(), the relational test is logical True, and a 1 is assigned into x. If the value returned from func1() does not match NULL, the test will be logical False and x will equal Ø. In either case, the only values x can assume are Ø or 1.

The correction is simple: you force the assignment to occur first with parentheses, as in

```
if ((x = func1()) == NULL)
```

Now x will be assigned the value returned from func1() before the test against NULL.

Plain Stupidity

Some errors have a way of becoming a challenge and lead to a sense of satisfaction when they are uncovered. Others are just plain stupid. You know better, and the error is so obvious that you don't see it. These errors come under the "it's time to go to bed" category. Code fragment 9.6 is a good (?) example of a stupid mistake that I made while writing this book. Take a moment or two to find the error before you continue reading.

Although the error may be obvious to you, it wasn't to me at the time.

Now that you have studied the program, take a close look at the putc(CLEARS) function call. Obviously, I wanted to clear the screen before printing a message to the user. That is, I should have used putchar(CLEARS) instead of putc(). I was trying to write to a file that wasn't opened yet. In my case, the program simply "went west" (the poetic term for locking up the system).

Because the program involved several different data files, I assumed that something was wrong in the (more complex) code which dealt with the file I/O. Only after I had checked through the file I/O section completely did I see the error.

```
#include <stdio.h>

#define CLEARS '\014'
#define MAX 200

main(argc, argv)
int argc;
char **argv;
{
    FILE *fp, *fopen();
    char c, let[MAX];
    int i, x, j;

    putc(CLEARS);
    if ((fp = fopen(argv[1], "r")) == NULL) {
        printf("\nCan't open file %s\n", argv[1]);
        exit(1);
    }

    puts("The purpose of this program is to...");
        .
        .
        .
}
```

Code fragment 9.6.

Note: The functions getc() and putc() work with files, whereas getchar(), getch(), and putchar() are usually relegated to the screen and keyboard. Operating systems may vary, and other possibilities exist. (See Appendix 8.)

Such errors do occur and can be very difficult to find because you refuse to believe that you could make dumb mistakes. You may tend to assume that there must be a complex reason for an error, particularly as you gain experience with the language. If an error is difficult to find, you should probably take a break. A few minutes away from the code can make even the most well-concealed error obvious.

Debugging

Someone once called a "bug" an undocumented feature of a program. Regardless of what an error is called, it *is* an error that must be isolated and corrected. There are three fundamental steps in this process: (1) detecting the error, (2) isolating the error, and (3) correcting the error. The first two steps are the most difficult.

Kinds of Errors

An infinite variety of errors can exist. The following sections present several different kinds of errors as well as ideas for detecting and fixing them.

Syntax Errors

The easiest errors to detect are those we discussed at the beginning of this chapter. Syntax errors fall into this category. In most cases the compiler will both detect and isolate the error for you. Most compilers will also tell you the line number in the source program where the error occurred. Error correction is reduced to editing the source file and recompiling it. Such syntax errors fall into the "oops" category and are easy to correct.

Program Errors

The more serious type of error is one that goes undetected by the compiler and results in a program that executes but produces the wrong results. In this case the source of the error must be detected and isolated by the programmer. Error correction is still fairly simple because you know an error exists in the program. Detection of the error is equally simple: the results of the program are incorrect. Isolating the error is usually the most difficult aspect of debugging in these situations.

Latent Bugs

The most pernicious bug is the "latent bug"—one that lies dormant during testing but shows up only when a certain data set is supplied to the program. Detecting the error is the most difficult aspect of the latent bug. Once the data set that caused the error is known, isolation and correction of the error are usually fairly simple.

C can be made less error-prone than many languages, especially BASIC, provided that you understand C's strong points. The privacy given to data through function calls minimizes the unwanted side effects that interaction between variables can produce.

Beginning programmers, however, have a tendency to defeat this inherent protection by avoiding function calls. Because such programmers are uncomfortable with how functions work (pointers in particular), the programmers tend to place code that should be a function call into `main()`. Unfortunately, when you place data in `main()`, you make that data available to other elements in the program; therefore, isolating an error becomes more difficult.

A preventative measure to lessen the need for debugging is *defensive coding*, which means pushing the busy work out of `main()` and into function calls. When you use function calls to do the busy work, you minimize interactions between variables. The fewer the data manipulations in `main()`, the less likely the chance of contaminating other data in the program. This is also an argument for keeping external storage class variables to a minimum. The greater the privacy afforded to the data, the easier it will be to isolate the error in the debugging process.

Most programs are composed of a series of smaller tasks, or intermediate steps, that build up to a final result. Each small task is probably a candidate for a function call. "Divide and conquer" has real meaning in C; push the busy work out of `main()` if possible. Divide and separate the work into smaller, more manageable, function calls.

Outlining the program and its underlying algorithm in a pseudo-language form is beneficial because it makes the smaller tasks readily identifiable. Once the individual tasks are known, each task can be coded as a function call and tested separately. If errors do occur, at least you will have a smaller section of code to examine.

Error Detection and Isolation

Error detection is done by the compiler, the programmer, and (sadly) the user. The compiler can detect syntactic and semantic errors. It cannot, of course, detect a properly coded but faulty algorithm. With programmer experience, compiler errors tend to disappear.

The more difficult error is one in which the program executes but does not produce the desired results. In such a case, the programmer must check through the code for the error. (We are assuming that the algorithm is correct.)

The process of error detection begins with a set of check data (data that is known to be correct). The known data is fed into the program, and the program is "divided down" until the source of the error is isolated. Dividing down the program consists of placing

various printf() statements in the program to see intermediate results. Probably 90 percent of program debugging is done with
printf()s.

The process needs little elaboration; simply place the printf()s at
those spots that are causing problems and print the appropriate
values. This procedure works for both isolating and correcting the
bug. Most of you have no doubt already used printf()s for debugging your own programs.

If you have used printf()s for debugging, you've probably had the
following experience. You needed to debug an array, so you
placed a for loop that controlled a printf() to examine the contents of the array. When you found the error, you went back into
the source code and removed all the (now unneeded) code that
was entered in the debugging process. A little later, you found that
you still had a bug in the same section of the program and had to
reenter the same debugging code all over again. This experience
is common.

There's got to be a better way, especially if you have that nagging
feeling that you're going to have to come back and enter the debugging code again. Consider the following approach. Let's assume that some function [such as func1()] is giving you problems
and you need to print out an array x[]. The normal procedure is
shown in code fragment 9.7.

```
int func1(s)
char *s;
{
     int i, j, k;
     .
     .
     for (i = 0; i < j; ++i)          /* debug code to look at s */
          printf("%c ", *s++);

     .                                /* rest of function        */
     .
     .
}
```

Code fragment 9.7. Simple
debug code.

First, notice that the for loop does *not* have the normal level of indentation within the program. This inconsistency makes locating
the debug code easier when it is to be removed. Once we are convinced that the function is working properly, we usually delete the
for loop and the printf(), and that's that.

Now for the alternative. Why not toggle the debug code on and off according to our needs? One approach is presented in code fragment 9.8.

```
#define DEBUG 1
     int func1(s)
     char *s;
     {
          int i, j, k;
            .
            .
            .
#if DEBUG

for (i = 0; i < j; ++i)               /* debug code to look at s */
     printf("%c ", *s++);

#endif
            .
            .                          /* rest of function        */
            .
     }
```

Code fragment 9.8. Toggling debug code.

In this code fragment, we make use of the #if-#endif preprocessor directive to toggle the debug code "into" or "out of" the function. The #if says that if the symbolic constant DEBUG is currently logical True (that is, nonzero), compile the following line(s) up to the #endif into the program. If the symbolic constant is logical False (that is, 0), ignore the lines up to the #endif.

Stop and think about how this works. If you suspect s in func1() to be a problem and you want to examine the contents of s, all you have to do is activate DEBUG with a logical True value (that is, 1). The preprocessor will then compile the debug code into the program for compilation.

Once you are satisfied that you no longer need the debug code, all you have to do is change the #define to

```
#define DEBUG 0
```

Because the #if works much like a simple if, the

```
#if DEBUG
```

will be logical False, and everything between the #if and #endif is ignored by the compiler. Hence, you've turned off the debug code.

If the need arises to reactivate the debug code, simply changing the value of DEBUG to some nonzero value will toggle the debug code back on—with no retyping! Indeed, the debug code never needs to be removed (and may even improve the documentation and maintenance of the program). The same approach can be used to add or delete variables, program lines, and even entire functions if necessary.

Some compilers simplify the debug process even further by use of the -d (reads as "dash d") switch. For example, if you were compiling func1() and it did not have the #define DEBUG 1 in it, but the debug code was there, the command line

```
cc libfile -dDEBUG=1
```

in effect places a #define DEBUG 1 at the start of the file named libfile. Thus, if a debug code is present in the file, the code will be turned on.

Note that you do not have to use the DEBUG symbolic constant. You might have something like that presented in code fragment 9.9.

If you used the command line

```
cc libfile -dVERIFY=1
```

only the debug code in func2() would be activated. If func1() and func2() both used VERIFY to toggle the debug code, it would be toggled on in both functions. However, since most compilers allow multiple uses of the debug switch, you could toggle the debug code on in code fragment 9.9 with

```
cc libfile -dVERIFY=1 -dDEBUG=1
```

You should check to see whether your compiler supports such a switch. For example, the UNIX C compiler uses -D instead of the lowercase -d. (The switch might be found under some other name than -d.)

Obviously, you can use the -d compile switch to toggle "permanent" code (that is, code that is always part of the program) on or off, too. If, for example, you have a French and English version of a program, you might see the following:

```
#if FRENCH
     printf("avez un bon jour");
#else
     printf("have a nice day");
#endif
```

```
        int func1(s)
        char *s;
        {
                int i, j, k;

                .
                .
#if DEBUG

                for (i = Ø; i < j; ++i)              /* debug code to look at s */
                        printf("%c ", *s++);

#endif
                .
                .
                                        /* rest of function        */
        }

        int func2(i)
        int i;
        {
                .
                .
#if VERIFY

printf("%u ", i);

#endif
                .
        }
```

Code fragment 9.9.

If the command line is

```
cc programfile -dFRENCH=1
```

the French translation is used; otherwise, the English version is compiled. If you use a little creativity, all kinds of possibilities are available with the debug compile-time switch.

Extreme Value Testing

One final suggestion is that for each new program, you try using extreme values for the data. Things may look fine until the data is stretched to the limit. For example, consider a subcalculation in statistics where the sums-of-squares of two variables are multiplied together, and then the square root of the product is taken:

```
i_val = sqr(sum_sq_x * sum_sq_y);
```

Code similar to this worked for three years without failing in a program used by several thousand users. Then someone plugged in a very large data set by using Gross National Product (in dollars) for both variables. The program failed because the number was larger than the compiler could handle (in other words, what occurred was numeric overflow). The correction was simple: take the square root of the numbers *before* multiplying them.

The (latent) bug was there all the time, but it never showed up until the data was pushed to its limit. Machine overflow and underflow are always potential problems. The best you can hope to do is to minimize the chances that such problems will occur.

Some Concluding Thoughts

If you have gotten this far, it's probably because you recognize the power and advantages offered by C. As you gain experience with C, you will become even more convinced. And a growing number of people agree with you. Although C is not perfect, it is a lot better than many of the alternatives.

This text used simple examples to convey the fundamentals of the C programming language. Now that you're ready to set out on your own, you will need more complex examples to study. C has many subtleties that are not covered in this book. One way of discovering them is to examine the code of other C programmers.

To that end, I strongly urge you to join the C Users' Group. The nominal cost (presently $15.00 per year) includes a subscription to the group's newsletter. Equally important is the growing library of C programs that are available for a nominal copying charge (less than $10.00 per volume, including the disk!). The programs on these disks are a great source for learning new coding techniques. There are also other benefits. For further information, write to

C Users' Group Newsletter
415 East Euclid
McPherson, KS 67460

Who knows, before long *you* may be contributing programs to their library.

Appendix A
ASCII Codes

The codes for the American Standard Code for Information Interchange, or ASCII, are listed below. These codes are given for those numbering systems commonly used in C. A control character is abbreviated as ^. A Control-C is shown as ^C.

Table A.1

Decimal	Hex	Octal	Binary	ASCII	
0	00	000	00000000	null	(NUL)
1	01	001	00000001	^A	(SOH)
2	02	002	00000010	^B	(STX)
3	03	003	00000011	^C	(ETX)
4	04	004	00000100	^D	EOT
5	05	005	00000101	^E	ENQ
6	06	006	00000110	^F	ACK
7	07	007	00000111	^G	(bell) BEL
8	08	010	00001000	^H	(backspace) BS
9	09	011	00001001	^I	(tab) horizontal HT
10	0A	012	00001010	^J	(linefeed) LF
11	0B	013	00001011	^K	(vertical tabs) VT
12	0C	014	00001100	^L	(formfeed) FF
13	0D	015	00001101	^M	(carriage return) CR
14	0E	016	00001110	^N	SO
15	0F	017	00001111	^O	SI
16	10	020	00010000	^P	DLE
17	11	021	00010001	^Q	DC1
18	12	022	00010010	^R	DC2
19	13	023	00010011	^S	DC3
20	14	024	00010100	^T	(DC4)
21	15	025	00010101	^U	(NAK)

22	16	026	00010110	^V	(SYN)
23	17	027	00010111	^W	(ETB)
24	18	030	00011000	^X	(CAN)
25	19	031	00011001	^Y	(EM)
26	1A	032	00011010	^Z	(SUB)
27	1B	033	00011011	Escape	
28	1C	034	00011100	FS	
29	1D	035	00011101	GS	
30	1E	036	00011110	RS	
31	1F	037	00011111	US	
32	20	040	00100000	Space	
33	21	041	00100001	!	
34	22	042	00100010	"	
35	23	043	00100011	#	
36	24	044	00100100	$	
37	25	045	00100101	%	
38	26	046	00100110	&	
39	27	047	00100111	'	
40	28	050	00101000	(	
41	29	051	00101001	)	
42	2A	052	00101010	*	
43	2B	053	00101011	+	
44	2C	054	00101100	,	
45	2D	055	00101101	-	
46	2E	056	00101110	.	
47	2F	057	00101111	/	
48	30	060	00110000	0	
49	31	061	00110001	1	
50	32	062	00110010	2	
51	33	063	00110011	3	
52	34	064	00110100	4	
53	35	065	00110101	5	
54	36	066	00110110	6	
55	37	067	00110111	7	
56	38	070	00111000	8	
57	39	071	00111001	9	
58	3A	072	00111010	:	
59	3B	073	00111011	;	
60	3C	074	00111100	<	
61	3D	075	00111101	=	

62	3E	076	00111110	>
63	3F	077	00111111	?
64	40	100	01000000	@
65	41	101	01000001	A
66	42	102	01000010	B
67	43	103	01000011	C
68	44	104	01000100	D
69	45	105	01000101	E
70	46	106	01000110	F
71	47	107	01000111	G
72	48	110	01001000	H
73	49	111	01001001	I
74	4A	112	01001010	J
75	4B	113	01001011	K
76	4C	114	01001100	L
77	4D	115	01001101	M
78	4E	116	01001110	N
79	4F	117	01001111	O
80	50	120	01010000	P
81	51	121	01010001	Q
82	52	122	01010010	R
83	53	123	01010011	S
84	54	124	01010100	T
85	55	125	01010101	U
86	56	126	01010110	V
87	57	127	01010111	W
88	58	130	01011000	X
89	59	131	01011001	Y
90	5A	132	01011010	Z
91	5B	133	01011011	[
92	5C	134	01011100	\
93	5D	135	01011101	]
94	5E	136	01011110	^
95	5F	137	01011111	_
96	60	140	01100000	`
97	61	141	01100001	a
98	62	142	01100010	b
99	63	143	01100011	c
100	64	144	01100100	d
101	65	145	01100101	e
102	66	146	01100110	f

103	67	147	01100111	g
104	68	150	01101000	h
105	69	151	01101001	i
106	6A	152	01101010	j
107	6B	153	01101011	k
108	6C	154	01101100	l
109	6D	155	01101101	m
110	6E	156	01101110	n
111	6F	157	01101111	o
112	70	160	01110000	p
113	71	161	01110001	q
114	72	162	01110010	r
115	73	163	01110011	s
116	74	164	01110100	t
117	75	165	01110101	u
118	76	166	01110110	v
119	77	167	01110111	w
120	78	170	01111000	x
121	79	171	01111001	y
122	7A	172	01111010	z
123	7B	173	01111011	{
124	7C	174	01111100	|
125	7D	175	01111101	}
126	7E	176	01111110	~
127	7F	177	01111111	del, rubout

Appendix B
Commercial C Products

This Appendix lists several commercially available C compilers. Most of those listed use either the CP/M or MS-DOS operating systems, although a few compilers are available for other operating systems. It is encouraging to note that, since the first edition of this book, a number of firms are marketing add-on products for various C compilers. These products include C debuggers, windowing, and other special-purpose library functions.

Letters were sent to many companies that produce C products. A number of these companies have supplied copies of their software, and a brief description of each company's products is given. What follows is not an endorsement of any of the products but rather a source for further information.

C compilers are divided into two classes: (1) full C, which means that all data types are provided, with the possible exception of bit fields and the enum data type, and (2) subset C, which normally means that the long, float, double, struct, and union data types are not provided. Structure passing should not be expected (although a few compilers do support it). Register storage class may or may not be supported on a full C compiler. (For example, register declarations may be recognized, but a register is not actually used.) Most subset compilers require that the source file reside in memory during compilation.

For compilers running under MS-DOS, "small" and "large" models may be available. The small model is limited to 64K of code and 64K of data. The large model uses 4-byte pointers and can address a much larger code-data area (usually up to one megabyte). Also note that most MS-DOS compilers will run under the 80186 and 80286 CPUs.

Compilers

Aztec C   (Full C)   (8080, 8088, 6502)   (CP/M, MS-DOS)

A copy for review was promised but not sent. However, Aztec does have a compiler for a variety of systems. Prices begin at $200.00. Manx Software Systems, P.O. Box 55, Shrewsbury, NJ 07701 (800) 221-0440.

BDS C   (Subset C)   (8080, Z80, 8085)   (CP/M)

Although listed as a subset C, this compiler does support structures and unions. The `static` and `register` storage classes and initializers are not supported. BDS C has fast assembly and link times and generates good code. (Published benchmarks place BDS C at or near the top of the list for subset compilers.) Documentation consists of approximately 180 pages, including information about a debugger that is available for use with the compiler. The library provided has over 90 functions. BSC C is available for the 8080 or Z80 CPUs using CP/M 80. Price is $150.00. BD Software, P.O. Box 2368, Cambridge, MA 02238 (617) 576-3828.

C86   (Full C)   (8086, 8088)   (MS-DOS)

The C86 compiler supports both large and small models. The documentation is approximately 250 pages, including a discussion of more than 180 library functions. The 8087 is supported along with software floating point. Considered one of the better MS-DOS compilers, the C86 does well on most benchmarks. The company also markets Introducing C, which is a C interpreter for the IBM PC (and "clones"). The interpreter is an improved version of Tom Gibson's Tiny c. Introducing C is not a full C (no structures or unions), it is a very good C learning tool. Price is $395.00 for C86 and $95.00 for Introducing C. Computer Innovations, 980 Shrewsbury Ave., Suite 310, Tinton Falls, NJ 07724 (201) 542-5920.

Eco-C   (Full C)   (Z80, 8086, 8088)   (CP/M80, MS-DOS)

Limitations: MS-DOS version supports small model only. Documentation consists of approximately 100 pages. Between 110 (Z80 version) and 160 (8086-8088 version) library functions are provided, including transcendentals. Error messages are in English, not numbers. Published benchmarks place it at or near the top for full C compilers in both the CP/M and MS-DOS environments. Both versions generate tight code and have fast floating point. The 8086-8088 version can sense the 8087 math co-processor at run time for either software or hardware floating point using a single library. (For example, users don't have to update software if they add an 8087 later on.) The price is $149.95 for the Z80 version (with assembler and linker). The price of the MS-DOS version has been dropped from $250.00 to $49.95 (generates OBJ files for use with the MS-DOS linker). Ecosoft, Inc., 6413 North College Avenue, Indianapolis, IN 46220 (317) 255-6476.

Hendrix Small-C   (Subset C)   (8080, Z80)   (CP/M80)

The package includes a copy of *The Small C Handbook*, written by Mr. Hendrix; the handbook also serves as the documentation for the compiler. When the compiler is invoked with no C source input file, the user can type in C commands and immediately see the resulting assembler code on the CRT. The compiler is based on Ron Cain's small c, but has a larger set of operators and statements. The book includes the source code for the compiler, contains a discussion of more than 80 library functions, and has an introduction to 8080 assembly language programming. Also available is Small-Tools (containing programs to copy, list, and merge, plus a small editor). Price is $42.95 for the compiler and $35.00 for Small-Tools. A macro assembler called Small-Mac is now available that produces Microsoft-compatible REL files and includes a linker and librarian priced at $30.00. Because Mr. Hendrix furnishes source code for virtually everything, these packages are both utilitarian and educational. J.E. Hendrix, Box 8378, University, MS 38677 (601) 234-7508.

Lattice C   (Full C)   (8086-8088)   (MS-DOS)

Although a request for a current compiler was not answered, the Lattice compiler is a good compiler with a complete library. The compiler generates good code and ranks high on published benchmarks. This product supports both large and small models. Contact the firm for current information and pricing. Lattice Inc., P.O. Box 3072, Glen Ellyn, IL 60138 (312) 858-7950.

Microsoft   (Full C)   (8086-8088)   (MS-DOS)

The compiler supports the full C language, both small and large models. Although late into the C market for the PC, the compiler promises to be a serious contender, as it generates tight and fast executing code. The standard library is complete, with good documentation. (The documentation consists of two manuals: a user's guide and a library reference manual, with a combined page count of more than 1,000 pages.) The compiler has a large number of compile-time options and comes with its own assembler, linker, and librarian. The price is $500.00. Microsoft Corp., 10700 Northup Way, Bellevue, WA 98009 (206) 828-8088.

Q/C   (Subset C)   (8080, Z80, 8086, 8088)   (CP/M80, MS-DOS)

Although listed as a subset, this compiler does have structures and unions. Documentation consists of over 170 pages (quite good, by the way), including a description of the internal workings of the compiler. Complete source code (8080-Z80 versions) for the compiler is included (based on a much-improved version of Ron Cain's small c), which makes Q/C an excellent source for learning compiler techniques. As is true of most small c compilers, the assembler file also includes the (commented out) C source that produced the resulting assembler code. The library includes over 80 functions. The company has just introduced a similar version for IBM PC (and clones). Price is $95.00 for the Q/C 88 and $50.00 for the IBM PC version. (Source code for the PC is available for a nominal fee.) Compile times are quite fast. Q/C is a good solid product. Published by The Code Works, P. O. Box 62136, Santa Barbara, CA 93160 (805) 683-1585.

C Support Product

Application Programmer's Toolkit   (8086-8088)   (MS-DOS)

The package contains a series of tools to speed applications programming and includes routines for user interfacing, direct and keyed-file access, data input and editing, screen generator, terminal driver, and report generator, plus a number of utility programs. The source code for the programs is provided, and the manual is on disk. The programs and utilities will make life much easier for those who wish to develop applications programs. Compiled versions are available for a number of different compilers; check for availability. Prices range from $295.00 to $395.00. Shaw * American Technologies, 830 South Second Street, P.O. Box 648, Louisville, KY 40201 (502) 583-5527.

Greenleaf Functions   (8086-8088)   (MS-DOS)

The library contains more than 200 functions for various C compilers. Most of the functions do not duplicate those you would normally expect to find in the standard library shipped with most compilers. The library contains a number of extended operating system, string, color, and file I/O functions. The documentation is approximately 230 pages. Source code (some of which is in assembler) is provided. Because some functions are hardware-dependent, inquire about availability for your compiler-hardware environment before ordering. Price is $200.00. Greenleaf Software Inc., 2101 Hickory Dr., Carrollton, TX 75006 (214) 446-8641.

Windows for C   (8088)   (MS-DOS)

The package provides a full complement of C functions designed for writing applications software, especially functions that use windows. The package also provides for manipulation of character graphics, menus, color, and contains ideas on animation, games, and other applications. Documentation is over 110 pages and has numerous examples of how the functions are called and used in programs. The package includes over 50 functions. Because Windows is written for the IBM PC and specific C compilers, check to see whether the functions work on PC clones and are compatible with your C compiler. Price is $195.00. Vermont Creative Software, 21 Elm Avenue, Richford, VT 05476 (802) 848-7738.

The information about these products was provided by the author. Que Corporation cannot attest to either the accuracy of this information or the availability of these products. All prices are subject to change without notice.

Appendix C
Syntax Summary

This Appendix summarizes the fundamental syntax features of C in one place for easy reference, but is not intended as a replacement for the information in the text. However, this Appendix should prove helpful if you forget a syntax rule with a given statement. (For example, does a `for` loop use a comma or a semicolon, or both?) Where applicable, a short example is given.

Objects, Data Types, Identifiers, and Storage Classes

Objects

An object is an area of memory in which a specific type of data is stored. There are four fundamental types of objects: `char`, `int`, `float`, and `double`.

char

A `char` is an area of storage that is large enough to hold one element of the computer's character set. The only valid modifier for `char` is `unsigned`.

For a microcomputer, the ASCII character set (see Appendix A) normally uses 1 byte of storage. (An 8-bit byte is used even though an ASCII character requires only 7 bits.)

int

An int is an area of storage that holds an integer number.

Typically, an int on an 8- or 16-bit computer is twice as large as a char (for example, 2 bytes). Valid modifiers include the categories short, long, and unsigned. On a 32-bit machine, an int is usually four times as large as a char (for example, 4 bytes).

float

A float is an area of storage that holds a single-precision, floating-point number.

Typically, a float requires an area that is 4 times that of a char (for example, 4 bytes).

double

A double is an area of storage that holds a double-precision, floating-point number.

Typically, a double requires twice as much storage as a float (for example, 8 bytes).

enum

The enumerated (enum) data type is a new data type that will most likely be added to the standard C syntax. enum is designed to constrain the variable to have only one value in the program. Therefore, enum data types are often used as "flag" variables.

void

void is a new data type that is used as a type specifier for a function which does not return a useful value from the function call. Trying to use the return value from a function that returns a void data type causes an error message to be issued by the compiler.

Data Types

The four types of objects may be combined into five derived data types:

1. Arrays of objects (such as an array of chars, or an array of ints)

2. Functions that may return an object (for example, a function returning int)

3. Pointers to objects (such as a pointer to ints)

4. A structure that holds two or more objects (for example, a structure of a char, an int, and an array of floats)

5. A union to store any size object. Only one object, however, can reside in the union at one time (for example, a union of char, int, and double, but with only one of these objects in the union at a time).

Identifiers

An identifier is used to name an object. The name references the object in a program (for example, variable and function names).

1. The letters A through Z (uppercase and lowercase are different), the digits 0 through 9, and the underscore (_) are valid characters for identifiers.

2. The first character must be a letter or an underscore (not a digit).

3. Variable and function names may be as long as you want, but no more than the first eight characters may be significant. (Check the documentation on both the compiler and the linker. Several major linkers are limited to six characters of significance.)

Storage Classes

There are four storage classes: automatic, static, external, and register.

Automatic

An automatic storage class is an object whose value(s) are local to a function or block in a program, as in the following:

```
fctn()
{
      int x;
      x = 7;
      while (1) {
            float x;

            fx2(&x);
            if (x == 1.375)
            break;
      }
      printf("%d\n", x);
}
```

1. The keyword auto is reserved for the automatic storage class.

2. The value of an auto variable is not available outside the function or block in which the variable is declared. (In other words, auto variables are not globally available throughout the program.)

3. The value of an auto variable is lost when you leave the function or block.

4. Unless otherwise specified or declared outside any function or block, all objects are of the auto storage class.

static

A static storage class is like auto, with the following exception:

The value that a variable had when the function was last exited is the value of the variable the next time the function or block is entered. For example, if variable col_2 is 7 when the cursor() function is exited, col_2 has a starting value of 7 the next time cursor() is called.

An auto, by contrast, will contain garbage on the second call to cursor(); an auto variable "dies" on leaving the function.

External

External (extern) variables are globally available throughout the program. They have values that "live" throughout the program.

register

A register is a variable that is stored in a register of the CPU. Typically, a register is used to store char, int, and pointer variables when execution speed is an important consideration in the program.

1. The data type cannot exceed the storage limitations of the register. That is, if the CPU has 16-bit registers, a (32-bit) float cannot be stored in a register.

2. register variables have an auto storage class.

3. You cannot take the address of a register variable.

4. Most compilers limit the number of register variables that can be used at one time. There is no guarantee that requesting a register storage class will actually result in the variable's being placed in a register. If no register is available, the object is placed in memory. The compiler will try to place the object in a register if one is available.

Attributes, lvalues, rvalues, Pointers, and Indirection

Attributes

Each identifier is of a specific type and storage class. The attributes of the identifier, therefore, are its type and storage class.

Collectively, the declaration of the identifier sets its attributes. For example,

```
register int i_Loop;
```

declares the variable i_Loop (that is, the identifier) and is an integer variable of the register storage class.

lvalues and rvalues

Each object resides at an address in memory, which becomes the object's lvalue, and has something stored at that address, which is the object's rvalue. Therefore, the lvalue is the object's address, and the rvalue is what the object contains.

For example, let's suppose that the character 'A' has been assigned to a variable named Let_r. Let's further assume that the variable has been stored at memory address 50000 by the compiler. The lvalue of Let_r is 50000, and its rvalue is 'A'.

Pointers and Indirection

The rvalue of a pointer variable is the address of another variable of a specified type. Notice the following example:

```
char Let_r, *ptr_Let;
Let_r = 'A';
ptr_Let = &Let_r;
```

Let's assume that Let_r is an object of type char stored at address 50000 and that ptr_Let is a pointer to type char stored at address 60000. The lvalue of prt_Let is 60000, and its rvalue is 50000. In this example, ptr_Let points to character 'A' through a process called indirection. That is,

```
printf("The character is %c", *ptr_Let);
```

prints the character A on the screen.

Expressions, Statements, and Braces

Expressions

An expression is a series of one or more operands connected by an operator. Some examples of expressions are

```
c = 25
y = (x * z) / n
y--
```

In the first example, the expression is the unary assignment operation, which assigns 25 to c. The second example involves three operations (multiplication, division, and assignment), whereas the third example uses only one operation (postdecrement). Unary operations (for example, postdecrement) have one operand, binary operations (for example, multiplication) have two operands, and ternary operations (such as x = (y == TRUE) ? 1 : 0) require three operands.

For complex expressions, the hierarchy of operators (see Chapter 7) determines the order in which the expression is evaluated. The precedence rules are strict, which is why an expression such as

```
x = y == 2
```

is a valid expression. Because the double-equal sign (that is, the test for equality) is of higher precedence than the single-equal sign (that is, assignment), the test for equality is performed first, then the assignment to x. What is assigned to x? If y equals 2, the expression is logical True; therefore, x is assigned the value of 1. If y does not equal 2, the expression is logical False, and x is assigned to equal 0.

Statements and Braces

Any expression in C that is terminated by a semicolon is a statement. Therefore,

```
c = 25;
y = (x * z) / n;
y--;
```

are now statements, whereas they were simply expressions before.

Statements can be grouped together into a single, larger statement (also called compound statements or blocks) with braces. Therefore, anywhere a single statement can appear in C, multiple statements can be used if they are surrounded by braces. One common example is the if statement:

```
if (expression)            if (expression){
    statement                   statement 1;
                                statement 2;
                                statement n;
                           }
```

If *expression* is True, then *statement* is executed. In the example on the right, if *expression* is True, *statement* is again executed. In this instance, however, the statement actually consists of *n* statements grouped together by braces. In other words, the use of braces in the second example forces the if to view the *n* statements as though they were a single statement.

Braces may contain multiple statements and declarations. Braces may also contain a single statement, but then the braces are redundant.

Keywords

Despite its power, C has relatively few keywords, which are listed here.

Keywords

Data Types	Storage Classes	Statements
char	auto	break
int	static	case
float	extern	continue
double	register	default
long		do
short		else
struct		for
union		goto
unsigned		if
enum		return
void		sizeof
		switch
typedef		while
		(entry)

(The entry keyword is not yet implemented, and typedef is really not a storage class in itself, but rather a shorthand form for existing data types.)

Statement Keywords

In this section, the expression is abbreviated as exp and followed by a number if statement uses more than one expression. The abbreviation id is used for identifier.

for

```
for (exp1; exp2; exp3)
        statement;
```

Typically, *exp1* initializes one or more variables, *expr2* performs a relational test, and *expr3* increments or decrements a variable. For example,

```
for (i = 0; i < MAX; ++i)      for (i = 0, m = 1; m == 10;
    s[i] = i + OFFSET;                ++i, m++){
                                      sum[i] = i * m;
                                      sumsq *= sum[i];
                               }
```

In the second example, both i and m are initialized as part of exp1, then incremented as part of exp3. (Note the compound statement and multiple subexpressions.)

if-else

```
if (exp)                          if (exp)

    statement    or                   statement 1;
                             else
                                      statement 2;
```

If the *exp* that follows the if is True (that is, nonzero), then *statement* is executed; otherwise, *statement* is ignored. When the if-else combination is used, *statement 1* is executed if *exp* is True, and *statement 2* is ignored. If *exp* is not True, *statement 1* is ignored, and *statement 2* is executed. Notice the following:

```
if (fd == ERROR)                   if ((c = getchar()) != '\n')
    put("Can't open file");            putchar(c);
                                   else
                                       putchar(CLEARS);
```

In the first example, if variable fd equals the symbolic constant for ERROR, the message is displayed. The expression in an if statement often uses a relational operator. The second example also tests for inequality between c and a newline character. If c is a newline character, then the screen is cleared through the else statement.

The if statement can also be used as

```
if (ptr)
      statement;
else
      puts("Not valid pointer");
```

If a pointer contains an address of zero, the pointer is invalid. A nonzero pointer value, however, is okay. The previous if statement tests for a nonzero rvalue for pointer.

break

The break statement is used to "break out" of a controlling for, while, do, or switch statement. One way break is used is for leaving a loop when a specified value of a variable is found. The following is an example:

```
for (i = 0;  i < MAXLOOP;  ++i){
      if (x[i] == MAXVAL)
            break
      statement 1;
      statement 2;
}
statement 3;
```

When variable x[] is equal to MAXVAL, the break statement is executed, which causes control to proceed to *statement 3*. If x[] does not equal MAXVAL, *statements 1* and *2* are executed, and the loop continues until i equals MAXLOOP.

continue

The continue statement, which causes a for, do, or while loop to repeat execution, is the opposite of a break statement in that continue sustains control of the loop. Notice the following example.

```
for (i = 0;  i < MAXLOOP;  ++i){
      if (x[i] == MAXVAL){
            ++count;
            continue;
      }
      statement 1;
      statement 2;
}
statement 3;
```

In this example, if x[i] equals MAXVAL, the variable count is incremented, and the continue statement causes the for loop to execute again. *statements 1* and *2* are ignored. Also, continue is used
to count the matches between x[] and MAXVAL and to ignore *statements 1* and *2* each time a match occurs.

switch, case, and default

Examine the following:

```
switch (exp1) {
    case constant exp2:
        statement;
    case constant exp3:
        statement;
    default:
        statement;
}
```

The switch statement uses the value of *exp1* to transfer control to
one of the case statements for execution. The constant expression
for each case must be an integer, and each constant must be
unique. If the value of *exp1* does not match any of the case constant
expressions, then the default is executed. The switch statement
may be used to replace a series of if statements, like an ON-
GOTO in BASIC. Study also the following:

```
switch (day_vaL) {
    case 1:
        puts("Monday");
        break;
    case 2:
        puts("Tuesday");
        break;
    case 3:
        puts("Wednesday");
        break;
    case 4:
        puts("Thursday");
        break;
    case 5:
        puts("Friday");
        break;
```

```
   case 6:
        puts("Saturday");
        break;
   case 7:
        puts("Sunday");
        break;
   default:
        puts("Invalid day of week");
        break;
}
```

In this example, the `switch` uses `day_vaL` to determine which `case` to whatever statement follows the `switch`. Note that braces are not used for compound statements within a `case`.

while, do-while

Compare the following:

```
while (exp)                do
     statement;                   statement;
                           while (exp)
```

For both `while` and `do-while`, `statement` is executed as long as *exp* evaluates as nonzero. The difference between a `while` and a `do-while` is that *statement* may never be executed with a `while`. If *exp* evaluates to zero in a `while`, *statement* is not executed; *exp* is evaluated before *statement*. In a `do-while`, *statement* is executed, then *exp* is evaluated. Therefore, even if *exp* is zero on entry into a `do-while` loop, *statement* is always executed at least one time. For example,

```
i = count = 0;                 i = count = 0;
while (x[i] != BADVAL) {       do{
     ++count;                       ++count;
     ++i;                           ++i;
}                              }while (x[i] != BADVAL);
```

On the left of the example, if `x[0]` equals `BADVAL`, both `count` and `i` equal zero on leaving the `while` loop. If `x[0]` equals `BADVAL` for the `do-while` loop, both `count` and `i` equal 1 on leaving the loop. The statements following the `do` are executed at least one time.

goto

In the example

    goto id;

the goto statement causes an unconditional transfer of control to the identifier that follows the goto. The identifier is a label in the program. Study the following example:

```
try:        puts("\nOutput to Screen or Printer (S,P):  ");
            c = getchar();
            if (c != 'S' || c != 'P')
                    goto try;
```

If you enter any character other than an uppercase S or P, the goto statement executes and sends control to the identifying label try.

The program repeats the prompt and requests the entry again. The label must be followed by a colon, which is not part of the identifier label.

return

In the following,

    return;   or   return exp;

once a function call is completed, the return statement returns control to the calling routine. A simple return statement without an expression returns an undefined value to the caller. A return followed by an expression returns the value of the expression to the caller.

If an expression is present, the data type returned is determined by the data type specified in the function declaration. See, for example, the following:

```
func1()                               double func2()
{                                     {
        .                                     .
        .                                     .
    return (x);                           return (x);
}                                     }
```

The call to func1() returns x as an integer because the default data type for a function is int. The call to func2() returns x as a double because the function is declared to be a double.

If a function with no `return` statement in it is called, an undefined value is returned to the caller. Program control "falls off" the end of the function, and the closing brace causes control to return to the caller.

sizeof

In the following,

```
sizeof (exp)
```

the `sizeof` statement returns an integer value that equals the size of *exp* in bytes. Take, for example,

```
y = sizeof (x);
if (y == 4)
     puts("x is a float");
```

When used with an array, `sizeof` determines the array size in bytes.

Macro Preprocessor and Control Lines

C has a number of control line commands that cause the compiler to include files, do macro substitutions, and do conditional compilations. For example,

```
#include "stdio.h"
#define CLEARS 12
```

tells the compiler to include the standard I/O file in the program and to define CLEARS (for example, a clear screen code) to be 12. Control line codes are introduced with a # sign and are not terminated with a semicolon. A newline character in the source code file signals the end of the control line. (If a `#define` is sufficiently long to warrant continuation on the next line, the backslash [\] may be used to continue the definition.)

#undef

If an identifier has been `#defined` in a program, such as `#define` MAXVAL 200, the preprocessor substitutes the value of 200 at every point in the program where MAXVAL appears. However, if the control line

```
#undef MAXVAL
```

appears in the program, MAXVAL becomes undefined from that point on.

#if

Control lines can also be used to alter compilation, depending on specified conditions. Examine the following:

```
#ifdef CLEARS
    putchar(CLEARS);
#else
    for (i = 0; i < 24; ++i)
    putchar('\n');
#endif
```

If the symbolic constant CLEARS is defined (for example, #define CLEARS 12) at this point in the program, the putchar(CLEARS) code is compiled. If CLEARS has not been defined, the for-loop code is compiled. The #endif marks the end of the conditional compilation.

The same results can be achieved with

```
#ifndef CLEARS
    for (i = o; i < 24; ++i)
        putchar('\n');
#endif
```

If CLEARS has not been defined, the compiler will include the code between the #ifndef and the #endif.

Finally, an #if can be used to include or exclude a section of code, depending on the evaluation of a constant expression. For example,

```
#if MAXVAL < 80
    puts("\nMaximum value is less than 80. ");
#endif
```

If the constant expression evaluates to nonzero, then the code for the message is included in the program; otherwise, the code is ignored.

Parametized Macros

If a program has the control line

```
#define MAXVAL 80
```

the preprocessor will substitute the value 80 wherever MAXVAL is found in the program. Let's suppose that a program has the following control line:

```
#define sqr(X) (X * X)
```

In this case, we have a macro substitution involving a parameter that is passed to the square function.

Note what macro substitution does: At any point in the program where the sqr() function is used, the compiler will substitute the square root code. In other words, there is no function call to sqr(). Because "in-line" code is faster than a function call, program speed is increased. The price of this increased speed is increased memory requirements for the program because the sqr() code is duplicated with each use of sqr().

When you use macros, make sure that there is no space between the name of the macro and the opening parenthesis of the argument list (if any). That is,

```
#define sqr (X) (X * X)
```

is incorrect because there is a space between the r and (.

Appendix D
Prototyping

What Is Prototyping?

The C language is undergoing a number of changes. These changes are being guided by the X3J11 Committee of the American National Standards Institute (ANSI). The goal of the Committee seems to be to remove some of the gray areas left in the language definition section (Appendix A) of Kernighan and Ritchie's *C Programming Language* and to correct some of the perceived shortcomings of the C language.

Some changes are minor, but others constitute major modifications to the language. One of these major changes involves prototyping, a language enhancement first appearing in AT&T's C++ compiler.

The first printing of *C Programming Guide Second Edition* did not discuss prototyping simply because the dust had not yet settled. No one knew the specific form prototyping would take in C. Indeed, while most of the dust has now settled, prototyping may still change before the proposed standard becomes an actual standard. However, prototyping is such a major enhancement to the C language that a discussion of prototyping is desirable at this point, even though some specific details are not established.

The purpose of prototyping is to add data-type checking and conversions in function calls. For example, the current definition for fseek() is

```
int fseek(fp, offset, direction)
FILE *fp;
long offset;
int direction;
```

313

The classic mistake in using `fseek()` is using an integer or integer constant for the second argument in the function call. For example, you might enter

```
fseek(fp, 0, SEEK_CUR);
```

instead of

```
fseek(fd, 0L, SEEK_CUR);
```

Another mistake is using the following sequence:

```
int readarec(rec)
int rec;
{
     int position;

     position = rec * REC_LENGTH;
     fseek(fp, rec, SEEK_BEGIN);
     .
     .
     .
}
```

In this sequence, the naked integer `rec` is passed instead of being converted to a `long`.

To reduce the problems associated with badly formed function arguments, the X3J11 Committee has proposed prototyping. An example will help illustrate what prototyping is and how it works.

Given the definition of `fseek()`, a function declaration in prototype form for `fseek()` is

```
int fseek(FILE *, long, int);
```

This declaration tells the compiler several things: (1) the function returns an `int` data type; (2) the first argument is a pointer to FILE; (3) the second argument is a `long`; and (4) the third argument is an `int`.

Prototypes may also use identifiers. For example, a prototype declaration for `fseek()` could be

```
int fseek(FILE *fp, long offset, int direction);
```

In this example, the prototype declaration includes identifiers to help the programmer recall what the variables are. With prototype declarations, the identifiers are for documentation purposes only. The prototype declaration does not define the variables `fp`, `offset`, and direction. These three names "disappear" as soon as the compiler reads the prototype. Adding identifier names to a prototype declaration is a recent innovation by the ANSI committee and is not honored on all compilers that support prototyping.

Now suppose you have the erroneous code fragment that appeared earlier in your program:

```
int readarec(rec)
int rec;
{
      int position;

      position = rec * REC_LENGTH;
      fseek(fp, rec, SEEK_BEGIN);          /* line 459 */
      .
      .
      .
}
```

The integer rec in line 459 would automatically be promoted to a long in the function call to fseek(). The compiler would perform an implicit cast of the integer to a long integer according to the prototype for fseek().

Prototyping also helps correct missing argument functions. For example, the correct definition for fputc() is

```
int fputc(c fp)
int c;
FILE *fp;
{
                .            /* Function details */
                .
}
```

The prototype declaration for fputc() is

```
int fputc(int, FILE *)
```

Given this prototype declaration, most compilers display an error message when fputc() is used in the following manner:

```
fputc(c);
```

In the preceding statement, the second argument, fp, is missing. Prototypes ensure that missing arguments are caught.

As these examples illustrate, prototyping provides tighter type checking than C originally provided.

Prototyping Functions with No Arguments

What would the prototype be for a function that has no function arguments? An example of this kind of prototype is

```
int getch(void);
```

This statement says that getch() should never be called with an argument. If you later (incorrectly) use getch() as

```
c = getch(stdin);
```

the compiler generates an error because the prototype states that getch() cannot have an argument.

Consider another prototype example:

```
void func1(void, int);
```

This prototype is incorrect. The function translates as "func1() is a function that returns nothing useful from the function and has no arguments followed by an int". This statement makes no sense because the void in the parentheses means that the function has no arguments, and yet the prototype goes on to state that the function has an integer argument. Therefore, illegal prototypes include

```
void func1(void, int);
```

or

```
void func1(int, void);
```

or

```
void func1(int, void, int);
```

Once void has been used in a prototype, any other data-type specifier appearing as an argument will be flagged as an error.

Prototyping with Pointers to Functions

What if you need a pointer to a function that returns an int? For example, consider the prototype for a bubble sort function:

```
void bsort(unsigned, int (*)(), int (*)() );
```

This prototype states that bsort() requires three arguments: one unsigned int and two pointers to functions that return an int. In this example, identifiers would help make the prototype more easily understood. Therefore, you might use

```
void bsort(unsigned nelem, int (*compare)(), int (*swap)() );
```

With this statement, you can more easily understand what bsort() is all about. Again, keep in mind that nelem, compare(), and swap() are not "defined" in the declaration and so cannot be used as "real" variables or function calls in the program unless the three have "real" definitions.

Prototyping with Variable Arguments

Some functions have a variable number of arguments, the data type and number of which cannot always be known at compile time. The printf() function is a common example. How can you prototype such functions?

For prototyping functions with variable arguments, the standards committee created a new symbol, the *ellipsis*, which consists of a comma followed by three periods (, ...). The ellipsis is used to designate functions for which you have no information about the number or type of arguments that are going to be used. Using the ellipsis, the prototype for printf() becomes

```
int printf(char *, ... );
```

This prototype says that printf() returns an int and that its argument(s) will always include at least a pointer to char and may have other unspecified arguments with unknown data types. When an ellipsis is used, the compiler does not check the arguments following the ellipsis. In the case of printf(), the compiler checks the first argument to see whether the argument is a pointer to char. Remaining arguments, if any, are not checked.

Creating Your Own Prototypes

When you write your own functions, you may wish to use a prototype form. This form enables you to get the benefits of type checking that prototyping offers. For example, suppose that you formerly defined a function as

```
char *func1(c, fp, num)
char *c;                        /* Argument declarations */
int num;
FILE *fp;
{


    .
    .

}
```

The new prototype form is

```
char *func1(char *c, FILE *fp, int num)        /* Line 1 */
{


    .
    .

}
```

Note that argument declarations are part of the prototype definition. You do not give the argument declarations on separate lines. Also notice that line 1 of the prototype can be "block-moved" into a header file for use as a prototype if the function definition is not in the file. (Don't forget the required semicolon at the end of the prototype if you use the block-move approach.)

Prototyping reduces certain types of bugs that used to be particularly difficult to uncover. If your compiler supports prototyping, use it. After you get used to the idea of prototyping, you will find that it will pay off handsomely.

During the Transition

Until the work of the ANSI X3J11 committee becomes a formal ANSI standard, most compilers will implement some "shade" of prototyping. The features and workings of the prototypes will vary slightly from compiler to compiler.

Currently, many but not all compilers offering prototypes allow an identifier in a prototype declaration. For compilers that do not allow an identifier in a prototype declaration, you must edit out the identifiers if you use the block-move approach.

Some compilers fully implement the automatic implicit conversions of prototyping. Those that do not perform the automatic conversions simply use prototyping as a "lint-like" predebugger tool for programmers. The types of automatic conversions supported in prototyping create a "gray area," but conversion is generally based on the rules for normal arithmetic conversions. For example, converting an integer argument to a long integer is generally allowed because precision is seldom lost in conversions from int to long. However, converting a long integer to an integer, where precision would be lost between 16-bit ints and 32-bit longs, is generally *not* allowed.

Minimally, all compilers using prototypes issue some diagnostic message when the arguments in a function call do not match the prototype. The diagnostic is either a warning message (program compiling continues) or an error message (compiling halts).

During the transition period, your best course of action is to use prototyping if it is available. Regardless of automatic argument conversions, correct your source code when any prototyping warning or error is given. Don't rely on prototypes automatically to cast function arguments. Write the function calls properly and make the C code right.

Index

More Computer Knowledge from Que

LOTUS SOFTWARE TITLES	1-2-3 for Business	$18.95
	1-2-3 Business Formula Handbook	19.95
	1-2-3 Command Language	19.95
	1-2-3 Financial Macros	19.95
	1-2-3 Macro Library, 2nd Edition	19.95
	1-2-3 Tips, Tricks, and Traps, 2nd Edition	19.95
	Using 1-2-3, 2nd Edition	19.95
	Using 1-2-3 Workbook and Disk, 2nd Edition	29.95
	Using Symphony	23.95
	Symphony: Advanced Topics	19.95
	Symphony Macros and the Command Language	22.95
	Symphony Tips, Tricks, and Traps	21.95
DATABASE TITLES	dBASE III Plus Applications Library	19.95
	dBASE III Plus Handbook, 2nd Edition	19.95
	dBASE III Advanced Programming	22.95
	R:base 5000 Techniques and Applications	19.95
	R:base 5000 User's Guide	19.95
	Reflex Tips, Tricks, and Traps	19.95
	Using Reflex	19.95
	Using Paradox	19.95
	Using Q & A	19.95
APPLICATIONS SOFTWARE TITLES	Excel Macro Library	19.95
	Multiplan Models for Business	15.95
	Using AppleWorks	16.95
	Using Dollars and Sense	14.95
	Using Enable	17.95
	Using Excel	19.95
	Using Javelin	19.95
	Using Smart	22.95
WORD-PROCESSING TITLES	Using DisplayWrite	18.95
	Using MicroSoft Word	16.95
	Using MultiMate	18.95
	Using the PFS Family: FILE, WRITE, GRAPH, REPORT	14.95
	Using WordPerfect, Revised Edition	18.95
	Using WordStar 2000	17.95
IBM TITLES	Networking IBM PCs: A Practical Guide, 2nd Edition	19.95
	PC DOS Workbook	14.95
	Using PC DOS	21.95
COMPUTER SYSTEMS TITLES	Amiga Programming Guide	18.95
	CP/M Programmer's Encyclopedia	19.95
	Managing Your Hard Disk	19.95
	MS-DOS User's Guide	19.95
	Using NetWare	24.95
PROGRAMMING AND TECHNICAL TITLES	Advanced C: Techniques and Applications	21.95
	C Programmer's Library	21.95
	C Programming Guide, 2nd Edition	19.95
	C Self-Study Guide	16.95
	Common C Functions	17.95
	Debugging C	19.95
	Turbo Pascal for BASIC Programmers	14.95
	Turbo Pascal Program Library	19.95
	Understanding UNIX: A Conceptual Guide	19.95
	Understanding XENIX: A Conceptual Guide	19.95

Que Order Line: **1-800-428-5331**
All prices subject to change without notice.

LEARN MORE ABOUT C
WITH THESE OUTSTANDING BOOKS FROM QUE

C Self-Study Guide
by Jack Purdum

This self-directed study guide uses a unique question-and-answer format to take you through the basics and into advanced areas of the C programming language. The book includes complete programs for testing new functions and for illustrating tips, traps, techniques, and shortcuts. A perfect companion for the *C Programming Guide*, this book will help you teach yourself to program in C. A companion disk is available.

Advanced C: Techniques and Applications
by Gerald E. Sobelman and David E. Krekelberg

Advanced C focuses on the more complex areas of the C language. This book emphasizes advanced programming features, including coding style, pointers, structures, and recursion; implementation of complex data structures; and advanced applications, including graphics, windows, and advanced user interfaces. If you know the basics and are eager for more, *Advanced C* is for you.

Common C Functions
by Kim J. Brand

This book displays dozens of C functions that are designed to teach C coding techniques to provide useful building blocks for program development. Learn the elements and structures of C programming by studying C code written by others. If you want to gain a stronger understanding of C code and how it works, *Common C Functions* is a superb guide. All the C code in this book is available on disk.

C Programmer's Library
by Jack Purdum, Timothy Leslie, and Alan Stegemoller

The most advanced book about C on the market today, this best-seller will save you hours of programming time and help you write more efficient code. Author Jack Purdum discusses design considerations in writing programs and offers programming tips to help you take full advantage of the power of C. A disk containing all the programs in the book is available.

Mail to: Que Corporation • P. O. Box 50507 • Indianapolis, IN 46250

Item	Title	Price	Quantity	Extension
176	C Self-Study Guide	$ 16.95		
284	Companion Disk, IBM PC format	39.95		
148	Common C Functions	18.95		
280	Companion Disk, IBM PC format	49.95		
179	Advanced C: Techniques and Applications	21.95		
229	Companion Disk, IBM PC format	49.95		
45	C Programmer's Library	21.95		
270	Companion Disk, IBM PC format	49.95		
		Book Subtotal		
	Shipping & Handling ($2.50 per item)			
	Indiana Residents Add 5% Sales Tax			
		GRAND TOTAL		

Method of Payment:

☐ Check   ☐ VISA   ☐ MasterCard   ☐ American Express

Card Number _____ Exp. Date _____

Cardholder's Name _____

Ship to _____

Address _____

City _____ State _____ ZIP _____

If you can't wait, call **1-800-428-5331** and order TODAY.

All prices subject to change without notice.

REGISTRATION CARD

Register your copy of *C Programming Guide, Second Edition* and receive information about Que's newest products relating to the C programming language and the UNIX operating system. Complete this registration card and return it to Que Corporation, P.O. Box 50507, Indianapolis, IN 46250.

Name _____

Address _____

City _____ State _____ ZIP _____

Phone _____

Where did you buy your copy of *C Programmiing Guide*?

_____

How do you plan to use the programs in this book?

_____

_____

_____

What other kinds of publications about C and UNIX would you be interested in?

_____

Which C compiler do you use? _____

Version number _____

Which operating system do you use? _____

Which computer? _____

THANK YOU!

FOLD HERE

Place
Stamp
Here

Que Corporation
P. O. Box 50507
Indianapolis, IN 46250

& : "address of"